THE SOUTH
COAL IND

THE SOUTH WALES COAL INDUSTRY 1841–1875

BY

J. H. MORRIS

AND

L. J. WILLIAMS

CARDIFF
UNIVERSITY OF WALES PRESS
1958

PRINTED IN GREAT BRITAIN

The years of which we write... were the days of the pioneer.... When we come, therefore, as we must, to point out the mistakes which were made in these early years of the coalmining industry, let us beware of merely being wise after the event, or of withholding the meed of praise due to a great race of men, employers, mining engineers, workmen and machinery makers alike. For whatever their faults, they were fit to rank with the greatest of Britain's industrial pioneers

Coal Mining
Report of the Technical Advisory Committee, 1945

PREFACE

THIS study was originally planned to cover the history of the South Wales coal industry from the early 1840's to the eve of the First World War. As work progressed, however, it became apparent that a volume could suitably be devoted to a shorter period. The mid-seventies of the nineteenth century stood out as a clear dividing line, witnessing, as they did, the formation of a powerful owners' association, the introduction of a sliding scale to regulate the wage rates of the majority of the workers in the mines, and the collapse of the first trade union movement of any strength amongst the colliers. The shorter period covered has a unity of its own. During it the value of the steam-coal resources of the region became apparent and the coal industry won the industrial predominance which had previously been enjoyed by the iron industry. At the end of it the individual capitalist or partnership was losing ground in face of the rise of the limited liability company, and the Aberdare valley was yielding pride of place to the Rhondda as the main producing area.

Our work has benefited greatly from help given by our colleagues at Aberystwyth. Our chief indebtedness, and one which can be only inadequately acknowledged, is to the Head of our Department, Professor Arthur Beacham, who not only read the typescript and made valuable suggestions but also facilitated our work at every stage. Professor David Williams and Dr. E. T. Nevin both read early drafts of the opening chapters and helped to remove some of their defects. Mr. Morlais Hughes, Senior Cartographer of the Department of Geography, kindly drew for us the two maps which illustrate this volume.

Of the members of the coal industry who have helped us we wish to thank particularly Mr. R. W. Burgess, who was instrumental in arranging for the records of the Monmouthshire and South Wales Coal-owners' Association to be deposited at the National Library of Wales. We are also grateful to the editors of the *Economic History Review* and of the *Journal of the National Library of Wales* for permission to use some material which was first published in their journals.

In the course of collecting material for this volume we have made especial use of the printed and manuscript sources housed at the National Library of Wales, the Cardiff Central Library, the Newport Public Library, and the County Record Offices of Glamorgan and Monmouthshire. We wish to acknowledge the unfailing co-operation and assistance which we have received from the staffs of all these institutions. From amongst so many it is, perhaps, invidious to single out one person for specific mention; but Mr. Walter Morgan, of the National Library of Wales, has placed us so heavily in his debt, both as a librarian and as a friend, that the risk must be taken.

Finally, we wish to express our warm appreciation of the interest shown in this book by our publishers and printers and of the helpful suggestions both have made. For the defects which remain we are alone responsible.

J. H. M.
L. J. W.

University College of Wales
Aberystwyth

CONTENTS

PREFACE vii

BIBLIOGRAPHY xi

I. THE EARLY 1840's
A period of change. An estimate of coal output. The regions of mining activity. Size of firms and collieries. Characteristics of the coalfield 1

II. THE MARKETS OF THE COALFIELD
The search for wider markets. The trade of the 1840's. The rivalry between South Wales and the north of England. The overseas and London markets. The demand for anthracite and bituminous coal. The iron industry 18

III. TECHNIQUE
Technique in the 1840's. Forces promoting change. The development of long-wall working. Ventilation. Haulage, winding, and mechanical coal-cutting. Productivity per head. Statistical note 50

IV. THE EXPANSION IN OUTPUT
The interaction of supply and demand. Sales of coal by the iron firms. The growth of output in the western part of the coalfield. The eastern region—Cardiff and Newport. The coal trade from the Aberdare valley. The rise of the Rhondda 77

V. LANDOWNERS AND COAL-OWNERS
Mineral leases. The landowners and the coal industry. The coal-owners 116

VI. THE STRUCTURE OF INDUSTRY AND CAPITAL FORMATION
The size of collieries and firms. The supply of capital. The banks and the coal industry. Limited liability companies 134

VII. COMMERCIAL ORGANIZATION
Variety of selling arrangements. Attempts at price control 163

CONTENTS

VIII. SAFETY
Growing disquiet about colliery accidents. The early years of mines inspection. The 1855 Act. The 1860 and 1872 Acts. Conclusion   179

IX. SOCIAL CONDITIONS
Introduction. Employment of women and children. The course of wages. Truck. Hours and regularity of work. Immigration and the mobility of labour. Housing conditions. Provision of schools and doctors; Benefit societies; the influence of religion   209

X. INDUSTRIAL RELATIONS
The principal industrial disputes before 1871. The main causes of unrest. Tactics of employers and employed during disputes. The slow growth of trade unionism   248

XI. INDUSTRIAL RELATIONS (*continued*)
The growth of employers' associations. The disputes of 1871-5. Conclusion—the sliding scale   274

INDEX   285

MAPS
The South Wales Coalfield   *facing page* 1
Aberdare Valley, 1874, Principal Collieries   105

BIBLIOGRAPHY

THE parliamentary papers and most of the other printed sources that have been utilized are indicated in the footnotes. The following list is restricted to the most important manuscript collections, newspapers and journals that have been consulted.

National Library of Wales (referred to in footnotes as NLW).
Bute MSS.
Clemenstone MSS.
Cyfarthfa MSS.
A. Stanley Davies MSS.
Dunraven MSS.
Evans and Bevan MSS.
Ewenny MSS.
Haverfordwest (Williams and Williams) MSS.
Llandinam MSS.
Lucas MSS.
Maybery MSS.
Merthyr of Senghenydd MSS.
Nevill MSS.
Penrice and Margam MSS.
South Wales Coal Owners MSS.
Astle, Ivor, *History of Aberdare*. NLW MS. 28788.
Lewis, E. D., *The Industrial Development of the Rhondda Valleys to 1910*. Unpublished M.A. thesis of University of Wales.

Cardiff Central Library (referred to in footnotes as CCL).
Bute MSS.
Cardiff Library MSS.

Glamorgan County Record Office.
Dowlais MSS.
Vivian MSS.

Monmouthshire County Record Office.
Bythway MSS.

Newspapers and Journals.
  Cambrian.
  Colliery Guardian.
  Merthyr Guardian.
  Mining Journal.
  Monmouthshire Merlin.
  South Wales Coal Annual.
  Western Mail.

The place of publication of the books referred to is omitted for those published in London.

Key to abbreviations.
  CG   *Colliery Guardian.*
  MG   *Merthyr Guardian.*
  MIR   Mines. Inspectors' Reports.
  MJ   *Mining Journal.*
  SWIE Transactions of the South Wales Institute of Engineers.

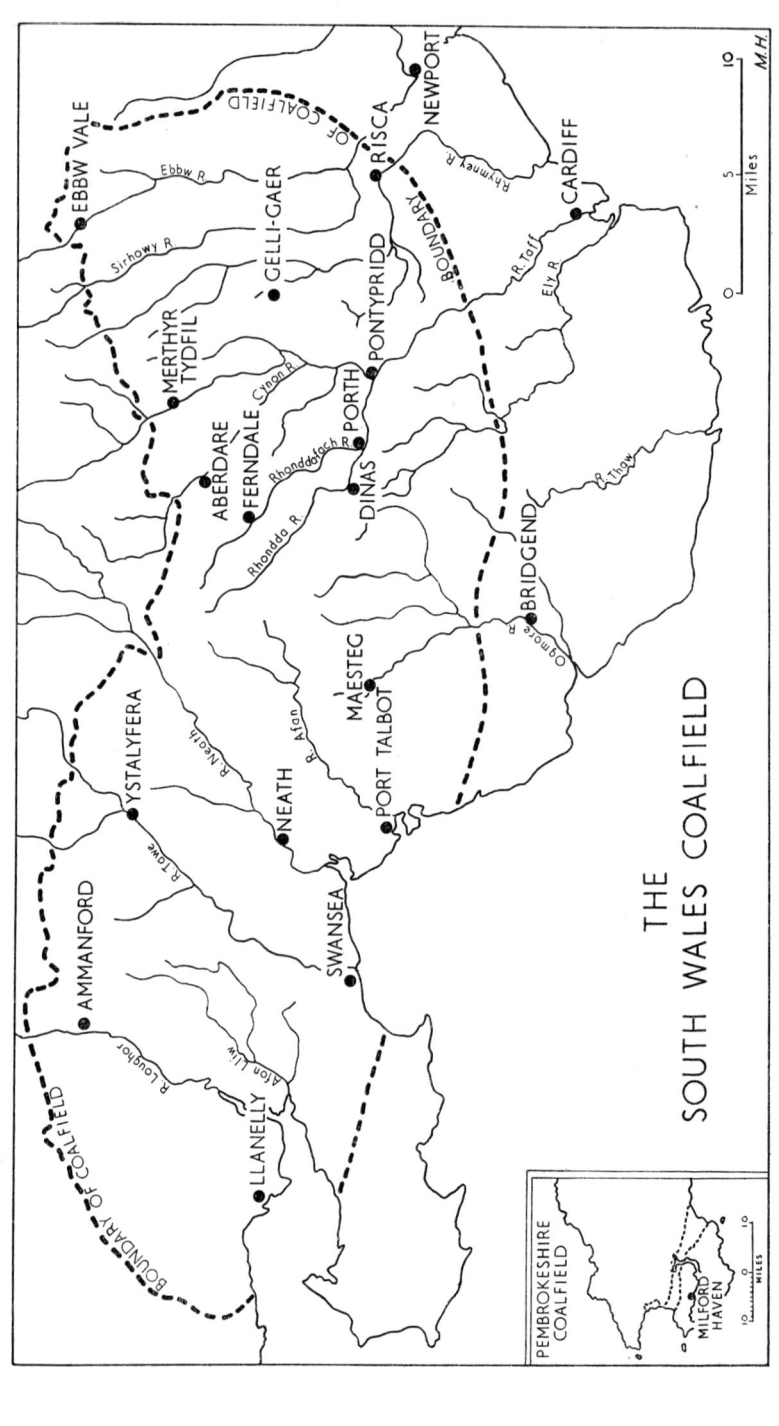

I

THE EARLY 1840's

WHILE economic development is usually a steady process, devoid of startlingly rapid transformation, occasions occur when it is clear that a definite turning-point has been reached. In the story of the South Wales coalfield the years about 1840 marked such an occasion. These years witnessed the growth of a new interest in access to more extensive markets, the construction of the first railways in South Wales, and the building of new docks at the ports. After 1840 the expansion of production in the coalfield rested on bases which differed significantly from those which had prevailed in the opening decades of the century. Thus the historian, in starting his account with the early years of Victoria's reign, feels that he is tracing a fresh phase from its beginnings rather than unceremoniously breaking into the middle of a continuous story. That 1841 was the year in which the two Children's Employment Commissioners, Robert Hugh Franks and Rhys William Jones, investigated conditions of employment in the South Wales coal industry, provides a further inducement to choose this year as a starting-point because the report of their inquiries furnishes an amount of information which has no parallel in earlier periods.[1]

In the early decades of the nineteenth century the South Wales coal industry had been expanding, but this growth had been, in the main, along lines which could have been anticipated.[2] During these years the greatest stimulus to production

---

[1] *Children's Employment Commission. Appendix. First Report of Commissioners. Mines. Part II, P.P.* 1842 (382), xvii. (Hereinafter referred to as *Children's Employment*.)

[2] For the history of the coal industry in the 1750–1850 period see A. H. John, *The Industrial Development of South Wales* (Cardiff, 1950).

had arisen from the home demand and this was dominated to an overwhelming degree by the growing needs of the local iron industry which, by 1840, accounted for more than a hundred furnaces. The remaining industrial demand came mainly from the various tinplate works and from the copper industry, a greedy consumer of coal, concentrated in the Swansea–Llanelly region. Supplementing this industrial demand were the requirements of the local household consumers, a demand growing *pari passu* with population, and other minor needs, such as the demand for coal by the farmers for lime-burning.

While the quantity of coal shipped to outside markets, either coastwise or overseas, still remained comparatively small, it was nevertheless growing perceptibly, shipments increasing during the decade of the thirties, for example, from just over 1 million to $1\frac{1}{2}$ million tons. But this growth had not altered the salient characteristics of these shipments; they still consisted primarily of bituminous coal and anthracite, and the greater part of them, indeed still over 95 per cent. in 1840 and 1841, went coastwise. The markets mainly served were those geographically adjacent—the Bristol Channel and the south-west ports as far as Plymouth and the Irish ports to the south of Dublin. The Cornish trade, particularly, was safely in Welsh hands because the coal served as a return freight for the vessels bringing copper ore to the Swansea and Llanelly district, but beyond Plymouth the competition of the north of England coals became increasingly severe. In the great market of London, Welsh supplies played little part, the north of England reigning supreme.

This coastal traffic in Welsh coal was thus still confined to areas which offered little prospect of any rapid growth of demand in the future. All that could be expected from these areas, non-industrial as they were, was a slow increase in traffic as the population in them grew. Greater opportunities would arise, not through a continuance of the connexion with these traditional markets, but with the exploitation of new overseas outlets based primarily, not on bituminous coals for household and foundry purposes nor on the specialized demand for anthracite, but on the steam-raising capacities of Welsh coal. Despite some recent growth the amount of Welsh coal shipped overseas remained insignificant, less than 65,000 tons a year being exported in 1840 and 1841. The trends characteristic of the Welsh coal trade in the later nineteenth century had clearly not yet emerged, although it is true that these exports, slight though they were, had already penetrated to widely scattered markets, laying a slender but extensive foundation on which future progress could be based.

If the prospects of expansion were limited while the coal-owners were serving mainly the needs of the iron industry and of the coastal traffic, they were also restricted while the canal remained the basis for the transportation of coal. Before canal construction had started in South Wales, at the end of the eighteenth century, the coal trade had been largely confined to that part of the western sector of the coalfield where the coal measures adjoined the sea. In the east, the area behind Newport and Cardiff, the gap between the coalfield and the ports had proved an effective barrier to the emergence of any significant trade in coal. The construction in rapid succession of some half-a-dozen canals, with their networks of feeder tramroads, spread throughout the coalfield had greatly enlarged the area from which a sea-coal trade was economically feasible. These canals had both increased the volume of the coal trade and altered its sources of supply; by 1840 nearly one-half of the Welsh coal shipments originated from Newport and Cardiff, harbours where the coal trade had been almost non-existent a half-century earlier. Nevertheless, the conclusion is inescapable that this performance of delivering $1\frac{1}{2}$ million tons of coal to the ports for shipment, as well as catering for the needs of the iron trade, was virtually the peak of canal achievement. Unless some alternative emerged it was clear that the limited capacity of the canals would soon exert a dampening influence on the growth of the trade. It is for this reason that the introduction of the locomotive railway into South Wales at this time marked a change too decisive to constitute a mere extension of past trends.

Of the changes, occurring about 1840, which were destined to alter the pattern of the Welsh coal trade the most significant were those connected with transport. At Cardiff, on 9 October 1839, amid scenes of great rejoicing, the West Bute Dock had been opened and to the accompaniment of the strains of 'Rule Britannia' the steamer *Lady Charlotte* had been the first vessel to enter. Soon the coal trade of the dock was growing swiftly, increasing from the modest 3,641 tons that were shipped in 1840 to over 200,000 tons as early as 1843. This rate of progress was made possible by the building of the Taff Vale Railway which brought the coal to the dock from the hills. The first 15-mile stretch of this railway, from Cardiff to Navigation House, was opened on 18 October 1840, and by April 1841 the line was completed to Merthyr. At Newport, too, a new dock was under construction, to be ultimately opened in October 1842. Farther west, at Port Talbot, a new harbour was opened to the public on May Day 1841,[1] while to serve Llanelly a railway had been constructed by 1840 along the Loughor valley and the Aman valley to Cwmaman works, a distance of 17 miles, tapping a region where, as ironworks were few, the main traffic was expected to be anthracite for shipment. Along this line, on 10 March 1840, the proprietors of the Cwmaman works had sent 20 tons of anthracite, using horses to draw the wagons as the order was too urgent to wait until the locomotives were ready. This railway, also, threatened to divert trade from Swansea to Llanelly, the Garnant Stone Coal Company, which had previously shipped its coal at Swansea, sending its first load by this alternative route on 1 May 1840. In the same year the Copper Works Dock was opened at Llanelly, to supplement the small docking accommodation that had been provided in 1835, but the navigation of the approach to Llanelly harbour still

[1] Penrice and Margam MSS., No. 9261.

THE EARLY 1840's

remained difficult.[1] Besides these undertakings, there were other projects, which did not immediately materialize, engaging serious attention in the early forties—a railway for Newport, two railways and a dock at Swansea, and a further dock at Neath.[2]

Side by side with these improvements in transport, and inextricably mingled with them as cause and effect, went a new interest in the fuller exploitation of the coal resources of the district and, in particular, of the steam-coal measures. The first pit was sunk to the Four Feet vein of steam coal in the Aberdare valley by the Wayne family in 1837. It was in 1840, according to a speech he made twenty years later, that John Nixon, impressed by the smokeless qualities of the Welsh coal he had seen used on a Thames steamer, came to Thomas Powell who was sinking a pit in the Dyffryn estate, his first in the Aberdare valley, and made arrangements to introduce his coal to the French market.[3] These developments, together with the Bute Dock and Taff Vale Railway, were setting the stage for the outstanding feature of the following two decades, the rapid expansion of the production of steam coal in the Aberdare valley and the emergence of Cardiff as the leading port in the South Wales coal trade.

But activity was by no means confined to Cardiff and its hinterland. In Monmouthshire, at their Risca colliery, in 1841, John Russell and Company were sinking a new pit to the steam-coal measures and in the following year the firm secured a contract to supply the Royal West India Steam Packet Company with 72,000 tons of coal annually from their enlarged colliery.[4] There was parallel activity in the western sector of the coalfield where attempts were being made to find new uses for anthracite. In the Swansea valley at the Ynyscedwyn works, with the help of the hot blast, the first successful use of anthracite in the smelting of iron had been

[1] *Cambrian*, 21 Mar., 9 May 1840, 11 June 1842.
[2] Ibid., 21 Feb. 1840, 30 Jan. 1841, 6 Aug. 1842, 25 Feb. 1843.
[3] *MG*, 12 May 1860.   [4] Ibid., 8 Oct. 1842.

achieved by George Crane in 1837. By 1841, when a third furnace was about to be blown in at the expanding Ynyscedwyn works, the new process had been adopted at other ironworks recently established in the Vale of Neath, in the Gwendraeth valley and at Ystalyfera.[1] Buoyed up by the hope that, in addition to its new use in iron-smelting, anthracite would find a substantial new outlet as a fuel for steamships, contemporaries believed that the anthracite resources of the coalfield had acquired a new value.

Before the effects of these various new ventures on the subsequent history of the coalfield are considered, an attempt will be made, in the remainder of this chapter, to depict some main features of the coal industry in the early forties. Any estimate of the quantity of coal mined in South Wales at this time must lack precision because an assessment of the amount produced to cater for the internal demand, both industrial and household, involves so much guesswork. There can be no doubt, however, that the iron industry was the largest consumer. Mushet estimated that South Wales produced 453,880 tons of pig iron in 1839, while Porter's estimate for a year later was 505,000 tons.[2] Since Mushet mentioned that thirty-two furnaces were building in 1839 and since the demand, particularly for railway iron, could lead to an appreciable increase from one year to another, these estimates agree reasonably closely. Porter considered that 1,436,000 tons of coal were used in the production of this pig iron and that a further 600,000 tons were used in the conversion of pig into wrought iron. The amount of coal consumed in making iron varied, depending on whether the older cold blast or the newer Nielson's hot blast method was used at the furnaces, but the substantial accuracy of Porter's figures receives confirmation from a newspaper account of the coal used at the

---

[1] *Children's Employment*, pp. 667 et seq.
[2] D. Mushet, *Papers on Iron and Steel* (1840), pp. 414–15; G. R. Porter, *The Progress of the Nation* (1851 edn.), p. 269.

Dowlais works in 1839.[1] Here, where five out of the fifteen furnaces were employing the hot blast, 3 tons of coal were needed to produce one ton of pig iron and a further 1½ tons of coal were used for each ton of pig which, by the refining, puddling, and rolling processes, was converted into bar iron. At Ynyscedwyn George Crane claimed that, using the hot blast, he could produce one ton of pig iron with 27 cwt. of anthracite, one-third of the amount of coal previously used.[2] Accordingly the amount of coal used in the South Wales ironworks in 1840 was something between 2 and 2¼ million tons.

Of the remaining industrial demand the most important was that of the copper-smelting works. Rhys Jones, the Children's Employment Commissioner, was unable to get accurate statistics but he estimated that between 130,000 and 150,000 tons of copper ore were smelted annually in South Wales, producing some 15,000 to 16,000 tons of fine copper and using from 180,000 to 200,000 tons of coal in the process. This may well have been an underestimate as others believed that from 17 to 22 tons of coal were used in the production of one ton of pure copper.[3] Perhaps when the demands of the tin-plate works, the brewers, brickmakers, lime-burners, blacksmiths, and other minor industrial users are added, a further half million tons of coal were used in industries other than the ironworks.

It is even more difficult to evaluate the household consumption in South Wales at this time as contemporary evidence gives less guidance. As the canals in South Wales merely connected the upland regions of the coalfield with the coast and as the only tramroad serving the interior was that from near Brecon, at the head of the Brecon and Abergavenny Canal, to Kington, Leominster, and the rural parts of Herefordshire, it was unusual for coal to be carried any distance inland from the coalfield. While coal was the common fuel in the southern parts of Brecknockshire, for example, in the northern parts,

---

[1] *Cambrian*, 29 June 1839. [2] Ibid., 3 Mar. 1838.
[3] *Children's Employment*, p. 682; *MJ*, 12 Aug. 1843.

where coal could be obtained only by tedious and difficult land carriage, peat was the fuel normally used.[1] The population of the five counties into parts of which the coalfield extended was, according to the census of 1841, 555,516. A great part of this population lived within comparatively easy access to some colliery, even were it only a tiny level or 'colehole'. Also this population included numerous collier families who were customarily allowed free or cheap coal, and the scale of their consumption is suggested by the clause in later leases restricting the amount of royalty-free coal for this purpose to 14 cwt. a month for each collier.[2] Any figure for the household consumption of coal carried inland on and near the coalfield, nevertheless, must remain a guess rather than a reasoned estimate, but perhaps an amount of half a million tons annually at this time may not be far from the mark.

For the remaining demand, from the markets served by the coastwise and overseas trade of the South Wales ports, reasonably reliable figures are available. These show that in 1840 the coastal shipments were 1,374,419 tons, while a further 63,857 tons were shipped overseas.[3] Thus, while it must be conceded that any figure put forward will be liable to a generous margin of error, the total output of coal in South Wales at the beginning of the 1840's was roughly $4\frac{1}{2}$ million tons of which something over 2 million tons were used by the ironworks, 1 million tons were used by other industries and by domestic consumers served by inland transport, and nearly $1\frac{1}{2}$ million tons were accounted for by coal shipments.

The nature of this demand naturally did much to determine the location of coal-mining activity in South Wales at this time. The most important ironworks were situated in the eastern sector of the coalfield. Here they stretched in a line

[1] S. Lewis, *Topographical Dictionary of Wales*, 4th edn. (1849). See 'Brecknockshire'. [2] NLW Bute MSS., Box 106, Mineral leases.
[3] *Coal Shipments*, P.P. 1841 (259), xxvi.

following the north-eastern outcrop—where the coal measures dipped gently and were generally accessible at fairly shallow depths—from Hirwaun to Pontypool. In this region the head of each valley was commanded by at least one ironworks. At the top of the Taff valley, for example, was the great iron centre of Merthyr, the largest town in Wales at this time. The glare of the furnaces from its four giant works— Cyfarthfa, Dowlais, Penydarren, and Plymouth—fascinated tourists and served as a lurid symbol of the extent to which the iron industry dominated the valley. In the Monmouthshire valleys—the Rhymney, Sirhowy, Ebbw, and Afon Lwyd —the same general pattern was repeated. A series of ironworks—of which the Rhymney, Tredegar, Sirhowy, Ebbw Vale, Victoria, Nant-y-glo, Blaina, Clydach, Blaenavon, and Varteg were the chief—straggled across the Monmouthshire hills, generally at or near the heads of these valleys.

While the works of East Glamorgan and Monmouthshire were the core of the Welsh iron industry there were also numerous lesser works located in other districts of the coalfield. In the Llynfi valley, north of Bridgend, were the three ironworks of Llynfi, Ton-du, and Maesteg, while slightly farther to the west lay Bryn-du, on the Kenfig brook, Aberavon, Cwmavon, Ton-mawr, and Glyncorrwg. In the Vale of Neath were the newly-opened works of Messrs. Jevons and Arthur as well as the old-established Neath Abbey concern. In the Swansea valley were the Ynyscedwyn works, where the inconvenience of bringing bituminous coal from a distance by canal had led to the efforts to smelt iron with local anthracite, and the Ystalyfera works. In Carmarthenshire, too, there were a few scattered works; at Trimsaran and Pontyberem in the Gwendraeth valley as well as the Aman and Brynaman works.[1]

Wherever the ironworks had been established there had been a corresponding stimulus to the development of coal-mining.

[1] For the ironworks see the account in *MG*, 6 July 1839; also Sir John Lloyd, *Old South Wales Ironworks* (1906).

This mining, however, was merely a subsidiary section of the iron industry as nearly all the ironworks of South Wales were integrated concerns, obtaining their coal from their own pits and levels. The Dowlais collieries, for example, produced 1,500 tons of coal a day in 1841, all for use at their vast works with its eighteen blast furnaces.[1] But where the production of iron had developed the progress of the sale-coal industry was also aided. When sale-coal collieries were set up near the ironworks they could draw on a labour supply which was growing through the attraction exerted by the existing industrial development and they could use transport facilities initially created primarily for the iron industry.

The influence of the demand for coal by the copper industry was much more localized, the extensive copper-smelting works listed by Rhys Jones all being situated near Llanelly, Swansea, and Neath.[2] The amount of coal used by these works was so great that as many were employed in the pits as in the smelting works themselves. However, the major influence encouraging the development of coal-mining in this western sector was not the copper industry but the shipment of coal. In addition to the advantages that, from near Port Talbot to beyond Llanelly, the coal measures adjoined the sea and that freights were low owing to the return traffic in ore, a further stimulus to trade arose from the high reputation held by the coal of this region—particularly that from the Graigola and Llansamlet collieries—for its steam-raising qualities. Collieries thus clustered thickly in the Swansea region, and a similar picture was presented at Llanelly, ringed round as it was with collieries, none far from the coast. After the Neath (1791) and Swansea (1798) canals had been constructed coal-mines had also been opened farther inland. There was a line of collieries up the entire length of the Neath valley, while the coal and culm brought down the Swansea canal in 1841 amounted to about 520,000 tons a year. This, in conjunction with the lively copper trade, had given Swansea 'a commercial

[1] *Children's Employment*, pp. 639 and 649.   [2] Ibid., p. 682.

interest and importance' which seemed 'to be increasing at a rapid rate of prosperous progression'.[1]

By 1841, however, Swansea had already lost its former pre-eminence in the sea-coal trade, owing to the stimulus that the canals and tramroads, constructed initially to serve the needs of the iron industry, had given to the coal trade of Newport and Cardiff. At the end of the eighteenth century the Glamorganshire Canal had been built to link the Merthyr ironworks with their sea outlet at Cardiff, and the later Aberdare branch (1811) served a similar function for the Hirwaun, Aberdare, and Llwydcoed concerns. In the next county the Monmouthshire Canal and the Sirhowy tramroad had been built to bring the iron down from the hills to Newport for shipment. The coal-owners were not slow to take advantage of the new transport facilities offered and by 1840 on both canals the greater part of the traffic—in bulk, but not in value—consisted of coal. In that year 248,484 tons of coal and 132,781 tons of iron were brought down the Glamorganshire Canal; in Monmouthshire 558,104 tons of coal and 194,459 tons of iron were brought down by canal and tramroad to Newport.[2]

At first the increase in shipments had been most marked from Newport. Under the Monmouthshire Canal Act of 1797 coal shipped coastwise from this port had been granted a partial exemption from customs duties and this advantage had not lapsed until these duties were removed in 1831. During this period there had grown up a flourishing trade in coal from the Mynyddislwyn seam, a bituminous coal which was admirably suited to the needs of buyers in the days when the steamship demand was insignificant. By 1840 the coastal trade from Newport surpassed that of Swansea and by 1841 the aggregate shipments from Newport were greater than those of any other port in South Wales.

From Cardiff the shipments of coal still lagged far behind those of Swansea and Newport. As late as 1841, indeed, the coal trade of Llanelly exceeded that of Cardiff although in the

[1] Ibid., p. 682.   [2] Ibid., p. 636; *MG*, 4 May 1844.

following year the relative position of these two ports in the coal trade was to be reversed. But even before this there had been signs that Cardiff was not destined much longer to play a subordinate role among the South Wales ports and in the 1830's, after Newport had lost her customs privilege, the sale-coal trade of Cardiff had doubled. The vital causes that were to promote the later phenomenal growth of Cardiff, however, were the advent of the railways, the provision of adequate docking facilities, and the exploitation of the vast steam-coal reserves that lay in its hinterland. These were movements that came to maturity only after 1840.

These new developments, however, were to demand a considerable capital expenditure. The steam-coal measures were deeper-lying so that, in addition to the costs of constructing railways and docks, there was the greater expenditure required for the shafts that were now necessary to reach the coal. It is doubtful if the capital for such ventures was available in South Wales before the second quarter of the nineteenth century. The capital needs of the Welsh iron industry had been provided mainly from outside sources; by London merchants such as Anthony Bacon, Richard Crawshay, William Thompson, and Richard Forman, by the Homfrays from Staffordshire, and by a host of Bristol merchants amongst whom the Harfords, who were connected with the Ebbw Vale works, were merely the most outstanding. The coal industry, catering mainly for a local and restricted market, had, in contrast, attracted only a limited flow of external capital.[1] It is true that several Bristol merchants participated in the thriving Monmouthshire coal trade and that occasional instances occur of capitalists being attracted from farther afield, but in the main the coal industry was left in the hands of lesser capitalists who were emerging within the coalfield itself as its industrialization developed.

Accordingly the scale of operations of the typical unit,

[1] See A. H. John, op. cit., ch. ii: The Financing of Industry.

whether colliery or firm, in the South Wales coal industry remained small. The large iron companies were exceptions, each employing several hundred colliers, but in the coal industry proper only a mere handful of owners employed more than 200 workers. In the west the favourable conditions for trade had led to the emergence of three large concerns. The Swansea Coal Company, financed by copper-smelters, employed 448 people in 1841, while the numbers employed by C. H. Smith at his Llansamlet collieries were 421. The other large firm in this area, the Landore Colliery Company, employed 357 workers. Farther to the east there was Thomas Powell, a timber merchant of Newport, whose connexion with the coal trade had started about the year 1810. By 1841 at four collieries in Monmouthshire and on the eastern edge of Glamorgan—Gelli-gaer, Gelli-groes, Bryn, and, in partnership with Thomas Prothero, Buttery Hatch—he employed 431 men and boys. In the previous year he had sent down 62,130 tons of coal on the Glamorganshire Canal alone, one-quarter of all the coal it carried.[1] In the lower Rhondda valley Walter Coffin employed 414 workers at his Dinas colliery, while 315 were employed by Messrs. Russell and Company in their Risca collieries near Newport. Operations on this scale, however, were still exceptional; most owners, at the time of the visit of the Children's Employment Commissioners, employed fewer than 150 or 100 people. George Insole was just growing out of this group, employing 157 men and boys at his Maes-mawr colliery in the parish of Llantwit Fardre, but even at collieries producing coal of an established reputation—such as the Graigola colliery in the Swansea valley and Mrs. Thomas's Waun Wyllt colliery at Merthyr—the numbers employed were only 65 and 50 respectively. In Pembrokeshire there was no outstanding owner or collicry, the largest colliery being Landshipping, owned by Colonel Owen, employing 163 workers. While at one extreme

[1] *Children's Employment*, p. 636. This report gives employment figures for most of the collieries that were visited.

there were employers like Thomas Powell, already extending his operations from colliery to colliery and from valley to valley, there were at the other the owners of innumerable tiny levels, employing fewer than a score of workers, which make little impact on history except to survive as a name in a collection of leases; in between there was the average Welsh colliery, with fewer than 100 workers, and the average coal master owning usually one of these collieries or, at the most, two.

There were many other reasons accounting for the predominance of the small-scale unit. Much of the coal, for example, was easily accessible either by levels or by shallow pits so that mining could be undertaken by owners of limited capital resources. Most mining, too, was still in the hands of individual owners or small partnerships and normally the scale of their business could be expanded only slowly by the ploughing back of profits. Furthermore, growth in scale had often to wait on slow changes in the environment—the attraction of labour to isolated districts and the provision of houses, the development of transport facilities, the slow growth in demand leading to the realization that more coal could be sold could it only be produced. Standards of technique also sometimes set a limit to the size of the individual colliery. Extensive workings did exist—William David, a door boy in the Landore collieries, 'kept a door' 2 miles distant from the entry to the mine, and the longest tramway at Craig-yr-allt colliery, near Eglwysilan, was $1\frac{1}{2}$ miles long—but often the simplest method of attaining an increased output was to start completely new workings, thus avoiding the technical difficulties of haulage, winding, and ventilation associated with large collieries. The Plymouth Iron Company, for example, won its coal by several separate levels and by three separate pits.[1] The effective ventilation of a large colliery, particularly

[1] *Children's Employment*, pp. 510 (Plymouth), 523 (Craig-yr-allt), 709 (Landore). A generation later an inspector of mines considered that the coming into general use of the safety lamp had been the most important single influence making the increase in size of the average colliery possible. MIR Report of Thomas Wales for 1867.

THE EARLY 1840's

a fiery one, often proved an intractable problem at a time when so little was known about mechanical ventilation, when 'splitting the air' to ventilate separately the different sections of a colliery was not yet a practice in South Wales and when the safety lamp was not in general use; it is not surprising that the workers at Craig-yr-allt colliery sometimes suffered a great deal of enforced idleness because bad air prevented work. One further factor limiting the scale of development in some regions, notably Pembrokeshire, was the occurrence of the coal in 'thin, exceedingly contorted and uncertain' seams. Because of this, it was noted in the early 1850's, the coal in Pembrokeshire was often worked by shallow and temporary pits, with a small number of workers, sometimes consisting only of the members of a family.[1]

The many advantages the South Wales coalfield offered when the new age based on railways and steamships began, however, were likely to stimulate efforts to exploit its resources on a far larger scale. The very extent of the field, stretching from Abersychan in the east to St. Bride's Bay in the west, a distance of over 90 miles, and varying in width from over 16 miles in Glamorgan to about 2 miles in Pembrokeshire, combined with the number of its seams, made its resources seem almost boundless. Coal from even the most remote colliery had to travel less than 30 miles to reach the nearest port. Moreover, the gradients from the valley heads to the sea outlets, which had proved an obstacle in the canal age, involving costly construction, numerous locks and a slow rate of transport, consistently favoured the load when the railways were constructed. The coal-laden trains ran cheaply and easily to the seaboard, leaving only empty wagons or wagons carrying pit props to be hauled back into the hills. Another advantage, as G. T. Clark, a trustee of the Dowlais Iron Company, pointed out in his report on the eastern half of the coalfield in 1869, was 'the very deep and extensive valley system by which the measures

[1] MIR Report of H. Mackworth for 1853.

are intersected. Here are none of those broad plains which elsewhere have rendered necessary for the winning of the coal shafts often of very great depth. Much of the coal here won has been obtained by levels driven upon the crop; and although this method of working necessarily becomes less and less applicable, the shafts required are less deep and therefore less costly than would be the case were the valleys less numerous ... It is mainly to the complete intersection of the field by the great valleys of the Nedd, the Afan, the Ogwr, Taff, Rhymney and Ebbw and their subordinates the Ely, Rhondda, Cynon and Sirhowy, and the Afon Llwyd which falls into the Usk, that are due the facilities for rapid and economical working which characterize the South Wales coalfield.'

The coal measures, besides being abundant and comparatively accessible, also had a variety—anthracite, bituminous, and steam—and a quality which fitted them 'in the highest degree for the purposes of manufacture, of commerce and of war'.[1]

Thirty years before Clark wrote this account the level or drift into the hillside had been far more common than the pit in the valley bottom, and the exploitation of some of the valleys he mentioned—the Rhondda and Ogwr (Ogmore), for example—had hardly begun. The demand for coal for steam raising had been comparatively insignificant and energy had mainly been concentrated on mining the bituminous and semi-anthracite coals to meet the needs of the industrialists and of the coastal shippers. Foreign shipments represented a minute element in the Welsh coal trade and little had been done to exploit the outstanding asset of the coalfield—its excellent deposits of steam coal. Yet in 1838 one observer, at least, found the future hopeful. He commented on 'the inadequate nature of the coal-winnings in this Basin, consequent on lack of capital', contrasting this with 'the superior facilities possessed by the ports of the other important Coal Districts, in accommodation for vessels of the largest class ... the grand scale in which their Collieries are conducted ... the force of their enormous capital'. But,

[1] *Report of Royal Commission on Coal Supplies, P.P.* 1871 (435), xviii, vol. i, pp. 9–10.

THE EARLY 1840's

he continued, 'there can, in fact, be no question that the district of South Wales is destined, and that at no very distant period, to become the chief seat not only of the coal trade of this kingdom, but also of all those manufactures in which large quantities of coal are consumed, and particularly of metals'.[1] This was written before any railway serving the coalfield had been constructed and when Llanelly was still the sole port with a proper dock. The faith shown in the potentialities of the region for the coal trade was to be justified when transport and dock facilities were improved there, when steam slowly ousted sail and new markets opened up overseas, and when it became clear that the coal-owners in South Wales had the enterprise to seize the new opportunities that were opening out before them.

[1] NLW MS. 6527 F (a newspaper cutting).

II

THE MARKETS OF THE COALFIELD

THE outstanding development in the South Wales coal industry in the decades after 1840 was the growth in the shipments of coal, particularly of steam coal to meet the overseas demand. By 1874 the production of coal in South Wales and Monmouthshire had risen to nearly 16½ million tons, an output which was between three and four times greater than that of the early 1840's, showing a rate of increase which diverged little from that for the United Kingdom as a whole. The foreign shipments of coal from South Wales, which had been a mere 63,000 tons in 1840, had by 1874 grown to nearly 4 million tons, thus showing more than a sixty-fold increase during this period. Whereas in 1840 the foreign shipments from South Wales had been an insignificant fraction of local output and less than 4 per cent. of the United Kingdom foreign shipments, in 1874 they accounted for over 24 per cent. of local output and nearly 30 per cent. of the foreign shipments of the United Kingdom. The basic cause underlying these changes was the growth of steam shipping; the steam tonnage entered at ports in the United Kingdom had been 0·4 million tons in 1840 and was 7·4 million tons in 1870.[1] Even though the tonnage entering the ports under sail in 1870 still exceeded that of the steamers and even though it was common for steamships still to be partially dependent on sail it is evident that there had been a significant growth in the demand for steam coal. The coals of South Wales proved well adapted to meet the needs of these steamers and it was their demand which accounted not only for the bulk of the foreign

---

[1] D. A. Thomas, 'The Growth and Direction of our Foreign Trade in Coal', *Journal of the Royal Statistical Society*, vol. lxvi (1903), p. 478.

THE MARKETS OF THE COALFIELD 19

shipments of Welsh coal but also for a considerable carriage of coal by rail to Birkenhead and Southampton. The growth of interest in wider markets had been obvious in the 1830's. One of the signs of this was the attempt to extend sales in the greatest domestic market, London, overwhelmingly the preserve of the north of England suppliers. Hitherto the cargoes of Welsh coal sent to London had been mainly isolated shipments, frequently of anthracite, but now there was an effort to establish a regular commerce and to base this largely on the steam-raising qualities of Welsh coal. It has been traditional to grant the main credit for this to a remarkable woman, Lucy Thomas of Waun Wyllt. In 1824 her husband, Robert Thomas, had taken a lease of the coal at Waun Wyllt, near Merthyr, on a yearly tenancy from the Earl of Plymouth.[1] Here he opened a level on the famous Four Feet seam from which he supplied the householders of Merthyr and Cardiff. The enterprise has come, however, to be particularly associated with Lucy Thomas because, after her husband's death, she and her son carried on the business. In 1830 the Cardiff agent for the Waun Wyllt coal, George Insole, shipped a small cargo to London. Although no great profit resulted from this particular venture the coal attracted attention owing to its smokeless quality and steam-raising power. As a result Insole was able to enter into a contract to supply Messrs. Wood and Company, London coal-sellers, with 3,000 tons of Waun Wyllt coal a year after 1831.[2]

It is largely on the basis of this transaction that Lucy Thomas has been dubbed the 'Mother of the Welsh Steam Coal Trade'.[3] It is, however, at least doubtful whether she had taken over the business as early as 1830 because at that time Insole directed letters to Robert Thomas and it was not

---

[1] Merthyr of Senghenydd Deeds, doc. 339.
[2] The references to Insole in this and the following paragraph are based on E. D. Lewis, *The Industrial Development of the Rhondda Valleys to 1910* (unpublished thesis submitted to the University of Wales, 1940). For this thesis Mr. Lewis had access to the Insole accounts and day books.
[3] C. Wilkins, *The South Wales Coal Trade* (Cardiff, 1888), pp. 72-73.

until 1835 that the account with the Glamorganshire Canal was transferred from Robert to Lucy Thomas.[1] Moreover, the financial risk of the first shipment was taken by George Insole which suggests that the initiative in sending it was also his. Wherever the credit lies, however, the significant point is that entry into the London market marked a crucial expansion in the horizon of the Cardiff coal trade. The process once started was cumulative since the use of Welsh coal by the tiny steamers plying the Thames brought it into wider notice. In 1831 Insole bunkered H.M. steamer *St. Pierre* with Merthyr coal and sent a cargo to Malta. A year later, referring to the London market, Insole wrote 'I am sure that if I could have obtained five times the quantity I could have sold every ton there', and, in 1833, that 'much of this Myrther Coal is used by Government Steam Packets at Woolwich and is found to answer extremely well'.

The later predominance of Cardiff in the steam-coal trade has led to the tendency to treat the early stages of the rise of the trade in this region as if they marked the original and outstanding effort to win a market for the steam coals of South Wales. To some extent this is misleading. Cardiff remained a minor source of steam coal until the Aberdare valley began to be opened out during the 1840's. Until 1840 Lucy Thomas's Merthyr coal was almost the only steam coal shipped from Cardiff, where the trade continued to be dominated by the house coals of Walter Coffin from Dinas and Thomas Powell from Gelli-gaer.[2] The really spirited attempts

[1] Merthyr of Senghenydd Deeds, doc. 343. John Nixon's account suggests that Lucy Thomas was not restlessly seeking new markets in 1840. Nixon used to relate that when he first realized the possibilities of Welsh steam coal he approached Lucy Thomas to obtain a supply; he was refused because she could sell all her present output and was afraid that if she extended her production the coal would soon be exhausted. J. E. Vincent, *The Life of John Nixon* (1900), pp. 108–10. Possibly legend gathered easily round the figure of a woman singular enough to operate a coal business.
[2] The Aberdare Coal Company shipped small cargoes of steam coal to London from the end of 1837. Lucy Thomas had moved from the Waun Wyllt level in the early thirties when the yearly tenancy was terminated and had leased the neighbouring Graig property.

to expand the market before 1840 came not so much from Cardiff but from the coal proprietors around Swansea and Llanelly. In 1824, six years before the first cargo of Merthyr coal had been dispatched, the Llangennech Company, for example, had entered the London steam-coal market.[1] In 1832, when 38,644 tons were sent from Wales to London, the three chief supplies from the western sector of the coalfield—Llangennech, Graigola, and Warde's Llanelly coals—between them accounted for 20,585 tons, while only 3,760 tons were sent from Merthyr.[2] These supplies from the west, too, were not simply an extension of the old trade in anthracite, for which a special demand existed, but consisted of semi-anthracite dry-steam coals.

The merits of Cardiff steam coals were only slowly realized and the shipments from Swansea and Llanelly continued to predominate for over a decade. Swansea shippers possessed an advantage because the coal trade had been long established at that port and contacts had already been made with the London dealers through the small sales of anthracite. Moreover, the transport facilities in the east of the coalfield were still insufficient to counterbalance the seaboard location of the coals in the west, while the regular traffic in copper ore between Cornwall and the ports of Neath, Swansea, and Llanelly made freights cheaper to obtain there at a time when the freight charge probably mainly determined the ability of Welsh coal to compete in the London market.[3]

Even if the ports of west Wales had advantages compared with Cardiff and Newport it still needed enterprise to push sales in the London market in the face of the supplies from

[1] *MJ*, 20 Feb. 1841.
[2] *Select Committee on Coals (Metropolis), P.P*, 1853 (916), xxii, app. ii. In 1840 out of a total of 60,069 tons from Wales, 9,771 tons came from Merthyr and 1,557 tons from Aberdare. The possible deficiencies of these official figures are not sufficiently great to invalidate the general argument.
[3] NLW Nevill MSS. Letter of R. J. Nevill to Samuel Rhode, 18 Dec. 1832. Nevill pointed out that it was impossible to get ships to carry coal to London at a freight of 11s. 6d. a ton and that the state of the coal market at this time made it imprudent to offer a higher rate.

Newcastle. The activities of R. J. Nevill provide a good illustration of this.[1] As the managing partner of the Llanelly Copper Works, Nevill's prime interest lay in the copper industry, but the dependence of this on local fuel supplies meant that he was also closely connected with the coal industry. In 1818 he became manager of General Warde's collieries near Llanelly and in 1829, in liquidation of a debt of nearly £30,000 owed him by Warde, he assumed ownership of these collieries.[2] Three years earlier he had gained control of the neighbouring collieries of Alexander Raby for a similar reason.[3]

The bulk of the output of these collieries, which Nevill held for a few years quite separate from his copper interests, continued to be sold to the copper works and in the customary markets of Cornwall and Ireland, but the colliery letter books also show that special attention was devoted to the development of new outlets. Thus for the first half of 1832 his London agent, Samuel Rhode, was paid commission at the rate of $2\frac{1}{4}d.$ a ton on the sale of 4,334 tons in the London market and, for the full year of 1834, on the sale of 14,189 tons.[4] That these

---

[1] Suitable records do not exist for the Llangennech Company, a partnership of London merchants, which was the largest single Welsh supplier of steam coal to the London market for the twenty years before 1846.

[2] Nevill MSS. Deeds 748, 817, 821.

[3] Raby was one of the outstanding pioneers of the industrial development of the Llanelly area. Starting in the last quarter of the eighteenth century he had not only opened collieries, built tramroads, and provided harbour facilities but also had made an unsuccessful attempt to establish ironworks. For these and other purposes he used the £175,000 realized by the sale of his estates at Cobham Park, Surrey.

[4] Nevill MSS. 8. 5 Nov. 1832, 18 Sept. 1834, and 17 Feb. 1835. According to the *Report of the Select Committee on Coals* (*Metropolis*), 1853, only 9,085 tons of 'Warde's Llanelly' and of 'Nevill's Llanelly' were sold in London in 1834. These were the two main types of coal Nevill sent. The difference between these figures and those of the Letter Books can hardly be accounted for by coals under the headings 'Stone' and 'Welsh' in the 1853 Report as Nevill did not work anthracite and the quantities of 'Welsh' are small. Possibly Rhode drew commission on coal sold outside the actual London market—perhaps to the government steam packets—and possibly some coal escaped official record if the payment of toll on it was evaded. (Both sources agree on the main points: that Nevill coals were selling in the London market, and that the quantities so supplied were increasing in the early thirties.)

sales were regarded as a novel venture is indicated by the special commercial arrangements made for them. The actual sale was conducted through Rhode and a London factor, William Metcalfe, except when an occasional direct order was received, but all the risks of loss, arising possibly from high freights or from a low final selling price, were borne by Nevill.[1] For his more customary sales Nevill did not bear these risks, his normal practice being to sell his coal f.o.b. at Llanelly in response to definite orders received.

Nevill was also prominent in the effort to establish yet another market for Welsh coal by supplying it to the government naval steam packets. Here again much of the credit for winning this market tends to be given to the Cardiff owners and shippers but there is much to suggest that they were largely consolidating and extending a position already substantially gained by their counterparts in the west. In this market, also, Nevill adopted the same commercial procedure that he employed for his London sales, his agent being authorized to submit tenders to the Navy Board at prices that included delivery at destination.[2]

The anxiety of Nevill to succeed with his government contracts is illustrated by one he obtained early in 1833 to supply 500 tons of coal for the West Indies.[3] This cargo involved special hazards because Llanelly harbour could not accommodate vessels of the size employed in the West Indian trade. The coal had to be loaded into small ships, taken to Bristol, and there trans-shipped into a larger vessel. This increased the risks of the transaction since careless handling would create a

---

[1] Ibid., 4 May 1833, 17 Feb. 1834. A letter to Rhode dated 1 July 1833 referred to a direct order. 'Pray mention this circumstance to Mr. Metcalfe it being our decided wish that all Warde's Llanelly coal for the London market should pass through his hands, but of course we cannot refuse to execute a positive order as in the present case.'

[2] Ibid., 18 Dec. 1832. Rhode is instructed to submit a tender for 'Nevill's Llangennech' at 29s. a ton delivered at Gibraltar and 34s. a ton delivered at Malta. The name 'Nevill's Llangennech' was doubtless given to the coal because the Admiralty advertisement invited tenders for Llangennech coals, which were already established in the market.

[3] Ibid., 2, 7 Feb. 1833.

great deal of small coal which the terms of the contract debarred from inclusion in the final shipment. Nevill wrote to the Bristol shippers emphasizing the need to avoid making small coal, stating that he was sending a special representative to supervise the trans-shipment and concluding with an expression of his desire that the final cargo should be good 'more particularly as this is I believe the first cargo that has been sent from this port to Barbados'.

Nevill was quick to exploit the prestige value that the government contracts conferred on his coal. 'I shall be happy', he wrote to a potential customer, 'to supply the Steamer you refer to with Coals of a Quality equal if not superior to any shipped for that purpose, as a proof of which I need only state that I am at present supplying (I believe exclusively) the Government Steamers from the Plymouth Dockyard.'[1] Also as the Llanelly coals became more established as a fuel for the naval steam packets Nevill tended to modify his method of dealing with government contracts. More and more he refrained from tendering direct, preferring to let London merchants undertake the freight risks involved and to restrict his own share to the provision of the coal at an agreed price, a policy feasible only when he was tolerably certain that these merchants would in fact turn to him for supplies. In May 1833 his nephew informed a correspondent that a recent naval contract had been 'taken by Robert Johnstone of Horse Shoe Wharf, London, who purchases the Coals off us at a price free on board here'.[2] A year later, referring to contracts for which he had himself tendered, Nevill wrote 'I do not at all regret to find . . . that Mr. Johnstone has taken the Deptford and Gosport contracts for my only object is the sale of my coal'.[3] His attitude is crystallized in two letters he wrote to Rhode. One announced his decision to tender for a government contract for coals for Malta because he feared that the contract might otherwise 'fall to a firm—like Jackson's—who will order the coal' from Swansea. But a week later he had

[1] Nevill MSS. 8. 18 Apr. 1833.   [2] Ibid., 21 May 1833.   [3] Ibid., 26 Apr. 1834.

decided not to tender because he did 'not want to compete with Mr. Johstone and Mr. Gillespie on any Government contracts' and he was sure that the other coals concerned—Graigola and Bryndewi—would not quote below his price of 8s. a ton.[1] Nevill's readiness to withdraw from making direct tenders, leaving the middlemen to bear the freight risks, was no doubt prompted by the knowledge of the advantages a London merchant possessed for securing vessels at the right time and freight, particularly when the contract involved overseas delivery.

Nevill's drive to dispose of his steam coal was not confined solely to these two markets. When he noticed an advertisement in a Scottish newspaper for coal for India he wrote to Rhode, asking him to inquire about the possibilities of this outlet. He urged Robert Johnstone, the London shipper, to send a trial cargo of Llanelly coals to Algiers as part of his contract with the French government. He persuaded a Ramsgate firm to take a cargo, confident that they would find it superior to the north of England coals they had previously used; and an advertisement for coals for French steam packets limited to north of England tenders spurred him to press on Rhode 'the propriety of seeing Mon. Andell, as surely the fact of our Government using Welsh Coals exclusively for Steamers would induce the French at all events to give them a trial'.[2]

No doubt other owners in the western part of the coalfield were showing similar enterprise as it was consistently from Swansea, Neath, and the Llangennech Company at Llanelly that Nevill expected to meet his main Welsh competition. The Nevill papers mention Cardiff only once in connexion with steam coals and Newport receives similar scant notice.[3]

[1] Ibid., 10, 18 Feb. 1834. In his second letter he asked Rhode to tell Johnstone and Gillespie of his decision not to compete with them, and to add a gentle reminder to these merchants that he could cut out the middlemen if they did not buy from him.
[2] Ibid., 24 June, 5 Oct. 1833, 3 May, 21 July 1834.
[3] Ibid., 24 Dec. 1834. Nevill recognized that Cardiff coals may be quoted lower 'but they are not as large or as durable nor do they emit so strong a heat'.

Competitors from Cardiff and Newport could be ignored, not because they were relatively remote compared with the Llangennech Company on Nevill's own doorstep and the other rivals in Neath and Swansea, but because they were as yet playing little part in the steam-coal markets. A London merchant told a Parliamentary Committee in 1837, for example, that while Welsh steam coal had come to be considered superior to north of England coal, that from Cardiff and Newport was not in such high repute as 'we do not find it answers for steam purposes'.[1] The advertisements inviting tenders for the naval steam packet contracts often specified only Bryndewi (Neath), Graigola (Swansea), and Llanelly coals. Moreover, the overseas shipments of coal from Swansea and Llanelly in 1840 were 52,000 tons compared with the 7,000 tons from Newport and 4,000 tons from Cardiff.

This pre-eminence of the western ports in the overseas shipment of coal, however, proved to be short-lived. The competitive possibilities of Cardiff and, to a lesser extent, of Newport, were transformed by the opening of the Bute West Dock in 1839, of the Taff Vale Railway in 1841 and of the smaller Newport Dock in 1842. These undertakings, particularly because they were not immediately paralleled by similar developments at Swansea and Neath, counteracted the advantages these western ports had hitherto enjoyed. The construction of the railway gave the coal in the hinterland of Cardiff comparatively easy access to the sea. The influence of improved docking facilities acted on another key factor in the coal trade—the level of shipping freights. The Bute Docks enabled vessels at Cardiff to be loaded afloat instead of— as at Swansea until 1852—their being forced to lie on the mud at low tide, with consequent hazards and delays. As foreign trade grew, and with it the size of vessels employed, this element increased in importance. Events at Llanelly, how-

[1] Evidence of George Jackson. *Select Committee on Coal Trade (Port of London) Bill*, P.P. 1838 (475), xv.

ever, where, despite the dock and railway, trade stagnated after 1840, suggest that transport considerations alone were not decisive. While Llanelly served a region where much of the coal was too anthracitic to be in great demand, Cardiff and Newport served an area which contained rich deposits of steam coal of the highest quality. As consumers came to realize this, so the demand grew, stimulating a new activity in both the valleys and the ports of the eastern sector of the coalfield. It was an age when the demand for steam coal was assuming new proportions. Already the steamer was competing successfully in the river and coastal services. The scale of the demand this occasioned at London alone is suggested by a report, in 1842, that there were '15 steam vessels working daily between Gravesend and London, the same number to Woolwich, 20 to Greenwich, numerous small steamers... [and]... 8 steam vessels constantly going up and down the river on their way to and from Dover, Ramsgate, Margate, Herne Bay, Southend and Sheerness. The General Steam Navigation Company muster 49 first class steamers... whose consumption of coal exceeds in value £50,000 per annum.'[1]

Steamships were as yet ill-fitted to compete widely in the carriage of merchandise overseas; their capital costs of construction per ton were higher than those of sailing-ships and their carrying capacity was limited by the inefficiency of their engines. When the Cunarder *Britannia* left Liverpool in 1840, for example, 640 tons out of her total carrying capacity of 865 tons were allotted to her coal. But steam could be used by shipping companies to carry passengers and high-class freight over the distant seas and this traffic was stimulated by mail subsidies as the government tended to withdraw from the direct carriage of mails in favour of receiving tenders from those companies to perform this service. In 1837 the firm that was later to become the Peninsular and Oriental Line contracted to provide a monthly service to Gibraltar. Later, after its contracts had been extended to Alexandria, Calcutta,

[1] *Cambrian*, 28 May 1842.

and Hong Kong, this company received an annual subsidy of £210,000.[1] The Cunard Line was founded on a similar basis to serve the Atlantic crossing while the Royal Mail Steam Packet Company provided a service to the West Indies and Havana. This latter company, which started its service in January 1842, had already spent £105,000 on coal by the end of August in the same year.[2]

As the opportunities for trade in coal broadened so did the predominance of the western ports fade. To some extent the new users still turned to the old sources. Of the eight types of Welsh coal that were supplied under Admiralty contracts for steam vessels between 1840 and 1844, for example, five were drawn from the western sector of the coalfield.[3] In 1843 the *Railway Magazine*, reporting on Llangennech coal, stated that 'the Royal Mail Steam Company have . . . used it in some of their vessels with much success; and why they have not employed it more largely seems to call for some explanation, particularly as the Peninsular and Orient Company and the Pacific Steam Company have found its employment advantageous'.[4] Two years later the Governor of the English Copper Company, which worked the coal at Cwmavon, could remark 'that the General Steam Navigation Company, having made a trial of our coal against some of the best north country coal, have found ours the better for their purpose of generating steam by 15 to 20 per cent.'.[5] But the steamships were also being supplied with coal from the valleys to the east. The *Great Western*, for example, after experiments had been tried with other coals, drew its supplies solely from Samuel Homfray of the Tredegar Coal Company, while a valuable contract to supply coal to the Royal Mail Steam Packet

---

[1] G. R. Porter, *The Progress of the Nation* (1912 edn.), p. 540. The East India Company repaid £70,000 of this subsidy to the government.

[2] *MJ*, 24 Sept. 1842. Report of first meeting of the Company. The stock of coal in hand was worth £30,000.

[3] *Return of Coal Supplied to H.M. Naval Establishments*, P.P. 1845 (600), xxx.

[4] Quoted in *MJ*, 16 Sept. 1843.   [5] Ibid., 19 Apr. 1845.

THE MARKETS OF THE COALFIELD 29

Company went to John Russell and Company, owners of Risca colliery, who were also supplying the Peninsular and Oriental Company. The East India Company too, which at one time had made some use of Llangennech coal, by 1849 included only one 'Welsh' variety—Risca Black Vein—in its list of acceptable coals.[1] The Admiralty, like the shipping companies, was recognizing the merits of the coal from the east of the coalfield, 'Powell's Duffryn', 'Tredegar', and 'Porthmawr Rock Vein' coals being included in the varieties of coal for which tenders were invited.[2]

The quality of the coal from the eastern part of the coalfield was also helping to increase its sale in the London market. Matthew Wayne related how, when the Aberdare Coal Company began, the difficulty had not been winning the coal but knowing where to find a market for it. However the company sent 'a barrelful to Mr. Lockett who, upon trying its qualities, highly approved of it and sent them an order for 20,000 tons'.[3] R. J. Blewitt, who shipped two or three cargoes to London soon after he had opened his colliery at Cwmbrân, hoped to gain a ready sale for his coal by issuing instructions that it should be advertised in the metropolitan papers as being similar to Tredegar coal in quality.[4] Perhaps the best illustration of how the quality of Welsh coal helped sales is provided by the details of an action brought against the London, Westminster and Vauxhall Steam Boat Company in 1846 by Williams, the sole agent for the sale of Thomas Powell's Duffryn coal in London. The company had been using Duffryn coal for some years and was buying £300 worth a week at a price of 23s. 6d. a ton when, after two coal merchants had joined its board, it cancelled the contract. Using the

---

[1] *Merlin*, 13 Feb. 1841, 1 Oct. 1842; *MJ*, 6 Jan. 1849.
[2] *MG*, 23 Mar. 1844, 21 Mar. 1845. The Admiralty lists also included 'Bettws Merthyr', mined in the Porthcawl district. 'Merthyr', as a description of coal, was now becoming an open sesame to markets just as 'Llangennech' had been a decade earlier.
[3] *MG*, 7 Aug. 1846. Wayne was speaking at a dinner held to celebrate the opening of the Aberdare railway and was referring to the events of 1837.
[4] *Merlin*, 20 Feb. 1841.

substituted coal each boat performed one journey a day less, involving the company in a loss of £120 a day and leading it to revert to the use of Duffryn coal. Williams, however, now charged the company £2 per ton and, arguing before the court that 'Duffryn' was scarce and in high demand, won the case that arose over the price difference.[1]

Supplementing the demand from these sources was that arising from similar requirements overseas. The effectiveness of this overseas demand was increased after 1834 when the export duty was virtually abolished for coal carried in British ships and the duty on coal carried in foreign ships was reduced to 4*s*. per ton. A further stimulus, particularly favourable to Welsh trade, was the reduction, in 1837, of French import duties on coal sent to ports lying between the Seine and Loire.[2] In 1842 there was a temporary set-back when Peel—as a revenue measure to counter his general reductions—revived the export duty of 2*s*. per ton on coal carried in British ships. The reaction to this showed the new Welsh interest in the coal export trade. At Swansea—still the main centre of the overseas trade of the coalfield—meetings of protest were held and a letter was sent to the Prime Minister calling on him to withdraw the duty. A committee was set up to communicate with coal exporters in ports in other parts of Wales and in the north, and a petition against the tax was addressed to Parliament.[3] 'It is to be regretted', wrote the *Mining Journal*, 'that an impost has been fixed which is partial in its application, for it must be remembered that it applies only to certain districts and does not affect the inland collieries —indeed, it may be said to be confined to the North and to Swansea.'[4] In 1845 this duty was repealed and the only remaining export duty was that of 4*s*. a ton on coal shipped in the vessels of countries that did not have a reciprocal treaty with Great Britain. In 1850 this was also abandoned.

Despite the importance of the various changes in duties,

[1] *MJ*, 5 Dec. 1846.
[2] *Cambrian*, 9 Dec. 1837.
[3] Ibid., 26 Mar., 16 Apr. 1842.
[4] *MJ*, 18 June 1842.

THE MARKETS OF THE COALFIELD

however, the most significant development in the sphere of overseas shipments was the effort of John Nixon to establish a trade in steam coal between Cardiff and France. Small quantities of anthracite had for long found their way across the channel but, if the experience of Nevill may be regarded as typical, the trade in steam coal had made little headway before 1840. Nixon, in 1860, gave his own account of his effort and, while the lapse of twenty years had perhaps added embellishment of detail to his story, there seems no reason to doubt its essential truth. When on a London steamer in 1840, he said, 'I saw stokers throw continuously coal into the furnace, and when I looked at the funnel I saw no smoke. This was a wonder to me.' Making inquiries, when his interest was still further aroused after he had been permitted to stoke the furnace himself, he found that the coal came from Merthyr, being supplied by Wood, a London coal merchant, who shipped about 150 tons a week from Cardiff, mainly for use on the Thames steamers. Nixon then went to Wales, where he found Thomas Powell sinking the 'Old Duffryn' pit.

'I went to Mr. Powell, and told him that if he wanted a market for his coal at Duffryn, I was willing to enter into some arrangements with him so as to introduce his coal into France, and that I was engaged in the trade of that country. After a great deal of negotiation we agreed that he should pay me so much per ton on all the coal exported to France, that he should at first give the coal, and pay the freight, and that I should go over there and give it away. I knew that was the only way to introduce it into that country.'

Nixon took the first cargo to Nantes, being given the coal only on the condition that he should show the recipients how to use it. First he induced the sugar-refiners, for whose work a constant steam pressure was essential, to use Welsh in preference to Newcastle coal and it was found that there was a considerable economy in labour as less time need be spent in cleaning the boilers. With more difficulty he then persuaded the owners of the French river steamers to give Welsh coal a trial and succeeded in getting a 'contract to supply them with 3,000 tons at an advance of 2s. 6d. on Newcastle coal'.[1] Finally Nixon was also successful in obtaining orders for Welsh coal from the French government in preference to that of Newcastle.

The influence of these developments on the South Wales coal trade by 1851 is shown in the following tables.

Coal Shipments (tons)

	Coastwise 1840	Coastwise 1851	Exported 1840	Exported 1851
Cardiff	162,283	501,002	3,826	249,001
Newport	482,398	451,491	7,256	151,668
Swansea	460,201	352,247	33,089	41,502
Llanelly	192,769	219,460	19,275	9,785
Milford	76,768	49,573	411	269
	1,374,419	1,573,773	63,857	452,225

(These figures are from the coal shipment tables in *P.P.* 1841 (259), xxvi, and 1852–3 (584), xcix. The figures include cinders and culm, and the Swansea shipments include those from Neath.)

The Metropolitan Market for Welsh Coals (tons)

	1840	1851
Total Welsh coal and culm sent to London	61,884	102,925
Graigola	5,491	—
Llangennech	17,692	7,616
Nevill's Llanelly	960	—
Merthyr	9,771	35,518
Aberdare	—	—
Powell Duffryn	—	10,830
Nixon's	—	11,929

(These figures are given in the report of the *Select Committee on Coals (Metropolis)*, 1853. 1851 is exceptional in that there were no shipments of Graigola coal; in other years a few hundred tons were still sent to London. In 1840 1,552 tons of 'Aberdare' coal were sent to London.)

[1] *MG*, 12 May 1860. Nixon's speech at the opening of Navigation colliery. Nixon was a Durham man who had been manager of a colliery and ironworks in France.

From these figures it is clear that the coastwise trade, although growing comparatively slowly, still overshadowed the export market in 1851. The amount of coal exported had, however, shown a striking growth, which was accounted for wholly by the increase in shipments from Cardiff and Newport. Above all it was Cardiff, now the leading Welsh port for both coastwise and overseas shipments, that had gained most from the developments of the 1840's.

As the markets for steam coal steadily grew there inevitably developed a keen sense of rivalry between the north country and the South Wales suppliers. In 1840, when an attempt had been made to form an association in London to encourage and protect the Welsh coal trade, one of the immediate objects had been to establish 'an effectual mode of testing the Coals of the Principality, in comparison with the North Country and other Coals imported into London'.[1] The results of such tests would provide a guide to consumers, freeing them from the liability to loss through experimental purchases, and would benefit producers by enabling them to overcome 'the prejudice which always prevails in opposing a new description of Coal, particularly if the slightest modification of flue or draft be a desideratum'. After an announcement, a fortnight later, that ' "The Cambrian Coal Owners Society"—A Metropolitan Association of Welsh Coal Owners' was in process of formation, this body is lost sight of, but the idea of official tests remained.

For users to hold private trials of competing coals was indeed a common practice. The Blackwall Railway, for example, which used stationary engines and an endless rope for the traction of the trains, had, in 1841, tried Llangennech coal 'for one whole day, in competition with a north country coal of high repute on a preceding day'. The Welsh coal, it was reported, showed a saving of over 30 per cent.[2] But tests of this nature usually received little publicity nor

[1] *Cambrian*, 31 Oct., 14 Nov. 1840.   [2] *MJ*, 20 Feb. 1841.

were their results regarded as authoritative. The first trials of real importance were those instituted by the Admiralty from the mid-forties onwards. Intended to serve as a guide to the Admiralty, itself becoming a more substantial customer and one involving no risk of bad debts, these tests acquired a significance which was hardly at first intended. 'From the form and ceremony, however, attendant upon the experiments, from the publication of details under the authority of Parliament, and from the importance attached to the results by the competing parties, the conclusions educed are equivalent to certificates of merit.'[1] Instead of holding their own trials the steamship companies and a host of home and foreign buyers now came to be guided, when making their purchases, by the results of those held by the Admiralty and, consequently, the inclusion of a coal in the 'Admiralty Lists' proved of inestimable value in extending its sales. The course of this rivalry over the privilege of supplying coal to the Royal Navy, a rivalry confined almost solely to the suppliers from Wales and from the north of England, merits some description, therefore, owing to its wide implications.

In 1845 Joseph Hume, M.P., wrote to the Lords of the Admiralty urging that 'without an accurate knowledge of the power of the coals to be used, the country may be paying the highest price for an inferior article, and depending on the power of the fuel the public service may suffer disappointment at a moment when the greatest interests of the country may be at stake'. The Admiralty, which had just bought the *Birkenhead*—its first iron steamship—responded by financing the tests which were carried out by Sir Henry de la Bèche and Dr. Lyon Playfair.

The results of these trials were published in three reports.[2] Tests were made on 98 varieties of coal, 37 samples being chosen from Wales owing to the scope for experiment offered

---

[1] *CG*, 12 Mar. 1864.
[2] *Reports on the Coals suited for the Steam Navy*, P.P. 1847–8 (915), xxviii; 1849 (1086), xxxii; 1851 (1345), xxxiii.

THE MARKETS OF THE COALFIELD

by the diversity of coals there, and 17 samples being chosen from Newcastle. As the samples were selected to secure a comprehensive test and included coals too bituminous or anthracitic for steam purposes the significant comparison is one between individual coals rather than between district averages. The following table, compiled from the reports, compares the five best coals—in terms of evaporative power—from both South Wales and the north of England.

Variety of coal	Evaporative power, or no. of lb. of water evaporated from 212 degrees by 1 lb. of coal	Rate of evaporation, or no. of lb. evaporated per hour	Weight in lb. of 1 cu. ft. of coal as used for fuel
Welsh			
Aberaman Merthyr	10·75	—	48·9
Ebbw Vale	10·21	460·22	48·9
Thomas's Merthyr	10·16	520·8	53·0
Duffryn	10·14	409·32	53·22
Nixon's Merthyr	9·96	511·4	51·7
Newcastle			
Willington	9·95	—	53·2
Andrews House Tanfield	9·39	351·2	53·1
Bowden Close	9·38	—	50·6
Haswell Wallsend	8·87	411·66	47·4
Newcastle Hartley	8·23	308·0	50·5

The suitability of Welsh coals for naval purposes was indicated, however, not only by these figures but also by the observations that were made on each type of coal. These showed that—apart from Ebbw Vale coal, which required more stoking and gave off rather more smoke—the best Welsh coals lit easily, blew steam up rapidly, produced a fine, clear fire with little clinker, and gave off very little smoke. The best Newcastle coals, on the other hand, all caked excessively, choking the draught and demanding constant attention, and gave off a dense black smoke. In face of this, the chief drawbacks of the Welsh coal—its friability and tendency to make considerable ash—did not seem enough to outweigh its merits.

As a result of these trials the reputation which Welsh steam coals had been slowly acquiring was dramatically enhanced and Admiralty orders were diverted to Welsh suppliers. During the Crimean War, when the Rhymney Railway Bill was being discussed in committee, Sir James Graham, First Lord of the Admiralty, stated that the supply of Cardiff steam coal was unequal to the naval demand and that any railway which would afford a new supply was an object of national importance.[1] In April 1856, on the occasion of a naval review, it could be reported that 'to obviate the chances of collision amongst such an immense gathering of ships, an Admiralty order has been issued directing the fleet to provide themselves with Welsh coals for the occasion; and all other ships that may be present are to adopt the same precaution. Any vessel making a smoke will be requested to withdraw.'[2]

The coal-owners of the north of England, hardly likely to accept the results of the Bèche–Playfair trials as conclusive, made unremitting efforts over a period of twenty years to stem the tide of orders flowing to South Wales. In this struggle the arts of parliamentary lobbying and press propaganda supplemented the attempts of deputations to the Lords of the Admiralty to secure fresh trials.

First the northern coal-owners had to find a solution to the greatest drawback of their coals—the amount of smoke they gave off during combustion. A prize of £500 was offered for the best method of preventing smoke when north country coal was used in marine engine boilers, and this was awarded to a Mr. Williams of Liverpool.[3] Using this new apparatus the northern coal-owners then, with two naval observers present, held their own trials and the results achieved were so favourable to northern coal that part of the naval contracts was diverted to the north. A challenge was issued by the Welsh owners that a practical test should be held in a transAtlantic steamer, one round trip between Liverpool and New

[1] *MG*, 2 June 1854.   [2] Ibid., 19 Apr. 1856.
[3] Address by Mr. Sherley, Cardiff Chamber of Commerce, 20 July 1870. CCL 5. 96.

York to be undertaken with Welsh coal and one with north country coal.[1] This the northern interest could afford to ignore, particularly as, in October 1858, an official report by a committee of officers confirmed the suitability of northern coals for naval use. This report brought forth a forceful letter to *The Times* from John Nixon and Thomas Powell, which asserted that the Newcastle tests had been impractical because 'the boilers and furnaces were peculiarly adapted for the consumption without smoke of the North Country coal, but of a construction not similar to any now in use in the Royal or mercantile steam navies'. Under practical conditions Welsh coal was superior, they argued, the purchases of the steamship companies being adequate proof of this.[2] Application was made to the Admiralty for new trials to be held and, in the meantime, the Welsh owners held their own tests at Cardiff which, not surprisingly, reversed the verdict of those held at Newcastle. When the official reports on these trials were published, in March 1859, no verdict was expressed in favour of either side, the superior evaporative power of Welsh coals being offset by the greater rapidity of combustion of those of Newcastle.[3] The Welsh owners remained dissatisfied, even though they were supplying 188,507 tons out of the 249,527 tons bought by the Admiralty in 1859.[4]

Further tests were held in 1860, this time in the more impartial environment of the naval dockyards, with results which were decisively in favour of Welsh coal. Even the *Newcastle Chronicle* was constrained to comment that 'the general result of these experiments, we regret to say, is favourable to the Welsh steam coals, and adverse to our Newcastle coals'.[5] Accordingly, when the Northumberland coal-owners memorialized the Lords of the Admiralty in 1863, they admitted the superiority of Welsh coal to their own when used alone but asked that tests should be made

[1] *MG*, 24 Apr. 1858.   [2] Quoted in *MG*, 30 Oct. 1858.
[3] *Reports on Evaporative Power and Economic Power of Hartley Coal and Properties of Welsh Steam Coal*, P.P. 1859 (116, sess. 1), xxv.
[4] *MG*, 16 June 1860.   [5] Quoted in *MG*, 22 Sept. 1860.

with a mixture of both coals. They cited the practice of the Peninsular and Oriental Company, which used a mixture of the two coals on occasions and, while using Welsh coal in the Mediterranean, did not use it in its Far Eastern stations.[1] They attacked the exclusive use of Welsh coal at its weakest point, its friability, which led to the creation of considerable quantities of small coal in transit, particularly to overseas stations. This small could be effectively utilized if combined with the better binding coals of the North and, provided the furnaces were modified to suit the northern coal, no great volume of smoke would be emitted. The north country coal-owners obtained their trials and, in part, a confirmation of their claims when the official report of the tests was published in March 1864. A mixture of Welsh and north of England coals, in equal proportions it was reported, 'would be attended with desirable results' in utilizing Welsh small and in producing more rapid evaporation. The Newcastle coal-owners had this report translated into several languages and gave it world-wide circulation.[2]

As a result of this report all ships of the fleet were ordered to conduct practical trials by burning a mixture containing one-third to one-half north country coals. In May 1864 a strong deputation of Welsh owners was assured by the Lords of the Admiralty that the dockyard tests had been mere preliminaries and that no final decision would be taken until the reports of these sea tests were received.[3] This met the claim,

[1] *MG*, 19 June 1863.
[2] *Reports on Trials of Welsh and North Country Steam Coal for use of Navy*, *P.P.* 1860 (485), xlii; 1864 (80–81), xxxvii. Before the official reports of 1864 were published the Welsh owners circulated the report of their observer, Tomlinson, claiming that the trials had shown Welsh coal to be superior to any mixture, and Thomas Powell, junior, wrote to *The Times* pointing out that the Nord Deutscher Lloyd Line of Bremen had ordered Welsh coal to be sent to Newcastle for two steamers although Newcastle coal was available at half the price. The northern reply was to wonder why Welsh owners appeared unwilling to wait for the official report and to point out that the second German liner had used Hartley coal, owing to the late arrival of Powell's second consignment, with a distinct improvement in performance. *CG*, 2, 30 Jan. 1864. Clearly the coal-owners attached great importance to these trials.
[3] *Hansard*, 3rd series, vol. 175, 6 May 1864.

made by the Welsh interest from time to time, that the artificial conditions of dockyard tests—short periods of stoking with small quantities of coal by specially selected stokers—diverged so greatly from actual voyage conditions as to impair the value of such tests. Certainly, while the pattern of deputations and dockyard trials still recurred after 1864, the outcome of the rivalry depended less on these than it did on the results of practical experience at sea.

In 1867, on the basis of reports from officers at foreign stations and particularly after the capture of a slaver off the coast of Africa had been attributed to the use of smokeless coal, orders were issued that the admixture with bituminous coals should be discontinued and that Welsh coal alone should be used in Her Majesty's ships. Pressure from the north of England led, in 1869, to a new order that a mixture containing a proportion of one-third north country coal should be used in all naval vessels, with the exception of those in the China and Africa stations. It also led to the carrying out of fresh trials.[1] The tests in Her Majesty's steamers *Urgent* and *Lucifer* at Portsmouth dockyard were held under terms of reference which largely prejudged the issue in favour of mixed coals, but once again the reports from officers at sea counteracted the guarded approval of a mixture based on the findings of dockyard tests.[2] The Vice-Admiral commanding the Channel Squadron reported, after an exercise, that 'the smoke produced by the present mixture of north country and Welsh coal, combined with that from guns in action, renders seeing

[1] Ibid., vol. 191, 30 Apr. 1868; vol. 195, 22 Apr. 1869. The mixture became derisively known to its opponents as 'Baxter's mixture', after the Liberal Secretary to the Admiralty who defended it with such fervour on the grounds of economy.
[2] *Results of . . . Trials . . . on Board H.M. Steamers 'Urgent' and 'Lucifer'*, P.P. 1870 (355), xliv. These trials were held to discover 'the best proportions in mixed coal, and the best form of furnaces to be used in the consumption of smoke'. The results showed a small saving when Welsh coal was used alone, if it was fresh-worked and of the best quality, but the advantages of a 50:50 mixture (less ash; the ability to consume the 'small' resulting from the disintegration of Welsh coal in foreign stations) more than compensated for this.

signals, or even ships, impossible'. The comment from the Commander in Chief, Mediterranean Squadron, was equally forceful: 'I consider it my duty to point out to their Lordships that, in case of war, north country coal is totally unfit for Her Majesty's service.' The blunt comment of a third officer, Captain G. O. Willes, was that Welsh coal was superior to a mixture 'in spite of theoretical trials'.[1]

At first the official attitude was that the dockyard trials were conclusive and these complaints were dismissed as being 'unscientific'. As their volume grew, however, it became impossible to write off the practical experience they embodied as being merely uninformed prejudice. In 1872 the government made a partial retreat. It was announced that, as soon as the stocks of north country coal were used up, 'My Lords will, in future, probably make provision for the supply of Welsh Coal only to the Channel Squadron'. In the meantime 'the coal may be stored in the ships in such a manner that some purely Welsh coal may be available for those occasions when . . . you have reason to apprehend any large amount of smoke, and when such an amount of smoke would . . . be attended with special disadvantages'. Similarly practical experience of the use of coals mixed in equal proportions on Indian troopships led the Admiralty to revise their fuelling arrangements to permit a greater use of Welsh coal. It was announced in 1872 that, while the coaling arrangements at Port Said and Bombay would be left unchanged, 'in future, the Indian troopships shall be supplied with Welsh coal on their outward journey from Plymouth and Queenstown, and with coal mixed in the proportions of one-third north country to two-thirds Welsh at Malta'.[2]

[1] *Reports as to the use of North Country Coal in the Navy, together with any remarks thereon, P.P.* 1872 (165), xxxix.
[2] *Reports of the Trials lately conducted in the Indian Troopships, P.P.* 1872 (165), xxxix. An Admiralty engineer had recommended an even more drastic revision in favour of Welsh coal; at Port Said two-thirds Welsh should be used for the outward voyage and all Welsh for the inward voyage. This engineer considered that the trials in *Urgent* and *Lucifer* had shown a greater advantage in using Welsh coal than had been stated in the official report.

THE MARKETS OF THE COALFIELD

The general result of the various trials held between 1846 and 1875 and of practical experience was that where Welsh coal was to be had 'fresh and good' it was superior to north country coal and to any mixture. It had excellent evaporative power, required little stoking, gave less smoke, and occupied less space per ton. In distant stations, on the other hand, the use of a mixture enabled Welsh small to be burned and counteracted the undoubted deterioration of Welsh coal over time and in transit. Even when a mixture was used, however, orders were not necessarily lost to the South Wales coalfield because, while the bituminous coals were usually supplied from Newcastle, there was a growing tendency for the Monmouthshire coal-owners to gain a share in this trade.

In 1840 the north-east had been pre-eminent in the coal export trade, accounting for 72 per cent. of all coal shipped overseas from the United Kingdom in that year. By 1870 the share of the north-east had fallen to 49·6 per cent. principally because of the encroachment of the South Wales trade, which then accounted for 31·2 per cent. of the country's coal exports.[1] Both areas derived advantage from the growth in demand associated with the development of steamships, and of the coaling stations established to increase their range and cargo-carrying capacity. Both, too, benefited from the stimulus of the growing demand from railways, industries, and increasing populations. Yet the greater gain of South Wales was partly the result of its excellent steam-coal resources and of the enormous prestige conferred by its success in the rivalry for winning Admiralty approval. Partly, too, it was the result of the locational advantage South Wales enjoyed for supplying many of the world's markets. This is illustrated by the table on page 42.

Any preference that was accorded to Welsh coal owing to its quality operated only within a narrow price range. To the final consumer the price of coal, a commodity of low value in

[1] D. A. Thomas, loc. cit., p. 496.

relation to its bulk, depended to a large extent on the level of freight charges. In this respect the Bristol Channel ports, once suitable docking facilities had been provided, were favourably

The Percentage of the United Kingdom Coal Exports to the Various Groups of Overseas Markets from South Wales and the North of England, 1869[1]

	South Wales (%)	North of England (%)	Total U.K. exports (000s of tons)
FRANCE (France, Spain, Portugal, Channel Islands, Azores, Canaries, Madeira)	49·4	43·4	2,562
MEDITERRANEAN (Austria, Italy, Greece, Turkey, Malta, &c.)	50·7	39·2	1,305
BALTIC AND NORTH SEA PORTS (Denmark, Norway, Sweden, Russia, Prussia, Germany, Holland, Belgium)	6·2	76·8	3,261
SOUTH AMERICA	63·3	10·2	628
AFRICA (West, East, and North Africa, Ascension, St. Helena)	44·5	37·7	569
NORTH AMERICA (U.S.A., Canada, W. Indies, &c.)	44·5	16·9	691
INDIA AND FAR EAST (India, Ceylon, China, New Zealand, Australia, &c.)	36·1	27·5	706

situated for trade with France (west of Havre), Spain, Portugal, the Mediterranean, Africa, and South America.[2] On the other hand, for trade with the Baltic and North Sea ports the

[1] These figures are compiled from the *Report of the Royal Commission on Coal Supplies*, 1871. In the period 1871–5 the trade of South Wales was affected by acute industrial unrest, rendering the figures for those years less representative.

[2] For some time the British coal trade with France, with which South Wales was particularly concerned, was impeded by the French import duties. These were a serious obstacle to trade both because they were high and because they favoured Belgian land-borne coal at the expense of that brought by sea from Britain. Despite improvements in the 1850's it was not until the treaty of 1860 that the situation was remedied. This not only halved the duty on British coal but also secured an agreement that the French duties on coal brought by land and by sea should be made uniform within four years of the ratification of the treaty. *The Economist*, 18 Feb., 3 Mar. 1860.

THE MARKETS OF THE COALFIELD

north of England enjoyed a locational and freight advantage so decisive as to exclude Welsh coal almost completely from this area. This outlet was important, absorbing 2½ million tons out of the 4¾ million tons of coal exported from the north-east and accounting for its retention of the lead in the coal export trade of the United Kingdom, but it was also the sole area in which the lead of the north remained uncontested. A freight disadvantage also explains the limited success achieved by Welsh coal in the London market before 1875. Although the supplies from South Wales to London increased nearly ten-fold between 1840 and 1874—from 60,069 tons to 587,621 tons—they still formed even at the latter date only a small part of the total London import of nearly 7½ million tons.[1] Probably the circuitous sea route round Land's End tended to restrict the competition of Welsh coal to that part of the London market which needed high-quality steam coal. The completion of the South Wales Railway from Chepstow to Swansea in 1850 eased this position only slightly. This line, like its parent the Great Western Railway, clung to the broad gauge until the early 1870's but nearly all the feeder lines serving the Welsh valleys were narrow gauge. The railway route, besides involving a break of gauge, was also circuitous, Welsh coal being sent by way of Gloucester before the Severn tunnel was built, and the high freights charged by the Great Western Railway proved a further impediment to traffic.[2]

The favourable conditions that faced the Welsh steam-coal producers did not apply to the other broad types of coal that existed in the district—anthracite and bituminous house or coking coal. The demand for anthracite, indeed, showed little tendency to increase during this period. At the beginning

---

[1] R. Hunt, *Mineral Statistics*, 1875; *The Economist*, Commercial History and Review of 1875, 11 Mar. 1876.
[2] The rate for coal from the Aberdare valley to London in 1865 was 10s. 6d. a ton. *CG*, 16 Dec. 1865. E. T. MacDermot, *History of the Great Western Railway* (1927), vol. i, p. 581, states that during the years of the broad gauge one coal train a day sufficed for the eastbound traffic from Swansea to London.

hopes had been high after Crane's success in smelting iron with anthracite and the adoption of this method by other iron firms in the district. On the wave of new interest this aroused, a meeting of landlords and coal-owners held at Swansea in 1839 determined to form an 'Association for extending the use of anthracite coal'. Those present immediately subscribed nearly £1,000 and appointed a committee to further the use of coal for locomotives, marine engines, land engines, and foundry purposes.[1] To advertise the properties of their coal and win a place in the steam-coal market the Association supported a project to run an iron steamer, the *Anthracite*, on the Thames later in 1839. This vessel attracted considerable attention from marine and naval engineers and *The Times* correspondent who travelled on her trial voyage commented favourably on the lack of smoke, the little stoking required, and the compactness of the coal. Anthracite, selling in London at 27*s*. a ton, compared favourably for cost with other fuels.[2]

These hopes that the anthracite field had acquired a new value were destined to remain unrealized. Two foreign observers touring the ironworks of South Wales about 1860 found those in the anthracite area in a far from flourishing state. In the Vale of Neath the Venallt works were in ruins and at Aber-nant only one furnace was in blast out of three. Between Neath and the Swansea valley the two smaller works of Banwen and Onllwyn were often idle. In the Vale of Swansea itself, Ynyscedwyn confined itself to the smelting of pig iron, sold mainly to the tinplate works; Abercrave had only one blast furnace; Ystalyfera, with furnaces, forge, and tinplate works, was the only fully integrated works in the district. Almost all the works in the anthracite region were, these observers commented, unfavourably situated for raw materials and means of communication.[3] The future was to

[1] Bute MSS. CCL VII. 44; NLW, Box 141. A similar Association had been formed in 1837 but had speedily languished. *Cambrian*, 1 Feb. 1840.
[2] *MG*, 30 Nov. 1839, quoting *The Times*.
[3] *CG*, 16 May 1863, based on an account by Gruner and Lan in *Annales des Mines*, 5th series, vol. xx.

THE MARKETS OF THE COALFIELD

see a further decline, Ystalyfera and Ynyscedwyn being the only two active ironworks with anthracite furnaces in 1874. Even here only seven of the thirteen furnaces were in blast, and the output of pig iron—23,760 tons—would not have kept the single works of Dowlais busy for more than a few months.[1] There was also a similar lack of success in the efforts to secure the acceptance of anthracite in the steam-coal market. Despite its smokelessness and high evaporative power, anthracite had, as Bèche and Playfair pointed out, 'disadvantages which, under ordinary circumstances, preclude its use'.[2] It was difficult to light and cohered badly, some of the fuel tending to fall through the bars unburnt. When properly alight it generated so great a heat that it ate away the bars and boilers. Had the incentive been strong enough, as it was in America where no obviously better fuel was readily available, these disadvantages could have been overcome by extra care and special furnaces. In Wales, however, anthracite was confronted with grades of coal which were better fitted for raising steam and, despite the occasional accusations of lack of enterprise levelled against the anthracite owners, it was their superiority that barred the entry of anthracite into the steam market.

The attempts to develop other outlets were equally discouraging. For ordinary household purposes anthracite was notoriously difficult to manage in an open grate as excessive use of the poker tended to put it out. Stoves to burn anthracite were patented from time to time but the cost of installing them was unlikely to be incurred while coal generally was cheap. Consequently the use of anthracite as a domestic fuel was predominantly local, being mainly confined to West Glamorgan, Carmarthenshire, Pembrokeshire, and parts of Cardiganshire. In the field of manufacturing the prime virtue of anthracite lay in its smokeless quality. Left to themselves, however, manufacturers were unlikely to change over to a

---

[1] R. Hunt, *Mineral Statistics* for 1874.
[2] *First Report on the Coals suited to the Steam Navy*, P.P. 1847-8, xxxviii.

smokeless—but more expensive—fuel without some compulsion. The London manufacturers thus strongly opposed the Smoke Nuisance Abatement (Metropolis) Bill of 1853, and they were supported by the north of England coal-owners who alleged that such measures 'would produce a total disarrangement of the northern coal trade'.[1] This Bill was pressed through by Palmerston as Home Secretary but, apart from a few prosecutions in 1854,[2] produced little result. In the absence of effective legislation anthracite made little headway in the market for general manufacturing purposes and, accordingly, in the late 1860's, its chief uses were still, as they always had been, for hop drying, malting, and lime-burning. These were demands which occasioned little expansion; indeed the scanty evidence suggests that the estimated production of anthracite in 1864—slightly over half a million tons—was smaller than the output had been a decade earlier.[3]

The trade in bituminous coal was somewhat more buoyant, the Welsh producers gaining from the general growth in population and expansion of manufactures, both in the coalfield itself and beyond its bounds. To some small extent—figures are not available to support a more precise statement—bituminous coal figured in the growing shipments overseas.[4] The railways not only extended the inland market but also were, for a time, themselves important consumers. The loco-

[1] *Hansard*, 3rd series, vol. 129, 9 Aug. 1853.
[2] *MG*, 1 Dec. 1854. When Sir Robert Peel pressed, in 1866, for general legislation on smoke prevention, although the idea commanded wide support it was not felt to be practical. *Hansard*, 3rd series, vol. 181, 9 Mar. 1866.
[3] Evidence of Thomas Evans, *Royal Commission on Coal Supplies*, 1871, vol. ii; *CG*, 18 May 1867. For estimates in the 1850's see Hunt, op. cit. Anthracite, which occurred in faulted seams and was a difficult coal to work, tended to have a higher cost of production, and thus generally sold at a higher price than other types of coal. This price differential further tended to restrict its sales to markets, such as the brewing industry, where other coals, cheaper in price but lacking the special qualities of anthracite, proved unsatisfactory. In the more rapidly expanding markets—for steam power and general manufacturing—the special qualities of anthracite were less important and its competitive ability was thus impaired by its higher production costs.
[4] Several of the cases cited in the *Report of the Royal Commission on Spontaneous Combustion of Coal in Ships*, P.P. 1876 [C 1586–1], xli, app. ii, concerned cargoes of Welsh bituminous coals.

THE MARKETS OF THE COALFIELD

motives in the early railway age in Wales generally burned coke made from bituminous coals, the Taff Vale Railway, for example, at first being supplied by Walter Coffin with coke made from his No. 3 Rhondda coal. The prospect of a growing demand here, however, faded when this market was lost to the steam coals. The first efforts to use steam coal in locomotives had been defeated by the rapid burning of the fire bars that resulted, but in 1857—when the Taff Vale Railway was forced to use steam coal owing to a strike of the Rhondda house-coal colliers—this difficulty was overcome by covering the bars with a layer of fire brick. The steam coals then, at a smaller cost, performed as efficiently as coke.[1] Thereafter, at home and abroad, the railway companies using Welsh coal tended to buy steam rather than bituminous coals.

There were also the needs of industry within the coalfield itself. There was an active demand for coal from the various metallurgical industries centred in the western sector of the coalfield. The advantages of a coastal site with free access to coal enabled the Swansea–Llanelly region to retain its importance in copper-smelting even when the Cornish ores, upon which the industry had been founded, were ousted by imported ores. In 1876 twelve out of the twenty-two copper-smelting works of the United Kingdom were located in this area, but the industry had passed its peak as it was proving more economical to smelt these imported ores near the mines.[2] The easy access to the sea, facilitating shipments to overseas markets, particularly the United States of America, was also an attraction to the growing tinplate industry. By 1875 fifty-seven of the seventy-seven tinplate works in the United Kingdom were situated in South Wales, mainly on the coast near Port Talbot, Swansea, and Llanelly.[3] Of lesser

---

[1] *MG*, 20 Nov. 1858. Report of a paper read by J. Tomlinson, locomotive superintendent of the Taff Vale Railway, 'On the burning of Welsh steam coal in locomotives'.
[2] Hunt, *Mineral Statistics* for 1876; D. T. Williams, *The Economic Development of Swansea and the Swansea District to 1921* (Cardiff, 1940).
[3] J. H. Jones, *The Tinplate Industry* (1914), app. D.

importance was the gravitation of a substantial portion of Britain's lead, zinc, and silver-smelting industries towards the same area. The steel industry was still a minor consumer as the new processes were only just beginning to make significant headway in South Wales by 1875. In the east both Dowlais and Ebbw Vale had introduced Bessemer converters in the 1860's, while in the west the Landore Steel Works, using the Siemens process, had started production only in 1869. By 1876 there were forty-two Siemens furnaces in the coalfield, mainly at Landore, near Swansea. The aggregate demand for coal from the metallurgical industries in the west could not have been of great dimensions, however, because the significant growth in the production of coal was taking place not in the Swansea district but in the valleys farther to the east.

By 1875 the relative importance of the iron industry as a consumer of coal had dwindled considerably. This was partly the result of fuel economies, such as the utilization of the waste gases from the blast furnaces at the ironworks. Dowlais had shown what could be achieved in this way, using only 25 cwt. of coal for each ton of pig iron in 1869, or considerably less than half the quantity required thirty years earlier. But Dowlais represented the best Welsh practice and elsewhere the economy had not been so great, the average amount of coal required to produce a ton of pig iron in South Wales still being $2\frac{1}{4}$ tons in 1874.[1] The more significant reason for the decline in the relative importance of the iron industry as a consumer of coal was the stagnation that became apparent in the production of iron in South Wales after 1860; in the period 1857–60 the annual production had averaged 950,000 tons while in the period 1867–70 it averaged only 890,000 tons.[2] When the finishing processes are taken into account, the iron industry was probably using rather less than 3 million tons of coal, or about one-fifth of the annual output in South

[1] Hunt, *Mineral Statistics* for 1874. For Dowlais, see evidence of W. Menelaus, *Royal Commission on Coal Supplies*, 1871. In 1869 17 cwt. of coal were used at Dowlais to make each ton of puddled bars.

[2] Figures derived from Hunt, *Mineral Statistics* for the years concerned.

Wales. In 1871 and 1872, during the temporary boom occasioned by the Franco-Prussian war, pig-iron production rose above the million ton mark, but the declining tendency then reasserted itself. The most prosperous days were over for the ironworks in the hills, but the growth of the coal industry was little affected because its progress was now linked more closely with the state of the world demand for steam coal than with the fate of any single industry at home.

III

TECHNIQUE

IN the 1840's the technique of Welsh mining retained many primitive traits. Some of the coal was still mined in 'patches' where it cropped out on the surface and where coal getting was more akin to quarrying than mining.[1] Only a very restricted production was possible by this method, however, because the dip of the seam, increasing the work of removing the surface soil covering the coal, soon made this process uneconomic. Moreover, 'patching' was fast disappearing as the damage caused to surface lands led lessors to insert clauses in mining leases forbidding the practice. 'Colliery to be worked in a proper manner and not by patchwork' ran one of the conditions of a lease in 1837.[2]

The most typical method of gaining access to the coal, however, was not by outcrop working but by levels driven into the sides of the hills. Where geological conditions permitted mining by level it was the natural method to adopt, as it needed only a small initial outlay of capital, avoiding the cost of sinking a shaft, and it also made for low working costs. These working costs were low because the level usually side-stepped the two basic problems of mining—drainage and ventilation. As the workings became too large for these problems to be easily solved, it was often both simpler and cheaper to abandon them and open out a new level.[3] It was, therefore, common to find that mineral advertisements and engineers'

---

[1] Diaries of W. S. Clark, 27 Aug. 1849. 'Went to Patches above Tyla Dowlais and got the workings of coal for the last two months.' Clark was mineral agent to the Marquis of Bute. The modern mechanized equivalent of 'patching' is open-cast mining.

[2] Penrice and Margam MSS., Doc. 7987.

[3] Evidence of J. Richardson, *Report from the Select Committee of the House of Lords. Accidents in Coal Mines*, P.P. 1849 (613), vii.

accounts stressed the possibility of working much of the coal by level as a particular attraction. 'From the depth of the Cwm Avon valley', stated a company report of 1842, 'many Millions of Tons of this excellent and varied fuel are easily obtainable, without steam power, by levels and drifts striking at once into the sides of the Hills.'[1]

But if levels were a natural method of gaining access to the coal, and not in themselves a mark of backwardness, their prevalence none the less retarded technical progress in other aspects of mining—ventilation, winding, pumping, and haulage—by making attention to these matters less urgent. The dominance of the level also meant that there was little accumulated experience in South Wales to help in solving the technical problems raised by the spread of shaft mining. There were a few collieries in the western part of Glamorgan and in Carmarthenshire worked by shafts of a considerable depth— 232 yards at Nevill's St. David's Deep Pit and from 180 to 200 yards at the Llansamlet collieries[2]—but normally shafts were less than a hundred yards deep and they had been sunk only where the coal could be reached by no other means.

Haulage depended on human or animal power. From the face the trams were man (or boy) handled to the main road where, two or three at a time, they were drawn to the mouth of the mine by horses, supervised by a haulier, who usually had a boy to assist him. Ventilation was equally rudimentary. Where the seams were not fiery reliance might be placed on natural ventilation, the warm air from the mine rising to the surface through an upcast shaft and being replaced by a current of cooler, fresh air flowing down the level from outside. Where this was patently inadequate, mainly in the fiery mines, a furnace, placed normally at the bottom of the upcast, would be used to speed the current of air. If the coal was reached by a shaft, often, to save expense, only one was sunk, this being

---

[1] Penrice and Margam MSS., Doc. 9261. Report circulated by the Governor and Company of Copper Miners in England.
[2] *Children's Employment*, pp. 560, 715.

divided into two by a brattice to form an upcast and downcast. Usually the current of air flowed through the whole mine in a single stream, without being split to give separate ventilation to different sections. Its course, in the larger mines, was thus long and tortuous, with the return air becoming a languid, highly vitiated current before it escaped through the upcast. The danger arising from poor ventilation was all the greater because, as the continual references in the Children's Employment Commission show, illumination was generally provided by candles, the use of the safety lamp being exceptional.

Contemporaries were clearly of the opinion that, in matters of mining technique, South Wales was lagging behind the best English practice. Many of the collieries of the kingdom were ill regulated, remarked Sir Henry de la Bèche in 1849, but 'some of the worst, at the present moment, are in South Wales; some of them, I think, are as bad as they can well be'.[1] The reference was primarily to the smaller collieries, but in South Wales it was these minor collieries which collectively accounted for the greater part of the output. Sir Henry excluded the ironworks collieries from his strictures; elsewhere technical retardation was associated with the lack of capital resources of the small units predominating in a coalfield which as yet was only partially developed.

Striking though the advance in technique in the ensuing thirty years was, it remained, nevertheless, partial and uneven. In 1878 the President of the South Wales Institute of Engineers could still lament that 'although we have in the district some very good examples of improved modes of working ... I fear that we must admit that much of our coal is worked in a very slovenly manner. In many places it may be noticed that the methods in use are extremely primitive and behind the improvements of the age.'[2] A body of trained

[1] Evidence of Sir Henry de la Bèche, *Lords Committee on Accidents in Mines*, 1849.   [2] *SWIE*, vol. xi, p. 6.

officials adequate to provide skilled supervision in all collieries had been slow to emerge and, in addition, much of the increased production emanated from small concerns lacking the capital as well as the knowledge to apply the more costly technical innovations.

Nevertheless, even if the improvement in technique was not sufficiently general to satisfy the more critical observers, there were many forces stimulating change. The most compelling of these was the necessity, as shallow mines and levels became exhausted and the pressure of demand remained insistent, of sinking pits to the deeper seams, particularly of steam coal. By 1875 not only had the pit replaced the level as the normal method of mining but the average depth of the shafts in the eastern part of the coalfield had increased to 200 yards, while the deepest sinkings—such as the Fochriw pit at Dowlais, or John Nixon's Merthyr Vale colliery—had a depth of over 400 yards.[1] An Act of 1862, moreover, had made it illegal for any colliery employing more than twenty persons to have only one shaft, thereby increasing the capital costs of sinking. These costs, and the costs of the more powerful machinery inevitably required, could be recouped only if spread over a large output and, in consequence, it became important to increase the area worked from a shaft or pair of shafts. Technical problems of extensive workings—the better application of steam power for winding and pumping, more economical methods of haulage and more efficient ventilation—could no longer be side-stepped but, instead, were thrown into sharper relief. The keenness of competition, accentuated by the rivalry with the north of England producers for markets, further stimulated this interest in more efficient machines and methods. Moreover, as coal was rarely produced for stock, the desire to be able to meet periods of peak demand also urgently impelled the search for more rapid productive methods.

[1] *Royal Commission on Coal, P.P.* 1871 (C 435), xviii, vol. i, p. 9; *Royal Commission on Accidents in Mines. Preliminary Report, P.P.* 1881 (C 3036), xxiv, pp. 299, 423.

The growth of deeper and more extensive collieries, especially those concerned with swelling the output from the fiery veins of steam coal, made it essential to improve methods of ventilation. Explosions, themselves the most devastating critic of inadequate ventilation, made this all the more evident and, after the appointment of Herbert Mackworth as inspector of mines in the South Western district in 1851, the advice of the government inspectors gave added urgency to the lessons they taught. Concerned primarily with safety, the inspectors nevertheless exercised a considerable influence on technique. Their work brought them into contact with developments throughout the district and, by disseminating knowledge and advice among the less progressive colliery managers, they served to raise the general standard, particularly after their powers had been increased by later legislation. Their influence, while affecting technique generally, revealed its results most clearly in the improving efficiency of ventilation where, even before the inspectors had the power to compel compliance, managers had every incentive to act on good advice when it was proffered. Catastrophic explosions, involving an appalling waste of life, not only shocked humanitarian feeling but also caused economic loss. Besides the loss of skilled colliers, and the burden of compensation payments accidents sometimes left in their wake, the more extensive the mine the more serious was the potential dislocation of production and damage to property.

The mining practice of other areas was another force affecting Welsh technique. Vivian, in 1849, said that they did not 'split the air' in his district, Swansea, but added that 'a short time ago I sent our head viewer to the North of England, and he has visited a number of collieries, and we shall introduce that system'.[1] There was also the continual trickle into South Wales of men who were familiar with technique elsewhere. Usually these men had acquired their engineering or mining skill in the north of England. Joshua Richardson, a mining

[1] Evidence of H. Vivian, *Lords Committee on Accidents in Mines*, 1849.

engineer, had served as a pupil with Robert Stephenson before he came south to Neath in 1842, while Samuel Dobson, who migrated to Wales about 1848 to become mineral agent to the Honourable Mr. Clive and other landowners, had previously had seven years' experience as mining engineer in north country collieries.[1] William Gray, too, had been doorboy, hewer, deputy, and sinker in the north before he was engaged by Vivian to sink and manage the Morfa pits near Port Talbot.[2] George Wilkinson, later to become the first manager of the Powell Duffryn Company, also had been long connected with collieries in Northumberland and Durham before coming to Wales to manage Thomas Powell's Duffryn collieries.[3] The important Navigation and Merthyr Vale collieries of Messrs. Nixon, Taylor, and Cory were sunk under the direction of their viewer, George Brown, who had previously been viewer at the northern Ryehope and Shotton collieries.[4] Some of the more important colliery owners, too, were skilled mining engineers who had gained their experience elsewhere, John Nixon and George Elliott in the north of England, and Archibald Hood in Scotland.

While Welsh mining technique bore the impress of the skill of these immigrants, the new-comers themselves were not unaffected, as they gradually realized that the geological peculiarities of the Welsh coalfield justified methods which had not been considered appropriate elsewhere. Welsh mines were, in particular, peculiarly subject to the phenomenon known as 'squeeze'. In most coalfields the crush of subsidence following the extraction of coal affected only the excavated areas and their immediate surroundings. In them, said a later authority,

'roads driven in the solid coal or in the undisturbed strata usually stand intact, and roads maintained through excavated areas soon

[1] Ibid., Evidence of J. Richardson and of S. Dobson.
[2] *Second Report from Select Committee on Accidents in Coal Mines*, P.P. 1852-3 (740), xx, p. 51.
[3] *Royal Commission on Accidents in Mines. Preliminary Report*, 1881, p. 292.
[4] *SWIE*, vol. xi, p. 371.

come to a state of rest. The characteristic of South Wales mining is that roads driven in the solid coal or in undisturbed measures do not generally stand intact, and are frequently more difficult and expensive to maintain than roads passing through excavated areas. The whole of the strata in Wales appears to be under compression, and being comparatively soft, an opening made in it, even of small dimensions, at once commences to squeeze or close up. It is this general characteristic that renders Welsh mining on the whole different from that of other areas.'[1]

These peculiarities, as is revealed by a reading of the various government reports and of the transactions of the South Wales Institute of Engineers, could not fail to evoke an occasional admission by the northerners of modification of views they originally held on entering Wales.

Another influence affecting technique was the South Wales Institute of Engineers, formed in October 1857, with Menelaus of Dowlais as its first president. It is true that the Institute attracted little support from the great mineral landlords and from the individual colliery owners, and that its membership, rising from 130 in 1858 to only 196 in 1876, showed no great expansion in this period. Moreover not all of these members were primarily concerned with coal and, in a region where there was so much heavy industry and where topography raised many engineering problems in railway construction, their discussions inevitably ranged over a wider field than the problems of one industry. Yet, despite these considerations, there is no doubt that the proceedings of the Institute, by inducing a questioning attitude to old-established methods, promoted change in coal-mining technique. There were papers and discussions about the best layout of collieries, the most economical methods of mining, the techniques of ventilation and haulage, and the relation of technique to safety. Even if few colliery owners attended these meetings, many of the managers, who controlled the day-to-day activities of the collieries, were present. These were able to acquire from

[1] H. Bramwell, 'The Economics of the South Wales Coalfield', *SWIE*, vol. xxxvi, pp. 325-6.

the deliberations of the Institute knowledge of the relative advantages of new methods and, what was perhaps more conclusive in a highly competitive trade, of instances of their successful adoption at rival collieries. Thus armed, they were better able to persuade owners to consent to innovations. Similarly the aloofness of the lessors was not significant as their agents—responsible for the surveying and overlooking of the collieries on the various estates—were generally members. Once the agent was convinced that any particular technical change would, by decreasing waste or by increasing the proportion of large coal, enhance the income from royalties he would be quick to impress this on his employer. In this respect the custom, after about 1840, of inserting a covenant in mining leases that the coal should be worked in accordance with the best mining practice of the area, played some part in raising the standards of mining.

The existing techniques of Welsh mining were, accordingly, subjected to pressure from several directions—the need to solve the inescapable problems of deep mining, the reforming zeal of immigrant mining experts, the standards imposed by the law and enforced by mining inspectors, and the attitude of self-criticism stimulated by debate at the Institute of Engineers. The effects of this pressure were seen especially in the change-over from the pillar-and-stall to the long-wall method of mining, in the improvements in ventilation and in the extension of mechanical haulage.

In the 1840's the pillar-and-stall system, with either single or double stalls, was the prevailing method of working coal in South Wales. The double-stall method involved the driving and maintenance of fewer cross-headings, but it was practicable only where the roof was strong enough to enable the longer stalls to be safely worked.[1] Under both methods main

[1] Evidence of S. Dobson, *Lords Committee on Accidents in Mines*, 1849, and diagram i, plan xxiv in appendix i to this report. Pillar and stall at Risca colliery is described in the *Report on Gases and Explosions in Collieries*, P.P. 1847 (815), xvi.

levels were driven into the coal and from them cross-headings were turned. These usually followed the coal to the rise (i.e. followed the uphill slope of the seam) since headings turned to the dip raised extra problems of drainage and haulage against the gradient. These headings, too, were usually not at right angles to the main level, but at an angle of about 75 degrees in order to lessen the gradient down which the coal had to be transported. The distance between cross-headings varied with the method of working, being about 120 yards with double stalls and about 60 to 70 yards with single stalls. From the cross-headings the working stalls were turned to run parallel to the main levels and were generally about 6 yards wide, and separated from each other by pillars of a similar width. With single-stall working the stalls were turned only from one side of the cross-headings and were driven to within 8 or 9 yards of the adjoining heading and then stopped. In double-stall working stalls were driven into both sides of the headings and continued until they holed into a stall being driven in the opposite direction. Once the colliers had driven the stalls, single or double, as far as they were to go they turned back, working the coal from the pillars as they went until these became too weak for prudent working. The coal that remained was lost.

There was considerable variety in the methods of pillar-and-stall working but most methods, however much they differed in detail, involved a considerable waste. Much coal had to be abandoned in the pillars or left to support the roadways and levels, whilst the coal that was worked from the pillars, owing to the pressure of the roof on them, contained a large proportion of small coal.[1] It was particularly the growing production of steam coal from the deeper seams that

[1] 'In many places in taking out pillars they lose more than 60 per cent. of the pillars by being crushed into small coal.' Evidence of M. Truran of Dowlais, *Royal Commission on Coal*, 1871, vol. ii. For this reason, in South Wales, as much coal as possible was obtained on the first working by driving wider stalls and leaving narrower pillars than was customary in the north of England, where the crush on the pillars was not so intense and where a higher percentage of large coal could be obtained by the later working of the pillars.

made this waste more obvious. The deeper workings necessitated leaving larger pillars, whilst it was in the steam-coal collieries that the economic loss of the greater proportion of small coal was most keenly felt. The small coal from the bituminous collieries could be used for coking but that from the steam-coal collieries was almost worthless. Although it could be made into patent fuel the method of conversion was not sufficiently economical to induce most steam-coal owners even to bring the small coal out from the pit. In addition the waste involved in small coal was increased after the 1850's by the insistence of purchasers that screens of a larger mesh should be used at the collieries and at the docks.

Growing dissatisfaction with this waste, reinforced by the feeling that the pillar-and-stall method made effective ventilation difficult, encouraged the search for alternative methods of mining and led to the adoption of the long-wall system. Under this method a given length of face—which varied widely with local conditions—was worked in a single line, all the coal being removed in one operation without any pillars being left. As the face advanced the roadway was moved forward, the excavated area being tightly packed with small and waste and the pressure from roof and floor entirely closing the gap. This method had much to commend it.[1] It made ventilation simpler and more effective. The tortuous direction of an air current around the numerous stalls by a complex—and thus dangerous—arrangement of doorways could be replaced by the more direct method of using the working face itself as an airway. Moreover, in the excavated area, unlike pillar and stall, no cavities were left where gas could accumulate. Besides facilitating ventilation, the long-wall method also led to economies in working. As the roof behind the collier was supported with tightly packed rubbish there was a saving in timber for propping, which the friable nature of the roofs made a particularly high cost in South Wales. The coal could be worked more economically because most

[1] *SWIE*, vol. ii, pp. 125-32.

of the waste of the pillars was avoided, a greater proportion of merchantable large coal was secured, and the even pressure of the roof on the long wall did much to loosen the coal for the hewer. In 1868 the manager of the Dowlais collieries estimated that the loss of coal—either as small or as coal abandoned in the pillars—had been reduced from 40 to 15 per cent. by the change to the long-wall method.[1]

It is not easy to date the introduction of long wall into South Wales. As early as 1837 R. J. Nevill offered to lend Sir John Morris two or three colliers 'who are used to long work ... for such time as may be necessary to instruct your men'.[2] It seems likely that this, and other early references, merely referred to variants of the old method whereby the coal was worked with unusually wide stalls. No conclusive evidence emerges from the various mid-century inquiries that long wall was worked in South Wales at that time, whilst the first reference to it in the mines inspectors' reports does not occur until 1857. Two years later the method could be described as being 'yet in its infancy' in Glamorgan and Monmouthshire.[3]

Both Richard Bedlington, the manager of Rhymney Ironworks, and John Nixon of Aberdare laid claim to having pioneered this innovation in South Wales,[4] no doubt the confusion arising through each having been a pioneer in his own district. Bedlington certainly initiated discussion of the long-wall method in the Institute of Engineers, reading a paper on it in 1860, based on his own practice at Rhymney where, copying the method from collieries in Derbyshire, he had already introduced long wall. In the Aberdare district, where Nixon

[1] Evidence of M. Truran, *Royal Commission on Coal*, 1871, vol. ii.
[2] Nevill MSS. 8. R. J. Nevill to Sir John Morris, Swansea, 12 Dec. 1837.
[3] MIR Thomas Evans's Report for 1857; Lionel Brough's Report for 1859. In 1849 Thomas Deakin of Blaenavon had commended the extra safety of long wall over pillar and stall. It is not certain that this was based on actual experience of working long wall at Blaenavon, although Galloway states that Deakin introduced the method into South Wales about 1840. *MJ*, 10 Nov. 1849; Galloway R.I., *Annals of Mining* (2nd series, 1904), p. 247.
[4] Evidence of R. Bedlington and of J. Nixon, *Royal Commission on Accidents in Mines*, 1881.

started long-wall work after he had studied its operation in Lancashire, all the coal was still being mined by pillar and stall in 1858. Nixon's efforts were, however, retarded by the opposition of his colliers, who were still resisting the innovation as late as the closing months of 1862.[1]

After 1860 the spread of the long-wall method was rapid. Following Bedlington's paper, three further papers were read to the Institute on long wall in the next three years, the discussions revealing that members were almost unanimously in favour of it.[2] The main obstacle to overcome was clearly the hostility of the men. Some members stressed the complications of maintaining a continuous working face when the men were so irregular in their attendance. 'Men would not shift out of their working places—one man would go ahead and leave another man in the lurch—and if he was told to go to another part of the pit he would not; and if he was told that his place should be stopped he said "Very well—I'll go home", and then the proprietor lost the services of a man, which was a most important thing now.' John Nixon related how he overcame the reluctance of his men by gradually reducing the thickness of the pillars until the colliers themselves had found it to their advantage to hole the stalls into one another.[3] The basis of the colliers' hostility was a fear that their earnings might suffer as a result of the revision in cutting rates and allowances that the new methods involved, but once it became clear that the gains to the landowner and colliery proprietor were not to be made at their expense serious opposition ended. By 1866 nearly all the Six Feet vein in the Aberdare district was worked by long wall and by 1871

[1] See *CG*, 8 Nov. 1862; *MG*, 24 Jan. 1863, for instances of Nixon prosecuting men who had left without notice because they objected to long-wall working.

[2] *SWIE*, vol. iii. G. Hedley, 'The Long Wall System', pp. 148-73; J. Nasmyth, 'The Pillar and Stall, Double Stall and Long Wall Systems of Working Coal in South Wales', pp. 185-93; J. Williams, 'The Long Wall System of Working Coal as practised at Lletty Shenkin Colliery', pp. 323-9. Detailed references have not been given where statements are based on these sources.

[3] Evidence of J. Nixon, *Royal Commission on Accidents in Mines*, 1881.

it had also become the normal method in the Six Feet and narrower seams in the Rhondda district.[1] In 1879 the mines inspector for the South Wales district (which excluded Monmouthshire) could assert that long wall prevailed in most workings in his area.[2] There is no evidence to suggest that conditions differed in Monmouthshire.

Each colliery and each seam presented its own problems, and long wall was not everywhere appropriate. More specifically its application during this period was limited by the thickness of the seam, since its operation depended on the availability of sufficient rubbish to fill the excavated area. In the thinner seams, where it was necessary to cut the bottom or rip the top to provide enough height for the horses, there were ample supplies of rubbish. But in the thicker seams—such as the Aberdare Nine Feet—the amount of rubbish was likely to be inadequate, and these seams continued to be worked by the pillar-and-stall method.

Reference has already been made to the difficulty of providing pillar-and-stall workings with effective ventilation and it was, indeed, the defects of this aspect of Welsh technique which occasioned the severest criticism in the 1840's. In a few mines all precautions were adopted, but there were also 'numerous others of which the condition is very defective and dangerous'.[3] Some, indeed, were 'altogether unprovided with anything to aid the mere natural action of the atmosphere'.[4] The collieries working the Mynyddislwyn vein in Monmouthshire, for example, often had only natural ventilation because of the confidence that no explosion would take place, but it was a 'common occurrence' for men to have to leave off work at these collieries when the direction of the

[1] Evidence of Thomas Evans, *Select Committee on Mines*, P.P. 1866 (431), xiv; A. Dalziel, *The Colliers' Strike in South Wales* (Cardiff, 1872), p. 176.
[2] Evidence of T. W. Wales, *Royal Commission on Accidents in Mines*, 1881.
[3] *Report on Ventilation of Mines*, by J. Kenyon Blackwell, P.P. 1850 (1214), xxiii, p. 10.
[4] *Lords Committee on Accidents in Mines*, 1849, p. v.

wind was unfavourable for the ventilation of the level. H. H. Vivian also relied on natural ventilation in his mines at Swansea, but sometimes in the summer, when the air was sluggish, he supplemented it by using the 'waterfall', that is by pouring water down the downcast to cool the air. However, by 1850, dependence on natural ventilation was becoming less common owing to the growing practice of assisting ventilation by means of a furnace. But in South Wales even this improved method was not applied to the best advantage. The reliance on coursing one single, undivided current of air through all the workings of a colliery, combined with the temptation to extend these workings beyond the limits of safe ventilation, often meant that insufficient fresh air reached the face, leading to dangerous working conditions. These dangers were aggravated by the numerous 'goaves', or old workings left by the pillar-and-stall method, where gas tended to accumulate, with the constant risk that it might foul the airways in other parts of the colliery. The defects of these primitive methods had, perhaps, not been serious 'in the working of tracts of small extent, and in which the coal had been drained of fire-damp, from its proximity to the outcrop and old workings'[1] but, with the growth in scale of mining, they could no longer be disregarded.

The validity of these strictures was confirmed by the growing prevalence of explosions, particularly those which accompanied the sinkings to the fiery steam coal of the Aberdare valley in the 1840's. Accidents clearly provided the strongest of all incentives to improve ventilation. As early as 1828 at Hendreforgan colliery, Swansea, when, an engineer remarked, 'we were driven to our wits' end for want of air', Stewart, a Newcastle man, had tried using steam jets to assist the ventilation.[2] Many accidents, too, at the Llansamlet collieries led to the employment there of a viewer from the north of England who both improved the air current and coursed it

[1] *Report on Ventilation of Mines*, by J. Kenyon Blackwell, 1850, p. 15.
[2] Evidence of J. Richardson, *Lords Committee on Accidents in Mines*, 1849.

more effectively.[1] Eaglesbush colliery, near Neath, was another colliery where explosions were frequent. 'If you were to allow this colliery to stand idle for twenty-four hours', observed W. P. Struvé, civil engineer and coal viewer for the Governor and Company of Copper Miners, 'all these stalls would fill with fire-damp.' The attempts made at Eaglesbush to improve the ventilation by means of a furnace at the bottom of the upcast had proved unsuccessful, and the colliery was still dependent on natural ventilation in 1848. In this year, on a warm April day when the air in the colliery had become stagnant, a further explosion occurred, causing the loss of twenty lives. Efforts to make Eaglesbush safer were renewed, and in February 1849 the first Struvé mechanical ventilator to be used at any colliery was erected there.[2]

There is no doubt that the generally low standard of ventilation in South Wales had arisen in part from the neglect and ignorance of the colliery owners, many of whom had no practical knowledge of mining and no competent officials to guide them. The necessity of improvement, however, became vividly clear with the rapid development of mining in the Aberdare valley, with its dangerous seams of steam coal. Yet at this time, as the evidence given in the series of parliamentary investigations into mining accidents between 1849 and 1854 abundantly showed, expert mining opinion was divided on how improvement could best be effected. Opinion in the north favoured the claims of the steam jet (which proved unfruitful) whilst furnaces, machines, and fans were also advocated. The age was one of experiment, and South Wales, as events showed, proved to be the venue for several of the most important experiments that were made.

Struvé's ventilator, a large mechanical air-pump, was both designed and first applied in South Wales. From Eaglesbush its use spread to two collieries in the Swansea valley—Mill-

[1] Evidence of Warington Smyth, *Lords Committee on Accidents in Mines*, 1849.
[2] Ibid., Evidence of W. P. Struvé and of J. Richardson; *MG*, 22 Apr. 1848. The cost of this machine was £300.

wood and Mynydd-bach-y-glo—and then to Thomas Powell's Middle Duffryn colliery near Aberdare where, after sixty-five lives had been lost in an explosion in 1852, two Struvé ventilators superseded a large furnace, forty steam jets and a water jet.[1] During the next decade Struvé's machine acquired considerable popularity in South Wales. John Nixon was another innovator, designing his own machine, similar to Struvé's in principle but original in construction, for use at his Navigation colliery, Mountain Ash, in 1861. Here the problem of ventilation arose in its most acute form because the colliery, the deepest in South Wales at that time, worked exclusively the Four Feet seam, a seam which 'gives off immense quantities of gas at a very great pressure, so much so, that at times it destroys the roof, and can be heard discharging immense blowers at a considerable distance'. The considerable number of mines inspectors and prominent colliery owners who watched the experiment testified to the keenness of the interest it aroused and, the machine proving successful, Nixon continued to use it at Navigation for many years.[2]

A more crucial development in colliery ventilation was the use of the centrifugal fan. In this South Wales again played some part, both the Brunton and the Waddle fans being evolved in the district. Brunton, an ex-employee of Boulton and Watt, secured the first trial of his fan at Gelli-gaer colliery in 1849;[3] Waddle, a member of the South Wales Institute of Engineers, initiated his fan in Pembrokeshire at Bonville Court colliery nearly twenty years later.[4]

At first, however, both machines and fans everywhere encountered considerable opposition. 'The liability to derangement in all machines appears to preclude their use in ventilation, in other than exceptional circumstances' was the verdict at mid-century.[5] There was much justification for this

[1] MIR H. Mackworth's Report for 1852-3; *MJ*, 7 Aug. 1852.
[2] MIR Thomas Evans's Report for 1863; *CG*, 23 Nov. 1861.
[3] Evidence of William Brunton, *Lords Committee on Accidents in Mines*, 1849. The fan cost £100. [4] *SWIE*, vol. v, p. 203.
[5] *Report on Ventilation of Mines*, by J. Kenyon Blackwell, 1850.

opinion. Struvé's machine was highly complicated and, working on the pump principle, was intermittent in its action; Brunton's fan, though continuous in its action and less complex, was not sufficiently powerful. Thus most of the early instances of mechanical ventilation in South Wales occur in collieries which, owing to some exceptional circumstance, were difficult to ventilate effectively by any other means; or occur in conditions such as those of Cwmsaerbren colliery, where a Brunton fan was used in 1855 simply as a temporary device while this fiery colliery was being opened up, the intention being to change over to furnace ventilation as soon as the workings became sufficiently remote from the shaft for this to be safe.[1] However, the later fans—the Guibal, the Schiele, and the Waddle—by their greater power, economy, and reliability led to a gradual change of opinion. In 1858 the assertion that mechanical methods were certain to replace furnace ventilation was still largely an act of faith; ten years later it was a generally accepted belief.[2]

Nevertheless, in South Wales, the furnace remained the normal basis of ventilation for a considerable time. The mechanical ventilation of Risca Black Vein pit could still be described as 'unusual' in 1860, the mines inspector remarking that nearly all the best managed collieries used the furnace. Indeed in 1861, after the question of the adequacy of the ventilation at Risca had been referred to arbitration, the arbitrator ordered a reversion to the furnace as he 'did not approve of ventilation by machinery'.[3] Such a view was soon to become outmoded, however, as the growing efficiency of fans made the defects of furnace ventilation more obvious. The furnace indeed had several fundamental disadvantages— the possibility that it might damage the sides of the shaft, the

[1] *SWIE*, vol. i, pp. 166, 179.
[2] See *SWIE*, vol. i, p. 180, and the various discussions on mechanical ventilation in vols. v and vi. By 1886 the view disparaging mechanical ventilation owing to its unreliability could be referred to as an antiquated curiosity. *Final Report on Accidents in Mines*, P.P. 1886 (C 4699), xvi, p. 9.
[3] MIR Lionel Brough's Reports for 1860 and for 1861.

TECHNIQUE 67

risks attached to relighting it after an explosion had occurred, and the danger that the furnace itself might originate an explosion. All these told against its retention, and by 1875 at least fourteen Guibal and twenty-four Waddle fans were in operation at some of the largest pits of the coalfield. By now the old-fashioned Struvé machine was being seldom introduced, while Nixon remained the solitary user of the ventilator of his own design.[1]

Side by side with the efforts to increase the power of the air current went general improvement in ventilation. The singlebratticed shaft became a thing of the past. A second shaft had often been sunk in collieries during the 1850's, although at the end of this decade one of the deepest mines in South Wales, the 390 yards deep Fochriw pit of the Dowlais Company, was still being worked with only one shaft.[2] By the Act of 1862, however, for all but the smallest mines or those nearing exhaustion, a second shaft became compulsory.[3] Although the chief object of this Act was to lessen the danger that men might be entombed alive after an accident, it also facilitated better ventilation. In addition, it was becoming more general for collieries to be divided into panels, separated from each other by barriers of coal, enabling the ventilating current to be correspondingly split and so utilized more effectively. The change in the tone of the mines inspectors' reports as the years went by is a measure of the progress achieved. Inadequate ventilation, which had figured so largely in the earlier reports, received comparatively slight mention by the mid-1870's. South Wales, starting with a low level of skill, had faced the challenge of exceptionally fiery mines and had met it with considerable ingenuity and with a steadily improving technique.

[1] Evidence of T. E. Wales, *Royal Commission on Accidents in Mines*, 1881; *SWIE*, vol. ix, pp. 89-91
[2] MIR Thomas Evans's Reports for 1860 and for 1861.
[3] 25 and 26 Vict., c. 79. Thomas Evans reported that there were only fourteen single shafts in South Wales in 1861, but Lionel Brough reported 'many' in Monmouthshire.

As the pits grew more extensive the problems of haulage also compelled greater consideration. Here the main change was the gradual replacement of human and animal by mechanical power, particularly for haulage along the main levels. In the 1840's once the coal had been moved from the face in trams by men or boys—or, before 1842, in the steep seams of Pembrokeshire by women working windlasses—the main haulage had been performed by horses. The costs were heavy, as may be inferred from one instance of the economies that could be achieved simply by the careful maintenance of tramroads. It was stated in 1850 that, in one level heading, an expenditure of £100 on relaying and ballasting three-quarters of a mile of tramroad had enabled two horses to do the work of five, saving £150 a year, without reckoning the decrease in the number of stoppages through derailing.[1] In 1849 the cost of the 300 horses used in the pits of the Blaenavon Iron and Coal Company was between £14,000 and £15,000 a year.[2] To this should be added the wages of the haulier and boy attending each horse and the costs of replacing horses. In 1878 it was stated that each horse represented an annual cost, with labour included, of £125 and that 30 per cent. of the horses had to be replaced each year.[3]

Mechanization could lead to cheaper and speedier haulage, but it needed power, and the difficulty was to find an effective and safe way of transmitting this. Stationary underground steam engines, such as the one made by George Stephenson in use at Hendreforgan colliery in the Swansea valley before 1840,[4] could be used generally only if sited near the upcast, while a constant limit to the wider application of steam power was the difficulty of transmitting it to the more remote part of the workings. The most promising alternative to steam was compressed air. It was wasteful but this was not prohibitive on a coalfield, where power was cheap, and the waste was offset by the facility with which the power of compressed air

---

[1] *MJ*, 5 Jan. 1850.   [2] Ibid., 5 May 1849.   [3] *SWIE*, vol. xi, p. 142.
[4] Evidence of J. Richardson, *Lords Committee on Accidents in Mines*, 1849.

TECHNIQUE

could be applied, however varied the conditions presented by different collieries. Probably compressed air was first applied in a South Wales colliery in 1857 at Dowlais—700 yards from the pit bottom.[1] Here, four years later, in one of the longest levels, from 30 to 35 trams (or about 36 tons of coal) could be hauled in a single trip.[2] That some other collieries were following the Dowlais example is shown by the references to the spread of mechanical haulage which begin to appear in the reports of the mines inspectors in the early 1860's. Of the two methods of mechanical haulage—the endless rope or the tail rope—the latter, which required only one line of rails, was the one usually adopted in South Wales. The cost of maintaining the double roadway necessary for the endless rope method was prohibitive, above all in collieries where the roofs were bad and in the steam-coal pits, where the use of large trams was considered commercially essential to enable the coal to be sent out as large as possible.

Mechanization of haulage became more general after about 1865. In 1866, no doubt thinking of the 3,000 yards long rope drawing its 30 to 35 trams along the Brewhouse level, Dowlais, Menelaus could say that the haulage methods in the other ironworks collieries had not improved much over those 'used to convey materials for the building of the pyramids'.[3] But old-fashioned methods could not be retained indefinitely in so competitive an industry, especially when it was claimed that mechanization might halve the former costs of horse haulage.[4] The boom demand of the early 1870's provided at once the incentive and, from inflated profits, the finance for more rapid change. There is no evidence that the colliers offered any objections, no doubt because the youths no longer required as hauliers were merely promoted more quickly to work at the coal face. By 1872 the Powell Duffryn Company anticipated that it would shortly be working one

[1] *SWIE*, vol. i, pp. 4, 41.　　[2] *CG*, 28 Sept. 1861.
[3] *SWIE*, vol. v, p. 26.　　[4] Ibid., vol. iv, pp. 174, 183.

pit without any horses at all, and by 1875 it could be affirmed that the underground haulage in the main roadways at most of the larger collieries was 'done by machinery. ... Within the last few years compressed air has come very much into use as a motive power for underground engines.' The trams were, however, still generally brought from the face of the work to the different stations by horses.[1]

Once the coal had been hauled to the bottom of the shaft it was raised to the surface either by water balance or by steam power. The water-balance pit, used where there was an abundant supply of water, was peculiar to South Wales. An example of it, used at the Cwm Bargoed pit of the Dowlais Iron Company, where 300 tons of coal were raised up a shaft 154 yards deep from the Upper Four Feet seam in a twelve-hour day, was described by the mines inspector for South Wales.[2] 'The tram containing about 20 cwt. of coal is placed on the top of an empty water bucket at the shaft bottom; and the empty tram on the bucket at the top; this bucket upon being filled with water descends, raising the full tram of coal and the empty bucket from the bottom. A valve is placed at the bottom of each bucket, and, immediately on its arrival at the shaft bottom, the valve is lifted and the water let off.' Beneath each bucket was a chain to aid the balance. The speed of working depended on the rate at which the bucket could be filled with water: at Cwm Bargoed the buckets held about 2 tons of water and each complete winding operation took about 1 minute 20 seconds. The water might, as at Cwm Bargoed, be pumped to the surface to be used again, or might, where there was free drainage, be allowed to flow away, possibly to another balance machine. In 1862, in Glamorgan alone, there were about sixty of these machines at work, all the pits of the great Cyfarthfa works being operated on this basis.

[1] T. Forster Brown, 'The South Wales Coalfield', *SWIE*, vol. ix, p. 91.
[2] Thomas Evans, 'Description of Water Balance Machines', *Trans. Manchester Geological Society*, vol. iii, 1862, pp. 334–9.

Such machines were cheap to erect and, provided the chains were good, needed little repair. For mines not exceeding a depth of about 180 yards, with free drainage, and raising not much more than 250 tons a day, they were a cheap means of winding. But at greater depths the machine became too cumbrous, and the limits to the rate of winding made it unsuitable for pits with a large output. Periods of drought, too, were liable to interrupt production. 'Engines will take the place of Water Balance pits if we have more such summers as this', wrote William Crawshay to his son in 1864.[1] Winding from the deeper and more extensive pits needed the power, speed, and regularity of steam, and by 1874, when the Griffin pit, Nant-y-glo, changed over to steam winding, the water balance could be referred to as 'old-fashioned'.[2] By now the steam engines had become more powerful, wire ropes had replaced hempen ones and, at the larger collieries, double-decked carriages raising two trams at a time had come into use. What could be achieved was shown by the claims put forward, in the closing months of 1874, as examples of exceptional performance from a single shaft. Over 1,000 tons were raised in a twelve-hour day from Ferndale colliery, in a ten-hour day from Fforchaman colliery, and in less than nine hours from Cwmaman colliery (managed by John Daglish of Tynemouth), where the winding engines could raise 120 tons up the 232 yards deep shaft in an hour with ease.[3]

Coal-cutting by machinery had hardly emerged from the discussion stage by 1875. This was true for all districts but conditions in South Wales were particularly unfavourable to the operation of machines. The geological conditions of poor roofs, dipping seams, and numerous faults offered obstacles to the use of machines, while the pipes transmitting the power

---

[1] Cyfarthfa MSS., Box VI. William Crawshay to Robert Crawshay, 11 June 1864. [2] CG, 4 Dec. 1874.
[3] Ibid., 30 Oct. 1874, 13, 27 Nov. 1874. At Abercarn colliery on 8 Feb. 1867 in a twelve-hour day the colliers had raised 1,369 tons from the Prince of Wales pit, about 300 yards deep. The men were cheered on their way home and later treated with 'home brewed' at the drill hall. Ibid., 16 Feb. 1867.

were liable to be damaged by the numerous falls of roof. Also the machines tried merely 'holed' or undercut the coal to loosen it and were thus less valuable in South Wales where the natural pressure of the roof did much to loosen the coal. Aware of these difficulties and limitations, the members of the Institute, when they discussed coal-cutting by machinery in 1863, were doubtful whether any economy could be achieved by it. A few machines were being tried out in the early 1870's, and in one instance, at Nant-y-glo, the men took one machine sufficiently seriously in 1873 to object to its introduction, but it still seemed likely, as members of the Institute had been told in 1863, that 'coal cutting by machinery in South Wales was a long way off'.[1]

Altogether the experience of South Wales largely confirms Clapham's general judgement that, apart from a few important innovations, the tendency was for everything to get bigger, deeper, or stronger, and for the best practice of the later 1840's to be more widely spread.[2] Local peculiarities, however, gave this seemingly unspectacular transition greater significance in South Wales than in most other areas. The predominance of mining by level, for example, had unduly depressed the general standard of technical competence in South Wales in 1840; the decline of this method thus made the improvement all the more pronounced. Again the unusual condition of the roof in South Wales marked off the considerable extent to which long wall replaced pillar and stall as a substantial technical advance in that it greatly reduced the waste in working and increased the proportion of large coal that was obtained; while the fiery nature of the coals lent added value to the improved methods of ventilation that were evolved. The individual steps bringing these changes about often left little record—perhaps merely a comment by a mines

---

[1] *SWIE*, pp. 95–118, 136; *CG*, 3 Oct. 1873.
[2] J. H. Clapham, *An Economic History of Modern Britain* (Cambridge, 1932), vol. ii, p. 100.

inspector that 'greatly improved machinery has of late years been introduced' by some particular owner[1]—but their cumulative effect was considerable. The fact that 'many of our Monmouthshire collieries are a long way in from the bottom of the pit' led Lionel Brough to remark, in 1873, that 'in the case of collieries, as years pass away, difficulties increase'.[2] As time went on coal was being mined not only from areas increasingly remote from the pit mouth but also from the deeper lying seams. In these less accessible places, too, atmospheric conditions naturally tended to become worse. The changes in technique may be envisaged as a struggle to counteract the depressive effect of these difficulties on the return to the collier's labour and the following table indicates very approximately the outcome of this struggle.[3]

	South Wales and Monmouthshire		U.K.
Coal output (million tons)	Male coal-miners	Tons per miner	Tons per miner
1851 —	31,373	—	264
1854 8·5	34,000	250	277
1861 10·7 (average 1860–62)	39,976	268	300
1871 14·2 („ 1870–72)	48,985	290	373
1881 22·1 („ 1880–82)	64,326	343	403

The above figures have their limitations. Apart from the dubious accuracy of some of the statistics of annual output, the figures may be distorted by the abnormal course of production in a particular year and thus may give a misleading impression of the rate of change in productivity. But for the strike of 1871, for example, the average output of coal per miner in South Wales would have been higher in that year and the advance of productivity in the sixties correspondingly greater. Nevertheless two broad conclusions emerge. Throughout this

[1] MIR Thomas Evans's report for 1862, referring to Nevill's collieries.
[2] Evidence of Lionel Brough, *Select Committee on the Causes of the Present Dearness and Scarcity of Coal*, P.P. 1873 (313), x.
[3] See statistical note at end of chapter.

period output per head in South Wales remained appreciably below the national average. Partly this reflected the depressing effect on the Welsh figures of the low productivity per head in the anthracite region; but only partly, because in Monmouthshire, where output per head was highest, not more than 370 tons per miner were produced in 1881. Partly, too, it reflected the more than usually difficult mining conditions of the South Wales coalfield. Second, in South Wales as elsewhere, until the 1880's more skilled management, better machines, and a larger capital investment were, despite increasing depths and difficulties, raising the yield to the miner's effort. This was all the more noteworthy because during this period the working day of the miner was tending to become shorter, a nine- or ten-hour day, with Saturday a half-day, having become general by the early 1870's.

Statistical Note

Coal-mining statistics become more accurate after 1872 when returns of the quantity of coal raised and the numbers of persons employed, both above and below ground, became compulsory (Coal Mines Regulation Act, 35 and 36 Vict., c. 76). Earlier figures, whether those in the mines inspectors' reports or those in Hunt's *Mineral Statistics*, were based partly on voluntary returns and partly on guesswork.

The inaccuracy of the inspectors' estimates of numbers employed in the 1860's became apparent when the 1871 census figures were published. Accordingly, the numbers of male coal-miners in the above table are derived from the various census reports and, in making an estimate for 1854, it has been assumed that the rate of increase in numbers employed remained constant during the intercensal years. The table does not include the few 'South Wales' coal-miners returned for the counties of Cardigan and Radnor, nor does it allow for the possibility that some of the small numbers of 'miners unspecified' in the census returns of 1861 and 1871 were coal-miners.

There are no statistics available to indicate how much voluntary and involuntary underemployment there was, but it is certain that throughout the period irregularity of work was a feature of the collier's life. Fluctuations in demand caused underemployment particularly among colliers working for the house-coal and steam-coal markets, while for all it could be said in 1873 that men did not work on Mondays, and sometimes not on Tuesdays.[1]

Colliery figures of output, owing to the necessity of making royalty payments if for no other reason, were likely to be accurate, although probably coal used at the colliery itself and colliers' concessionary coal were not always included. But while returns were voluntary many coal-owners, particularly those owning the smaller collieries, did not make them, so the output of a district could be arrived at only by a more or less well-informed guess. A further complication arises because the collieries of Monmouthshire and a few collieries in Glamorgan and Brecknockshire lay outside the South Wales mines inspector's district. For these collieries, forming part only of the South Western inspection district, separate figures of output are not available before 1860.

The table of output given below is based on the following sources:

1854–9. Total output of the coalfield, R. Hunt, *Mineral Statistics*; output of the South Wales mines inspection district 1856–9, MIR Thomas Evans's Report for 1861.

1860–9. *Report of Royal Commission on Coal*, 1871, vol. iii.

1870–7. Output of South Wales mines inspection district, Mines. Inspectors' Reports; output of Monmouthshire, including a few collieries in Glamorgan and Brecknockshire, *Appendix to Report of Select Committee on Coal*, 1873, for the years 1870–1; W. G. Dalziel, *The Monmouthshire and South Wales Coalowners' Association* (1895), p. 610 for the year 1872; Mines. Inspectors' Reports, for the years 1873–7.

[1] Evidence of Lionel Brough, *Select Committee on Coal*, 1873.

76   TECHNIQUE

It may be noted that for the three years 1861–3 the Commission of 1871 accepted an estimate of the production of the South Wales district which was lower than that of the mines inspector (see the figures in brackets in the table below), but no explanation of this difference is given. The estimate of the production of Monmouthshire for 1861 accepted by the Commission seems excessively high; no corresponding jump for this year is shown by the figures for iron production or for coal shipments from Newport.

Annual Output of Coal in the South Wales Coalfield 1854–77

Year	South Wales district	Monmouthshire &c.	Total output South Wales	Percentage of U.K. output
		(*million tons*)		
1854	—	—	8·5	13·2
1855	—	—	8·6	13·3
1856	5·4	—	8·9	13·4
1857	5·2	—	7·1	10·9
1858	5·7	—	7·5	11·5
1859	6·0	—	9·7	13·5
1860	6·25	4·0	10·25	12·8
1861	6·7 (6·8)	5·0	11·7	13·4
1862	6·5 (6·9)	3·75	10·3	12·7
1863	6·9 (7·2)	4·1	11·0	12·8
1864	6·9	4·0	11·0	11·9
1865	8·5	4·1	12·7	12·9
1866	9·4	4·4	13·8	13·6
1867	9·1	4·6	13·7	13·1
1868	9·0	4·25	13·25	12·9
1869	9·2	4·3	13·5	12·6
1870	9·3	4·4	13·7	12·4
1871	9·1	4·9	14·0	11·9
1872	10·1	4·75	14·9	12·1
1873	11·5	4·7	16·2	12·6
1874	11·5	5·0	16·5	13·0
1875	10·0	4·2	14·2	10·7
1876	11·7	5·3	17·0	12·7
1877	11·7	5·2	16·9	12·5

IV

THE EXPANSION IN OUTPUT

DURING the period from 1840 to 1875 improved technique was merely one of many factors which were contributing to the increase in the output of coal from South Wales. The lucrative opportunities the industry offered, or seemed to offer, not only stimulated men of enterprise within the coalfield itself to embark upon or to extend production but also attracted men from outside into the ranks of the coal-owners. The hope of profit stimulated capital investment and in the 1860's, as limited liability was slowly adopted, capital was attracted in from farther afield. The labour force grew, being recruited both from local sources, particularly from colliers' families, and from the immigrants who came to the coalfield in search of employment. A railway network grew up in the coalfield, enabling old districts to be exploited more fully and new areas to be opened up, and improved harbours were constructed, facilitating shipment from the ports. The landowners, rarely themselves playing any direct part in the exploitation of the wealth that lay under their estates, readily granted mineral leases for the sake of the royalty income they yielded. All these factors contributed to increase the output of coal in the area from about $4\frac{1}{2}$ million tons in 1840 to nearly $16\frac{1}{2}$ million tons in 1874.

The course of this increase in supply, however, was by no means regular. In the trade in household coal, where coal served as a consumption good, the dominant fluctuation was not so much that occurring from year to year as that occurring seasonally within the year. The main variation in the supply of anthracite, too, was governed by the changes in the demand for its use in malting and hop-drying which resulted from fluctuations in the state of the harvest. One of the most marked trends in the Welsh coal trade after 1840, however, was the substantial decline in relative importance of both house coal and anthracite. The more important sections of the industry—the bituminous coal used particularly by the iron and copper industries for smelting, and the steam coal which was in demand for industrial and commercial purposes at home and abroad—were much more sensitive to the general movements of economic activity. The effects of these general movements on the coal industry as the trade cycle ran its course were seen partly in changes in the level of production of coal and partly in changes in its price.

In the short run there were obstacles in the way of fully adjusting supplies of coal to meet changes in demand. In times of active trade there was a limit to the extent to which the supply could be expanded by working more regularly and for longer hours and by opening out fresh working places. Once this limit was reached a further increase in supply could be attained by the sinking of new pits but this, particularly when it became necessary to sink deep, was a time-consuming operation. Beyond certain limits, it was hardly easier to effect a quick diminution of supply as trade slackened. It was often better to work a colliery—even at an unremunerative return on capital or at an actual loss—than stop production altogether. The shaft and workings of a colliery represented capital that rapidly depreciated if all work was discontinued; without constant pumping and the regular repair of headings and roadways—especially in South Wales where the roof and floor were subject to constant 'squeeze'—a colliery could rapidly become unworkable and might have to be abandoned, or restored to working order only at considerable cost. Thus, so long as the coal could be sold at a price which covered the variable costs (of cutting, transport, and so on) and also made some contribution to the essential work of keeping the mine in order, operations were probably continued.[1]

[1] See, for example, evidence of Thomas Brown, *Select Committee on Payment of Wages Bill*, *P.P.* 1854 (382), xvi. 'It is known to many Honourable Members that you cannot shut up a colliery.'

The result of the difficulties experienced by coal-producers in regulating production according to the state of the market was a tendency for prices to oscillate within a fairly wide range. In time of boom even a comparatively small deficit in supply could cause a sharp rise in price without choking off demand; 'if there is a scarcity of coal you are on your beam ends . . .', George Elliot remarked in 1873, 'you must have it at any price'. In time of slump, on the other hand, a reduction of coal prices would not immediately stimulate any marked extension of demand and the competition of producers eager to dispose of their output would drive prices down to low levels. It was, George Elliot commented, 'as difficult to keep down the price in the year 1872 as it was to get it up in the years 1869 and 1870'.[1]

While in the short run output responded only sluggishly to changes in demand with the consequence of disproportionate movements in prices, in the long run there was little difficulty in increasing supplies to meet the secular growth in demand. Existing collieries could be extended and, as there were considerable areas of the coalfield unleased, new pits sunk; the capital required, though rising, was for most of this period still comparatively small. The high prices, and the large profits that were associated with them, during the occasional years of full boom encouraged widespread investment in the industry at these times. Mackworth commented on 'the extraordinary and sudden activity infused by high prices, and excessive demand, into the coal trade' of South Wales in 1853, and a year later referred to 'the large number of new shafts and new collieries being opened within my district'.[2] The story was similar in 1866 when the mines inspector commented on the 'unprecedented' demand for steam coal and on the many shafts that had been or were being sunk in South Wales; the unusually prosperous years of 1872–4, too, led to

---

[1] Evidence of George Elliot, *Select Committee on Dearness of Coal*, P.P. 1873 (313), x.
[2] MIR Mackworth's Report for 1853, p. 163; for 1854, p. 119.

another outburst of activity when the number of new shafts sunk, some of them among the deepest in the area, was without precedent.[1] While the periods of good trade produced these spurts in the growth of productive capacity, the intervening years were not altogether devoid of activity, particularly for those who could see beyond the immediate prospect of depression and whose actions were governed more by the long-term upward trend in demand. Even in the poor year of 1869, it was noted, men of capital and ability were plodding on in extensive sinking speculations as if the coal trade had never been better.[2] Nevertheless this growth in productive power, at times steady and at times suddenly accelerated, produced periods of low prices and poor profits which lasted until the excess capacity was more than absorbed by the persistent upward trend in demand.

These were the broad economic conditions under which the industry was operating; any detailed chronological account of the movements of output and prices under the impact of these conditions, however, must be somewhat tentative, as it can be based on material that is only partially adequate. After 1854, when figures of annual estimated output first become available, there were three periods, each lasting for two or three years and beginning in 1858, 1864, and 1871 respectively, when the rate of increase in output was particularly rapid. There is one continuous series of yearly average prices for the period. This, however, relates solely to steam coal f.o.b. at Cardiff, and does not appear to be fully representative of the price movements of this branch of the trade even at Cardiff. It has, therefore, been supplemented by an examination of the references to prices in this trade which appeared from time to time in the contemporary press and trade journals. As these price figures may relate to different grades of coal they do not form a dependable guide to long-period price changes, but they are a reasonably reliable index

---

[1] MIR T. E. Wales's Report for 1874, p. 155; Lionel Brough's Report for 1875, p. 121. [2] *CG*, 30 July 1869.

of movements from year to year.[1] There were three periods after 1850 when the price of steam coal was rising; from 1852 to 1856, from near the end of 1863 to 1865, and from 1870 to 1873. In the first of these periods, superimposed on the growing demand associated with industrial activity, was the demand for steam coal arising out of the Crimean War. The naval estimates in 1854 included a supplementary estimate of £160,000 for the purchase of coal; the estimates in 1855 were still higher and, in addition, there were about 200 transports, 'most of them steamships of the largest size', in the pay of the British government.[2] These considerable purchases—some 430,000 tons of coal, treble the normal quantity, were sent to overseas depots in 1855[3]—were enough to send Welsh coal prices to a peak. After the war prices fell and remained at a low level until they began to rise again at the beginning of 1863. After two or three years of prosperity the story of decline was repeated, until prices reached their nadir in the early months of 1869.[4] In 1872 prices started to soar. The

[1] Average selling prices per ton of colliery-screened steam coal, f.o.b. at Cardiff, based on figures in circulars issued to their customers by Messrs. Tellefsen, Holst and Wills, Merchants, Cardiff. W. G. Dalziel, *The Monmouthshire and South Wales Coal Owners' Association* (1895—for private circulation), p. 108c.

Year	Prices s. d.	Year	Prices s. d.	Year	Prices s. d.	Year	Prices s. d.
1852	8 0	1858	8 9	1864	8 9	1870	9 3
1853	10 6	1859	8 3	1865	8 9	1871	10 6
1854	11 0	1860	8 3	1866	8 6	1872	19 3
1855	10 6	1861	8 6	1867	8 6	1873	23 3
1856	9 6	1862	8 7	1868	8 0	1874	16 11
1857	9 3	1863	8 9	1869	8 9	1875	14 3

The highest price in 1872 was 30s. in Sept. and Oct. The upward movement of prices in the early sixties was probably greater than the above figures suggest. Steam coal was selling f.o.b. Cardiff at 7s. 6d.–8s. in Nov. 1862; at 9s. 9d.–10s. in Oct. 1863; at 11s. in Oct. 1864. Apart from the prices quoted, the whole tone of the press references implies that these were years of rising prices or high prices. *CG*, 15 Nov. 1862, 17 Oct. 1863, 30 Apr. 1864; *Merlin*, 11 June 1864; *MG*, 7 Oct. 1864.

[2] *Hansard*, 3rd series, vol. 132, 5 May 1854; vol. 136, 16 Feb. 1855.

[3] *Report of Steam Coals purchased for the Navy and supplied to Depots Abroad*, P.P. 1860 (363), xlii.

[4] *CG*, 30 Apr. 1869.

boom following the Franco-Prussian war increased the demand, while the upward movement of prices was accentuated by rumours that the men intended to restrict output and by fears that the Mines Regulation Act of 1872 would increase costs of production.[1] At the beginning of 1874 it was still difficult to buy steam coal at Cardiff for less than 25s. a ton, but the break in prices came in the early months of this year and by September 1875 large steam coal was selling at Cardiff for between 11 and 13s. a ton.[2]

One potential source of instability in the sale-coal industry was the possibility that the iron and copper firms, nearly all extensive colliery owners, might decide to raise coal not only for their own industrial needs but also for sale in the market. Sales of coal, particularly by the large iron firms, attracted a considerable amount of attention at the end of the sixties, when they were growing in scale and, it was claimed, depressing coal prices to unremunerative levels. This development, because of its importance, merits close examination. In so far as these sales represent an addition to the activities of firms already raising coal for manufacturing purposes they help to account for the overall increase in the output of coal from South Wales; in so far as they represent a diversion of enterprise from manufactures which had entered on a state of decline they form part of the story of the changing balance in the industrial development of South Wales which culminated in the displacement of iron by coal as its leading industry.

Many of the copper companies were already actively engaged in the sale of coal in the forties. In 1843 the Company of Copper Miners of England, for example, was selling about half of the 45,000 tons of coal raised at its Graigola colliery in the Swansea valley, and a further 60,000 tons out of its production of 150,000 tons at Cwmavon.[3] The Llanelly

[1] See *Report on Dearness of Coal*, 1873.
[2] *CG*, 9 Jan. 1874, 3 Sept. 1875.
[3] Penrice and Margam MSS., No. 9261.

Copper Company, too, conducted a large coal trade from the collieries it owned in connexion with its copper works. The owners of the Morfa works, Williams, Foster and Company, united with Messrs. Vivians, also important copper-smelters, 'to work collieries for the supply of their works. Under the name of the Swansea Coal Company they also sell and export coal, but not in large quantities.'[1] The early entry of the copper companies into the coal trade was not surprising. In their works they could make extensive use of small coal, which had a negligible value in the open market, and this left them free to sell some of their large coal. In addition, their mineral takings were likely to include seams of different qualities, while the copper works were mainly restricted to the use of free-burning coal. Finally, the copper companies drew their ores from Cornwall and could utilize this commercial connexion to sell their surplus coal to the Cornish mine-owners. Most copper firms, thus, were engaged in the coal trade, but the scale of their participation was not great and, as the market easily adjusted itself to it, little dislocation was caused.

The ironmasters, who controlled vast stretches of mineral land, were potential suppliers of coal on a much greater scale. In the late sixties supplies from this source became considerable; in these years, too, when the local supplies of iron ore had become inadequate, the locational disadvantage of the string of ironworks sited at the valley heads along the northern outcrop was increasingly apparent. It would, however, be wrong to assign the beginnings of coal sales by the ironmasters to these years and to explain them solely by the ironmasters' fears about their future prospects in the iron industry. The coal trade exercised an attraction of its own and different ironmasters succumbed to this attraction at different times. The date of their entry into the coal trade often depended more on the circumstances peculiar to their firms than on the general state of the iron trade.

[1] *MJ*, 17 Aug. 1850.

As early as 1840 the Tredegar Iron Company was selling steam coal and it was from this source exclusively that the supplies for the steamship *Great Western* were drawn. The Company—trading as the Tredegar Coal Company—was one of the most substantial coal shippers from Newport about this time.[1] Later in the forties the Ebbw Vale Iron Company, when submitting samples for the Admiralty steam-coal trials, claimed that its coal was 'much in demand for marine and other steam purposes', particularly in the markets of the Mediterranean, the West Indies, and South America.[2] These iron companies and, no doubt, others in Monmouthshire where there were 'a good many sale collieries attached to the ironworks',[3] exploited the coal market as a source of extra profit; some companies, like the Blaenavon Iron Company, turned to the sale of coal with a touch of desperation. The reports of this company between 1844 and 1851 clearly indicate that its inability to compete in the iron market was pushing it into the coal trade. In 1850 the company was sinking a new pit solely for sale-coal purposes and was, at the same time, looking for an enlarged market on the completion of the railway to Hereford.[4] The new firms which attempted to enter the iron industry at this time usually aimed at combining the sale of coal with iron manufacture. Some of these firms, indeed, once their collieries were opened, abandoned their original intentions and concentrated on the coal trade, the Bryn-du colliery (1844) and the Cefn colliery (1852), both near Bridgend, originating in this way.[5]

Gradually more and more of the iron companies devoted part of their attention to the sale of coal. The Aberdare Iron Company entered the trade probably before 1858 as it was being sued early in that year for the under-payment of com-

[1] *MJ*, 7 Mar. 1840; *MG*, 30 Aug. 1845.
[2] *First Report on the Coals suited for the Steam Navy*, 1847–8, appendix, section ii.
[3] Evidence of E. S. Barber, *Lords' Committee on Accidents in Mines*, 1849.
[4] *MJ*, 27 Apr. 1844, 2 May 1846, 6 May 1848, 5 May 1849, 4 May 1850, 26 Apr. 1851.
[5] Penrice and Margam MSS., Nos. 9275–7, 9323.

mission on the sale of coal at Swansea, Briton Ferry, and Cardiff. This company had extensive mineral properties in the Ely and Rhondda valleys and in the following decade, when its coal sales had risen to over 150,000 tons a year, it was able to sell freely as one of its Rhondda collieries supplied most of the bituminous coal needed for the furnaces.[1] Although samples of coal were submitted by both the Plymouth and the Dowlais iron companies for trial by the Admiralty at the end of the forties, neither company was at that time selling coal. Both companies, however, entered the sale-coal trade in the fifties; by 1859, when the first sales were made by Dowlais, the Plymouth Iron Company was already selling 200,000 tons of coal a year.[2] The directors of the Rhymney Iron Company reported the first sales of steam coal by that firm in 1860: 'the development of this trade must, however, be gradual and will involve a considerable outlay for rolling stock; still the directors look forward to it being an important source of profit'.[3] With the entry of Cyfarthfa in 1866 and of Nant-y-glo and Blaina in the following year nearly all the Welsh iron companies had become sellers of coal.

One of the striking features of this general trend is the comparatively late beginning of the sale of coal by the Merthyr ironmasters and particularly by the giant firms of Dowlais and Cyfarthfa. But it would be wrong to infer that these firms delayed their participation in the coal trade until the stagnation of their iron trade compelled them to look elsewhere for profits. A more satisfying explanation emerges when the circumstances under which both the Dowlais and the Cyfarthfa firms carried on their business are more closely examined. Even when the growing demand for Welsh coal rendered obsolete the view held by William Crawshay in 1833 that 'the Coal Trade always was a lean one'[4] neither firm had, at first,

[1] *MG*, 10 Apr. 1858; *CG*, 13 Jan. 1866.
[2] Cyfarthfa MSS., Box 4. Wm. Crawshay II to Robert Crawshay, 20 Oct. 1859. [3] *MG*, 24 Nov. 1860.
[4] Cyfarthfa MSS., vol. 13. Wm. Crawshay II to T. H. Gwynne, 24 July 1833.

a surplus of coal for sale. Their existing winnings of coal were barely adequate to supply the needs of their ironworks and both held leases that for different reasons discouraged the sinking of new pits.

The old Dowlais lease expired in 1848. Its renewal, partly owing to the antipathy of the Marquis of Bute towards Sir John Guest,[1] was for long in doubt and, indeed, agreement was reached only at the eleventh hour. This long uncertainty discouraged investment in new coal workings, while the old workings had been roundly condemned as inefficient a full decade before.[2] Nor did uncertainty end immediately with the signing of the new lease as Dowlais, after working for nearly a century under a lease which had involved merely nominal payments, had to adapt itself to an agreement which reflected the commercial value of the property. This adaptation was not helped by the considerable withdrawal of capital from the undertaking which had taken place in the years before the old lease expired.[3] In 1852, in the midst of the reconstruction, Sir John Guest died; not until the appointment of G. T. Clark and H. A. Bruce as trustees in 1856 did the management at Dowlais display the energy that was needed if there were to be ventures into new fields. Indeed, so far removed was the possibility of selling coal from Dowlais at this time that the new trustees found themselves obliged to contract for a supply of 60,000 tons of coal a year to maintain the fuel supplies necessary for the production of iron.[4]

Efforts were made to improve the productivity of the Dowlais pits by equipping them with new engines and by mechanizing the underground haulage, and the sinking of two

[1] NLW Bute MSS., Box 70, Letter Book, vol. 2. Bute to R. Roy, 30 Mar. 1839, 14 May 1841.
[2] CCL Bute MSS. XIV. 84. Report by J. Gray, 6 July 1839; VI. 1. Report by R. Beaumont, 1839.
[3] Dowlais MSS., Section E. Report by Wm. Jenkins on accounts for 1862–3. The partners drew from Dowlais an average of £64,000 a year in the eighteen years before 1848.
[4] Ibid., Deeds, No. 310. Agreement between Dowlais Iron Co. and T. Joseph, 10 Dec. 1856.

large new pits at Fochriw was started—innovations, however, which could yield no quick results. A more immediate solution of the difficulties of Dowlais came when an opportunity occurred in 1859 for the company to buy the adjoining Penydarren mineral field. This purchase not only gave Dowlais control over additional supplies of good quality coal which could be worked comparatively cheaply[1] but it also, even after the closing of some of the more expensive Dowlais workings, enabled a small surplus of coal to be produced. The Penydarren lease actually passed to Dowlais in June 1859; at the end of May the Cardiff agent of the Dowlais Works was already 'taking steps to make well known our position as open to sell a "limited quantity of first class Steam Coals"'.[2]

Two years later, when the Fochriw pits were coming into operation, the Dowlais Company was able to consider a much larger participation in the coal trade. In urging this course Menelaus, the manager of Dowlais Works, brought forward a variety of arguments.[3] The current iron-making capacity of 2,000 tons of finished iron a week was, he considered, as much as one family ought to commit itself to in a risky trade. With the new Fochriw pits, however, the company could raise about 1,000 tons a day more coal than was needed by the ironworks for this production. The advantages of raising, and selling, this extra coal were that it would enable the company to derive the fullest benefit from its present lease, would not involve any large additional capital commitment, and would prove a source of profit. Working the coal at this rate would more or less exhaust the property by the time the current lease expired and this could be done, once the present sinkings were completed, without the necessity for

[1] Ibid., Section B. Report on value of Penydarren Mineral Field to the Dowlais Iron Works, by Wm. Menelaus, 27 Jan. 1859. In the Dowlais workings most of the coal was worked 'to the dip'; this involved the extra expense of underground haulage against the gradient, and extra pumping costs.

[2] Ibid., Cardiff Agency Letters. S. Howard to G. T. Clark, 25 May 1859.

[3] Ibid., Section D. Report on Dowlais entering coal trade, by W. Menelaus, 7 Nov. 1861.

any new pits. Nor would much capital be required for the disposal of this possible coal surplus; only the circulating capital, and this 'looking at the large business done by some of the Cardiff people who have been but a few years in the trade . . . must be a small matter to a concern like Dowlais'. Menelaus considered that the prospects of selling the coal at a profit were bright. Dowlais steam coal was as good as any and 'it is well known that the Iron master under the same circumstances can always work his coal cheaper than the Coal owner' because he gave more regular employment and because he could use the small coal. 'Now while the coal owner finds difficulty in getting rid of the small from his screens at 1*s*. per ton, we can use it in the works where it is worth upwards of 2*s*. 6*d*. a ton; this in itself is an element of profit which will enable us better to compete with the Aberdare coal owner.'

Menelaus realized that the lack of a direct rail connexion between the Dowlais collieries and the sea—they were served by a lengthy incline joining them to the Taff Vale Railway—increased transport costs. Even if this disadvantage remained, and even in the unlikely event of it converting a profit on the sale of coal into a small loss, he still thought that, in view of the labour tactics of the colliers, the trade would be worthwhile.

'Colliers have been at all times difficult men to manage and have become worse owing to the great demand for men in Aberdare and the adjoining districts. They are ever ready to take advantage of the masters on the slightest pretence. When an Iron works only raises sufficient coal for daily use in Iron making the men have always the power to inflict grievous loss upon the master by simply idling, keeping the Furnaces and the Forges short of coal. In good times if the master refuses to accede to the demands of the colliers, which are frequently most unreasonable, they attempt to gain their ends by keeping the works short of coal preventing the master making quantity when he would be able to realize large profits.'

If more coal was raised than was needed for iron-making alone this power of the colliers was eliminated, as the sale coal could be diverted to the works. 'The loss on sale coal would be nothing compared with the loss by small makes of iron in good times.' The enthusiasm of Menelaus for coal sales clearly did not arise out of any loss of faith in the future of iron.

At Cyfarthfa the Crawshays, as early as 1822, were asserting their right to sell coal in opposition to the view of their landlords that the lease allowed the working of coal only for use in the works.[1] This was a recurrent battle,[2] but one that is difficult to interpret as the coal-trade issue merged into a wider struggle over the terms of a new lease. Under their old ninety-nine-year lease, due to expire in 1864, the Crawshays paid only £100 a year in rent and no royalties. They were eager to force an early renewal of this lease for a long term, offering in return to accept an immediate increase in their rent and the payment of some royalty charge. Their claim to their right to enter the coal trade implied a threat, if the landlords refused to accept their terms, to exhaust the mineral property during the current peppercorn lease by selling coal on a vast scale. Even though their terms were rejected the Crawshays failed to implement this threat, perhaps because their interest in the coal trade was more apparent than real, perhaps because they believed that the conditions of their lease effectively debarred them from selling coal. In the fifties, particularly, the approaching end of the old lease discouraged the outlay of the capital required to secure a coal surplus that could be sold. The new lease was agreed in 1860, but it was not until six years later—when the Castle Pit sunk specially for the sale-coal trade was opened—that the first twenty wagons of coal were sent down to Cardiff from Cyfarthfa.[3]

[1] Cyfarthfa MSS., Box 1. Thomas Bold and E. P. Richards to Wm. Crawshay, Jun., 14 Oct 1822; Wm. Crawshay, Sen., to Wm. Crawshay, Jun., 23 Oct. 1822.
[2] Ibid., Box 3. Wm. Crawshay, Jun., to Hon. G. R. Trevor, Jan. 1832; Wm. Crawshay, Jun., to Thomas Bold, 9 Oct. 1838; E. P. Richards to Wm. Crawshay, Jun., 10 Feb. 1846; Wm. Crawshay, Jun., to E. P. Richards, 11 Feb., 18 Mar. 1846.
[3] *MG.* 28 Apr. 1860, 25 Oct. 1866. Cyfarthfa MSS., Box 7. Wm. Crawshay to Robert Crawshay, 26, 28 Oct. 1866.

It is true that by the end of the 1860's the Crawshays, like many of the owners of the other Welsh ironworks, were seriously considering the coal trade not merely as an auxiliary but as an alternative to the iron trade. 'I really think it would be wise to give up the Iron Trade entirely and sell the Coal', old William Crawshay, who at seventy still controlled the business from his seat at Caversham Park, told his son Robert in 1866.[1] It was becoming increasingly clear that, apart from the brief prosperity of the early seventies, for many of the hill works 'the star of the iron trade was fast setting'.[2] The timing of the entry of individual ironmasters into the coal trade, however, was only slenderly related to this broad economic trend. It depended more on the varied circumstances of the different firms; the extent of their mineral resources and the cost at which they could be worked; the restrictions placed by leases on coal selling; the accessibility to markets; and the enterprise of managements. There was no need for the ironmasters to wait until their works were in difficulties before engaging in a trade from which Anthony Hill of the Plymouth Ironworks claimed to be reaping a profit of £10,000 a year in 1859[3] and from which Dowlais derived a profit of £27,892 in 1868.[4] Nevertheless, sales of coal which might have been a mere bagatelle in prosperous years for the iron trade could expand when that trade was depressed and might ultimately oust the manufacture of iron altogether.[5]

Certainly by the beginning of the 1870's the scale of the intrusion of the ironmasters into the coal market had become formidable. In 1873, for example, when the iron firms were probably not using more than 3 million tons of coal for manu-

[1] Cyfarthfa MSS., Box 7. Wm. Crawshay to Robert Crawshay, 12 Nov. 1866. [2] The phrase was William Crawshay's.
[3] Cyfarthfa MSS., Box 4. Wm. Crawshay to Robert Crawshay, 20 Oct. 1859.
[4] Dowlais MSS., Section E. Financial report for 1868 by Wm. Jenkins. This profit represented nearly one-third of the total net profit of the works for that year.
[5] The Nant-y-glo and Blaina Ironworks Company Ltd. sold nearly 560,000 tons of coal in the year ending 31 Aug. 1875, when the firm was described as being little more than a coal-producing enterprise. *CG*, 3 Dec. 1875.

facturing purposes, their aggregate output of coal was rather more than 5 million tons. The repercussions of this were numerous. It made for a sharp cleavage between the coal-owners and the ironmasters, the coal-owners resenting the growing scale of this competition, particularly as the ironmasters enjoyed the competitive advantages of being able to utilize their small coal and of paying lower wage rates to their colliers. The attempts of the coal-owners to abolish or reduce this wage differential exercised a particularly baneful influence on the course of industrial relations in the early 1870's. For the moment, however, it need merely be noted that the invasion of the coal market by the ironmasters contributed substantially to the increase in the coal output of South Wales.

In the sale-coal industry proper the most striking feature of the increase in output that was fostered by the rising demand for coal was its uneven distribution over the coalfield. The regions where the development of mining activity was most intense were pre-eminently the valleys which found an outlet for their coal through the port of Cardiff and, to a lesser degree, those served by the port of Newport. The decisive nature of this change in the balance of production of sale coal from the west to the east—already the principal area for the production of coal for industrial purposes—is illustrated by the figures of coal shipments.

Coal Shipments from South Wales Ports. Coastwise and Foreign

	1840	1874
	(000's tons)	
Milford	77	34
Llanelly	212	222
Swansea	} 493	768
Neath		275
Cardiff	166	3,780
Newport	489	1,066

Three major influences determined the pattern of coal production over the area during these years. First, the rapid growth in the demand for steam coal stimulated production in the areas where the coal was best fitted for this purpose. Second, the geological structure of the various areas—the condition and the depth of the coal seams—governed the extent to which they were worked. Third, and not wholly independent of the first two influences, the relative adequacy of transport facilities—vital for the carriage of a bulky commodity—helped to determine the degree of the exploitation of an area. It remains to examine the interaction of these forces within the different sectors of the coalfield.

West of the Vale of Neath anthracite was the predominant type of coal, and the stagnation of the demand for anthracite is thus largely sufficient to account for the slower expansion of output in this region. There were, however, also substantial reserves of bituminous and of dry steam coals near the coast. The output of bituminous coal expanded soberly but steadily with the industrial needs of the area (arising from the location of the tinplate, copper, and other metallurgical works near Neath, Swansea, and Llanelly) but the steam coals of the region were generally inferior in quality to those found in the hinterland of Cardiff and thus secured only a minor share in this most rapidly expanding market.

The difficult geological conditions of this area also retarded its development. The faulted and disturbed nature of the coal seams added to the risks and costs of working, while the great fault running along the Vale of Neath depressed by some 700 yards all the coal seams that lay to the west of it so that the lower coal series were to be found only at considerable depths. Whilst these difficulties hampered the development of the western part of the coalfield generally, their effect was most evident in Pembrokeshire. This factor apart, Pembrokeshire should have suffered less than the rest of the anthracite coalfield from the failure of the demand for anthracite to develop; the anthracite in Pembrokeshire was of the purest and highest quality, whilst the collieries there were nowhere far from the sea. In opposition to the general trend, however,

THE EXPANSION IN OUTPUT

the output of the Pembrokeshire coalfield, never considerable at any time, declined both relatively and absolutely. There was no important local industrial demand to stimulate production; the shipments from Milford by 1874 had fallen to less than half the volume of those of thirty years earlier; nor could there have been any great increase in the carriage of anthracite by land, as the census returns showed a decline in the number of colliers in Pembrokeshire. The decline is primarily attributable to the highly complex geological structure of the area. The normally thin seams were 'frequently dislocated by over-thrusts causing large-scale horizontal displacements of strata', and the coal was often shattered by intense pressure.[1] By 1840 most of the easily won coal from the outcrops had already been worked to supply the trade of the preceding centuries. Pembrokeshire was thus becoming a high-cost region at a time when competition was intensifying. As the railways spread over South Wales the vast anthracite field behind Llanelly, Swansea, and Neath, where the coal could be more cheaply won, became more fully opened out; in general it was only in those restricted outlets where a high premium could be obtained for quality that the Pembrokeshire pits could compete.[2]

Perhaps some small part of the substantial decline in the relative importance of the western sector as a whole could be attributed to its failure to secure transport facilities suitable to the times. At Swansea, for example, the Canal Company was allowed to remain in uncontested control of the Swansea valley trade until the late 1850's, even though the effect of the opening of the Llanelly Railway in 1840 and 1841 in diverting the mineral traffic of the Cwmaman and Garnant areas away from Swansea had been evident.[3] The idea of a railway up the Swansea valley had, indeed, been mooted as early as

[1] *Regional Survey Report. South Wales Coalfield* (H.M.S.O., 1946), p. 10.
[2] Evidence of Thomas Evans, *Royal Commission on Coal*, 1871, vol. ii.
[3] W. H. Jones, *History of the Port of Swansea* (Carmarthen, 1922), p. 263. See also H. Pollins, 'The Swansea Canal', *Journal of Transport History*, vol. iii, May 1954.

1830, while a plan for providing the port of Swansea with a floating harbour had been formulated at about the same time, but there was a long delay before these plans came to fruition. Not until 1852 was the floating harbour completed, and a further seven years elapsed before the South Dock was ready; only in 1860 was the Swansea Vale Railway opened. The landowners, including the powerful Beaufort interest, with less vision than the traders, had generally heavily discounted future benefits in favour of immediate gains and a renewed plan for the floating harbour was thus held up for four years while claims for compensation were being settled. Both the South Dock and the railway suffered too, from the tangled rivalry between the landowners on the two sides of the river. Moreover the Swansea Corporation, dallying between the twin visions of Swansea as an industrial centre and as a fashionable watering-place, vacillated between support and opposition. As late as 1847 it decided—by the casting vote of the Mayor—to oppose the new Dock Bill because its interference with the promenade threatened to detract from the amenities of the town as a holiday resort.[1]

The development of the Neath district encountered similar obstacles. The Vale of Neath Railway was opened in 1851 and soon extended to tap the growing trade of the Aberdare valley. The company attributed its early barren years to the lack of a convenient outlet, claiming this as the reason why it obtained only the overflow traffic from the Aberdare valley while the Taff Vale Railway, which had 'a dock at its doorstep', could retain the bulk of the Aberdare coal trade.[2] A company had been formed in 1851 to build a dock at Briton Ferry, slightly lower down the river than Neath, and the shareholders of the Vale of Neath Railway agreed to take up

[1] *MG*, 18 Dec. 1847.
[2] Ibid., 19 Feb. 1859. In fact, Cardiff was the 'natural' outlet for the Aberdare valley, the Vale of Neath involving a longer haul partly against the gradient. But it is reasonable to suppose that with a suitable dock the Vale of Neath line would have secured more traffic for vessels bringing cargoes to Neath and anxious to take a return cargo of the 'matchless' Aberdare coal.

THE EXPANSION IN OUTPUT

one-third of its share capital of £60,000.[1] The dock, however, was slow to materialize and in its absence much of the Vale of Neath traffic was forced to travel on to Swansea. This journey not only involved extra mileage but also meant, until a second and more suitable line was constructed between Neath and Swansea, that the coal had to be carried from Neath by the South Wales Railway over gradients that were ill-suited to mineral traffic. Not until the Vale of Neath company agreed in 1860 to guarantee 5 per cent. on a further £40,000 was enough capital raised to complete the dock in 1861.[2]

Nevertheless the experience of Llanelly, the third major port in the west, helps to place these transportation problems in their proper perspective. A floating dock had been built at Llanelly in 1828, and a further dock was under construction in 1840 when the first section of the Llanelly Railway was opened. Although these improvements enabled Llanelly to avoid the fate of Swansea, where coal shipments actually declined during the 1840's, they failed to stimulate any marked rise in the trade of the port. In the five years from 1840 to 1844 the annual coal shipments from Llanelly averaged 193,000 tons; in the next quinquennium the average was 233,000 tons. There had been rosy hopes of a swifter progress, based largely on the belief—erroneous, as events proved—that anthracite would gain access to wider markets through its steam-raising qualities. A number of colliery enterprises, attracted into the area when the railway was being built, had contracted with the railway company to send down various quantities of coal; by 1843 it was already clear that these agreements could not be honoured. One firm had undertaken to send down coal sufficient to make up railway dues of £300 a year, but in two years their traffic had been worth less than £70 to the line; another had sent down only 746 out of a promised minimum of 10,000 tons. It was made clear by the colliery owners that these deficiencies arose not from a lack

[1] Ibid., 5 July 1851, 30 June 1860.   [2] *CG*, 24 Aug. 1861.

of capacity at the collieries but from the lack of an outlet for their product.[1] If the experience of Llanelly may be taken as a guide[2] it confirms that the delay in providing dock and railway accommodation at Neath and Swansea was not the decisive factor in the relative decline of the western sector in the Welsh coal trade; it merely accentuated a trend that arose naturally from the failure of the attempts to find new uses for anthracite coal.

In the eastern part of the coalfield the same forces were at work but their proportionate influence differed. Along the southern outcrop, in the basin south of the great Risca–Pontypridd–Maesteg anticline, unfavourable geological conditions put a sharp brake on development. The particular problem encountered was that of the steepness of the dip of the seams, although this was further complicated by their great irregularity in thickness and quality. Steeply inclined seams were costly to work not only because of technical difficulties but because a pit of a certain depth generally won less coal when sunk on steep than it did when sunk on flat measures.[3] Apart from the southern outcrop, however, the geological conditions in the coalfield east of the Vale of Neath did not present difficulties sufficient to deter expansion. Moreover this eastern sector possessed rich reserves of high-quality steam coal well adapted to meet the growing demand. Under these conditions transport played a significant part,

[1] *MJ*, 28 Jan. 1843.
[2] The example of Llanelly is not quite representative as the benefits of its dock and railway facilities would have been partly reduced—even if the anthracite trade had developed—by the sandbanks that made the approach to the port difficult to navigate. 'Within the last years ships which have come here to load coal . . . have actually been shut up in the dock where they took their cargoes aboard, by sudden accumulations of sand at its entrance and there were no means of enabling them to get to sea but by cutting channels thro' sandbanks which filled up almost as soon as they were made.' Nevill MSS. 9. R. J. Nevill to Earl of Cawdor, 25 Mar. 1843.
[3] T. Forster Brown, 'Caerphilly Mineral District', *SWIE*, vol. iv (1864). Owing to the geological difficulties, even in 1946 there were large areas still unleased, or leased only in the upper seams, in this region. The coal was usually gas or coking coal. *Regional Survey Report. South Wales Coalfield* (1946).

since its inadequate provision could seriously retard the expansion of output.

The importance of the factor of transport emerges when a comparison is made between the development of the area served by Cardiff and that of the area served by Newport. Undoubtedly the chief influence affecting the relative development of two areas was the more plentiful supplies of the best steam coals in the area commanded by Cardiff. Nevertheless, while the bituminous gas, coking, and house varieties were more characteristic of the coals of Monmouthshire, the tracts of good steam coal were sufficiently extensive there to suggest that the disparity in the rate of growth of shipments from the two ports cannot be explained on this ground alone. In the period between 1840 and 1874 the volume of coal shipments from Cardiff increased twenty-two fold while the shipments from Newport little more than doubled. More significantly, the contrast is still evident when attention is confined to coastal shipments in which the bituminous coals, with which Monmouthshire was well endowed, played a more important part. The coastal shipments from Cardiff rose five-fold during these years, while those from Newport increased by less than half.

These divergent rates of growth were closely related to the contrasting history of the provision of railways and docks to serve the two ports. Cardiff, with the opening of the Taff Vale Railway to Merthyr in 1841, secured a railway early. From the outset, too, it was expected that this line would carry an important coal traffic. It is true that Brunel, in assessing its financial possibilities, restricted his estimate to the carriage of iron, and that the first chairman of the line—Sir John Guest—was an ironmaster whose works at Dowlais were less conveniently sited in relation to the Glamorganshire Canal than were those of his chief rival at Cyfarthfa. However, two important members of the first Board were the coal-owners Thomas Powell and Walter Coffin, and the two branch lines that were included in the original scheme—the Llancaeach and the Rhondda—were specifically designed to serve their pits and those of other owners. These men, too, in assessing the prospects of the line about 1840, did not base their calculations solely on iron but budgeted for an annual coal traffic of 379,000 tons.[1]

It would be difficult to overestimate the impact of the Taff Vale Railway on the rise of the coal trade of Cardiff. 'Generally speaking, in railway matters', the Taff Vale chairman stated in 1846, 'a good railway dividend is like what charity is in religion—it covers a multitude of sins.'[2] The prosperity of the Taff Vale, however, once its initial difficulties were over, was firmly based on the vast mineral traffic that the line served to foster. This traffic was further increased by the later extensions of the line. In November 1846 the Taff Vale agreed to lease the newly-built Aberdare Railway in perpetuity. Two ironmasters, Sir John Guest and Crawshay Bailey, had provided most of the capital required for this short seven-mile line, but it was the coal trade that provided the bulk of its revenue. In the next decade, once the steam coal had been proved and won, the Taff Vale tapped another rich mineral region when it penetrated into the twin Rhondda valleys. The railway not only fostered the exploitation of the Aberdare and Rhondda valleys, but raised Cardiff to the status of the premier coal-shipping port of the area.

The history of Newport, which during the forties continued to be linked to its industrial hinterland only by canals and tramroads, presents a marked contrast. The dilemma that retarded the penetration of some parts of South Wales by railways—that it was difficult to raise support and capital for a railway to serve a region where industrial or mining development had not already begun, while it was risky for an entrepreneur to attempt to open out a new district in the absence of a railway[3]—clearly did not apply to industrialized Mon-

---

[1] CCL Bute MSS. V. 3.   [2] *MG,* 14 Feb. 1846.
[3] John Edmunds, for example, was said to have spent in the years after 1849 some £15,000 in attempting to conduct an extensive coal trade from the

THE EXPANSION IN OUTPUT

mouthshire. There the chief obstacle was rather the monopolistic position of the Monmouthshire Canal Company. This company controlled both the canal and the Sirhowy tramroad, the two main arteries of the Newport trade; it opposed early railway schemes, and saw no urgent need to undertake costly modifications to its own profitable system. It paid a regular 10 per cent., and its only liability was to keep the canal and tramroads in repair—the tramroad wagons and the horses to pull them being provided by the freighters. The discontent of the freighters, however, aware of the steady loss of custom to Cardiff where transport rates were cheaper and facilities better led to a project, put forward in 1842 by R. J. Blewitt, the member for the Monmouth boroughs, for a railway from Newport to Nant-y-glo. The foundation of the Newport coal trade was the Red Ash house coal which, lying in the topmost seams, was cheap to work but, owing to transport charges of $2\frac{1}{4}d.$ per ton mile compared with $\frac{1}{2}d.$ per ton mile levied on the rival Glamorganshire Canal, expensive to bring to port.[1] Despite the high charges the facilities provided by the Canal Company, Blewitt claimed, were poor. The bad state of the tramroads meant that coal carried on them deteriorated in value through the shaking and that the freighters were faced with a cost of wagon repair equivalent to $3d.$ per ton on the coal carried. The canal traffic was subject to all the delays incidental to periods of drought and frost and, in addition, to stoppages of a fortnight a year for canal repairs. These considerations were not only pricing the Red Ash coals out of the market but were hindering the attempts to establish a reputation for Newport steam coals in the market. 'It is found . . . that [the new steam coal trade] cannot be extended or even successfully maintained in competition with other places, unless the coal can be brought to market at all times, in the best order, with the greatest facility and by the cheapest possible means of transit.'[2] Even though a reduction in the

Ely valley. His failure was ascribed chiefly to the 'want of proper Railway Communication with the property'. Mon. County Archives, Bythway MSS., Doc. No. 0525. [1] *Merlin*, 14 Jan. 1843. [2] Ibid., 31 Dec. 1842.

Canal Company's charges was made at this time they still remained 50 per cent. higher than those of the Taff Vale Railway and the Glamorganshire Canal.[1]

The freighters, however, were experiencing the third of a series of depressed years for trade and despite the reality of their grievances the railway scheme languished for a time. The revival of trade in 1844 brought renewed proposals for a railway; the canal proprietors, too, were goaded into projecting a rival line to run from Newport to Pontypool. The bitter struggle that ensued ended in a compromise in 1845. The freighters withdrew their scheme and the Canal Company agreed to apply for powers to make the railway to Pontypool. The Canal Company agreed also to adapt all its tramroads to locomotive power; to become general carriers; and to reduce its charges by 25 per cent. in 1848 and by a further 25 per cent. in 1850.[2] Even then there were still delays in the carrying out of this agreement, the Canal Company securing a new Act in 1848 authorizing the raising of additional capital and extending the time allowed for the completion of the line; relieving the Company of an obligation to provide mineral wagons; and postponing the second reduction in rates till 1858 (but limiting dividends until then to 5 per cent.).[3] The first line—the Western Valley line through Newport, Risca, Abercarn, Newbridge, Crumlin, and Abertillery—was opened at the end of 1850; the completion of the Newport–Pontypool railway took a further two years.

The consequences of the full decade that Newport lagged behind Cardiff in the acquisition of railway facilities were momentous. In 1840 Newport had shipped three times as much coal as Cardiff (490,000 tons as against 166,000 tons); by 1848 Cardiff had overhauled its Monmouthshire rival to become the chief Welsh coal-shipping centre. By mid-century the shipments from Cardiff had reached 731,000 tons, well above the 552,000 tons sent from Newport. In assessing the relative part played in this transformation by the develop-

[1] *Merlin*, 28 Apr. 1843.   [2] *MG*, 1 Feb. 1845.   [3] Ibid., 10 June 1848.

THE EXPANSION IN OUTPUT

ments in transport and by the difference in the type of coal principally found behind the two ports it should be noted that in the foreign shipments—which were mainly composed of the steam coals with which the hinterland of Cardiff was richly endowed—Newport maintained its lead until 1848, while in the coastal shipments—which consisted more of house coals, the traditional basis of the Newport trade—Cardiff had by this time surpassed its rival. The supremacy of Cardiff, moreover, had already been established before the results of the Admiralty trials gave the excellence of its steam coals authoritative publicity. There is thus a strong presumption that the swifter growth of the coal trade at Cardiff at this time arose rather from the relative ease and cheapness with which coal could be brought to the port than from the type of coal involved.

This conclusion is strengthened when the consideration of transport changes is extended to include an examination of the docking facilities available. The natural facilities at Cardiff were poor, the river Taff being unsuited for all but the smallest vessels. The basin that formed part of the Glamorganshire Canal marked little improvement since ocean-going vessels still had to be loaded and unloaded by lighters. The extra handling this involved increased costs and—particularly injurious for the coal trade—the amount of breakage. It had been asserted in 1830 that the 'impediments and inconvenience to vessels using this Canal . . . necessarily occasion a great expense to them, which enhances the price of freights to and from the Port, while at the same time it prevents the Trade of the District from being carried to the extent of which it would otherwise be capable, more especially in the article of Coal'.[1] The deficiency was remedied by the construction of the Bute West Dock, opened in 1839. This was a bold and imaginative project, involving the second Marquis of Bute in an expenditure of nearly £300,000;[2] the future return was expected more

[1] CCL Bute MSS. XI. 1. J. Green, 'Observations on the Port of Cardiff, and Explanation of the Marquis of Bute's proposed Improvements there' (1830).
[2] NLW Bute MSS., Box 70. R. Roy to Lord Bute, 19 Oct. 1843.

from the resulting increase in the value of the 20,000 acres of mineral land and of the extensive real estate in the port and town of Cardiff, that formed part of the Bute Estates in Glamorgan, than from the revenue from the dock itself. The trade of the dock was, at first, disappointing but after the opening of the Taff Vale Railway its success was assured; by 1844 the shipments of the dock exceeded those of the canal.

At Newport activity was on a more modest scale, partly because improvement seemed less essential as the river Usk was deep enough to allow a substantial trade to be conducted from the riverside wharves. A Dock Company had been authorized in 1835 but when the dock was eventually completed in 1842 it covered only $4\frac{1}{2}$ acres compared with the $19\frac{1}{2}$ acres at Cardiff. In the outcome the dock did as much to retard as it did to encourage the expansion of trade. It was not only conceived on too small a scale but its charges—partly because its size was small in relation to its capital costs—were higher than those levied at Cardiff. Moreover, while the Taff Vale Railway had provided machinery for loading coal at the Bute Dock by 1842, the freighters on the Usk still complained in 1848 of the expense and breakage caused by hand-loading which involved the coal being taken from the trams, 'put into barrows and then wheeled along and turned over into the hold of the vessel without any shoot at all'.[1] It was the cumulative effect of all these shortcomings, together with those of the Canal Company, that largely explained such examples as the decline in the coal trade between Newport and Waterford during the 1840's from a level of 30–40,000 tons to one of a mere 1,000 tons a year.[2]

Once the main lines of development within the coalfield had been determined there was a marked tendency for trade to beget trade. By 1875 the coalfield, apart from the area west of Swansea, was generally well provided with railways. Yet, while nearly all the main valleys then had a rail connexion

[1] *MG*, 18 Mar. 1848.   [2] Ibid.

with at least one port, the network was finer in the east. Some of the more important districts, like the Aberdare valley, were served by several lines competing for their produce and providing outlets not only to all the major ports of South Wales but also to Liverpool, Southampton, and London. The course of dock construction revealed even more visibly the same disparate development. At Cardiff by 1875 the dock accommodation had expanded from the 19½ acres of the original Bute West Dock to 97½ acres.[1] Nearly all of this area was still owned by the Bute interest, although the opening of the Penarth Dock in 1865 pointed to the determination of the coal-owners to act on their own to supplement the accommodation provided by this family. Meanwhile the gap between Cardiff and the other Welsh ports had widened still farther. The only improvement to be brought into effective operation at Newport during this period was the extension of the Town Dock (by 7¼ acres) in 1858, and even then the bulk of Newport's coal trade continued to be conducted from the river wharves.[2] The total dock area at Newport remained much less than that of the original Bute West Dock until 1875, when the Alexandra Docks, covering 28¾ acres, were completed. At Swansea only the South Dock, opened in 1859, was provided to supplement the small North Dock or river float that had been opened in 1852.

In 1873 one observer commented that 'the world is stretching out its hands to us for coal, and a plethora of gold may be obtained in exchange'.[3] The clear lead Cardiff now enjoyed in the trade which arose to satisfy this demand rested primarily on the surpassingly rich reserves of steam coal which lay in the hinterland of the port. It was this steam coal which dominated overseas shipments, where the lead of Cardiff was

---

[1] The Bute West Dock (1839) 19½ acres; the Bute East Dock (1855 and 1857) 45 acres; the Penarth Dock (1865) 21 acres; and the Roath Basin (1874) 12 acres.

[2] *CG*, 6 Apr. 1867, cites the following figures for Newport coal shipments in 1864; from the docks, 322,646 tons; from the river wharves, 574,500 tons.

[3] Ibid., 11 July 1873.

overwhelming. This lead had been established, however, before the advantages Cardiff had in the steam-coal trade had been fully realized, and to this early rapid growth priority in transport improvements contributed in no small measure.

Within each of the broad sectors of the coalfield exploitation proceeded with a similar lack of uniformity. In Monmouthshire the Sirhowy and western valleys were more fully developed than the Rhymney and eastern valleys; in the west more attention was directed to the Neath and Swansea than to the Loughor and Gwendraeth valleys. This uneven growth arose, as it did in the wider divisions of the coalfield, from the complex interaction of a number of geological, technical, economic, and personal factors. Full illustration of this process lies beyond the scale of this book, and here attention will simply be concentrated on two valley systems—the Aberdare and Rhondda—which command attention because of the outstanding part they played in the expansion of output and growth in shipments that took place in South Wales at this time. In the two decades before 1875 the growth in production from these two valleys accounted for 37 per cent. of the total increase in output from the coalfield, while their share in the increase of coal shipments, coastal and foreign, from South Wales was probably over 60 per cent. in the period between 1840 and 1854 and about 70 per cent. in the following two decades.

The sinking and opening of the first important sale-coal colliery in the Aberdare valley took place in 1837. This pit did not, however, mark the introduction of industrialism into the district;[1] Crawshay's Hirwaun ironworks could already look back on a continuous history of three-quarters of a century and several other concerns—particularly the Aberdare and

---

[1] Referring to Aberdare, a writer in 1839 stated that 'the village has almost entirely lost its rural character, and now assumes the appearance and manners of its neighbour Merthyr Tydfil'. D. Jenkins, 'Material for Glamorgan History', NLW MSS., No. 7885 C.

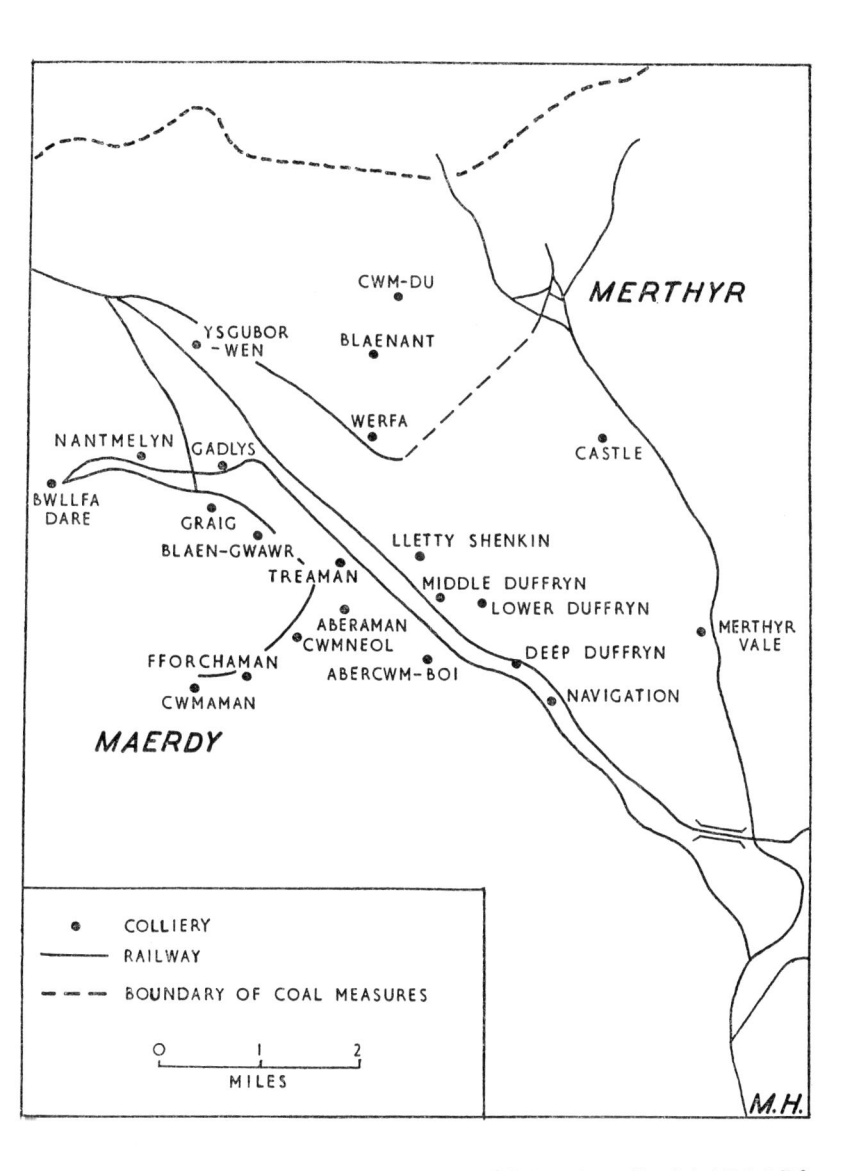

ABERDARE VALLEY 1874 PRINCIPAL COLLIERIES

The above map is based on the map of 'The South Wales Coalfield' used by T. F. Brown to illustrate his Presidential Address to the South Wales Institute of Engineers in 1874 and subsequently printed in vol. ix of the *Transactions* of that Society.

the Gadlys works—were also firmly established in the iron trade. To meet the needs of the ironworks the Aberdare Canal, a branch of the Glamorganshire Canal, had been constructed in 1811, so the exploitation of the coal resources had clearly not been delayed by lack of transport facilities. All that was needed to start a trade in the type of coal that was found in the valley was a market and this developed with the growth of the demand for coal for steam-raising purposes. At the same time, the small market that had been won during the 1830's for the same type of coal from Merthyr served to encourage similar ventures in the neighbouring Aberdare valley.

It was in response to these impulses that the first pit was sunk at Aber-nant-y-groes by the Waynes, owners of the small Gadlys ironworks. This sinking—specifically for steam coal for sale—was a novel venture, as it was unusual for the ironmasters of Glamorgan at this time, despite their knowledge of the coal of the area and their capital resources, to display an interest in the coal trade.[1] Once the winning had been made at Aber-nant-y-groes the Aberdare Coal Company, consisting of three members of the Wayne family and three local landowners, was set up as an undertaking entirely distinct from the Gadlys works. This company never attempted any great expansion by new leasings, remaining content with its single colliery, although further pits were sunk to serve it. Thomas Powell, who followed the Waynes in the Aberdare coal trade, was not so easily satisfied. He brought with him the same drive that had already made him the most substantial coal-owner in Monmouthshire and the largest shipper of coal at Cardiff. In 1840 he started sinking the Duffryn pit at Tyr Founder and two years later struck the Four Feet seam.[2] In the next decade or so Powell added the Plough, Lower Duffryn, Middle Duffryn, and Cwmpennar

[1] The moving spirit was Thomas Wayne; it was later asserted that his father and brother had at first objected to the new venture. See obituary notice, *MJ*, 13 April 1867.
[2] W. W. Price, 'History of Powell Duffryn in the Aberdare Valley', *Powell Duffryn Review*, 1942–3.

pits to form the nucleus of the greatest single undertaking in the South Wales coal trade. He undoubtedly aimed at—and succeeded in—dominating the development of the valley; indeed his leasing of mineral property was on such a scale that for a time he had to leave large tracts of it unworked. Nevertheless many others were showing similar enterprise, on a less ambitious scale, and already by 1846 six further pits were in operation or being sunk.[1]

Apart from the success of these undertakings two other developments stimulated the coal trade of Aberdare. One of the two projects occasioned by the railway boom of the mid-forties, but unlike many of them a modest and sound scheme, was that for a line down the Aberdare valley to link with the Taff Vale Railway and thence to Cardiff. This was completed in 1846, ending the long dependence on the old canal.[2] Of no less importance were the experiments on steam coals carried out on behalf of the Admiralty between 1848 and 1851 which demonstrated the superiority of the coals of South Wales, and particularly of those from the Aberdare Four Feet seam, over the north of England coals for steam-raising purposes. Together, these opened up wider markets and increased the ease of access to them.

These factors, and the general revival of trade after 1848, contributed to a new burst of activity. David Williams, who already owned the Ynyscynon colliery, opened further collieries at Aberaman, Deep Duffryn, and Cwm Dare. Samuel Thomas, whose son[3] was to create and preside over the Cambrian Combine, sank the Ysgubor-wen pit. Before 1854 two further undertakings—Fforchaman and Cwmneol—had been started. In a little over ten years, therefore, the fame of the Four Feet seam had led to the taking and opening out of much of the mineral property of the upper part of the valley.

[1] These were Lletty Shenkin, Blaen-gwawr, Gadlys, Aberaman, Ynyscynon, and Weifa. The opening of a new colliery can generally be traced from references in the contemporary press. See also NLW MSS. I. Astle, 'History of Aberdare'. [2] *MG*, 7 Aug. 1846.
[3] D. A. Thomas, who became Lord Rhondda.

In 1854, for the first time, the output surpassed one million tons; in 1862 it rose to over two million tons. This increase was achieved mainly by extending existing collieries, and especially by sinking to the deeper steam-coal seams. In 1851 the lower Nine Feet seam had been little worked, but ten years later it had been opened almost everywhere in the valley.[1] There were, however, some important new collieries started. Thus in 1856 David Davis added the Abercwm-boi colliery to his Blaen-gwawr undertaking, and by 1860 Dr. Roberts and Mordecai Jones had struck the coal at their Nantmelyn colliery in Cwm Dare at the head of the valley. More significant, perhaps, was the Navigation pit at Mountain Ash, which was opened in 1860. At this colliery, situated farther from the outcrop than those at the upper end of the valley, the coal lay deeper and, owing to the presence of hard rock, it was in fact won only after sinking operations had extended over seven years. The Navigation pit was an indication of the greater quantities of capital that were becoming necessary in the coal trade and, to cover these capital costs, it had from the outset been planned to command a large area and to handle a large output; its mineral taking extended over 4,000 acres and the shafts were capable of raising over 1,000 tons a day.[2]

The figures of the output of coal in the parish of Aberdare,[3] apart from two years of stagnant production in 1857-8 (years

Parish of Aberdare. Coal Output in 000's of tons

1844	. 177	1854	. 1,009	1864	. 2,048	1874	. 1,963
1845	. 193	1855	. 1,204	1865	. 1,976		
1849	. 434	1859	. 1,633	1869	. 2,142		
1850	. 477	1860	. 1,755	1870	. 2,071		

marked by a financial crisis and a major strike), were rising year after year in the period between the early 1840's and the

[1] *MG*, 18 Oct. 1851, 21 Dec. 1861. [2] Ibid., 12 May 1860.
[3] R. Hunt, *Mineral Statistics*. The production figures for the Aberdare valley would be slightly higher, as some of the coal of the valley was raised in the parish of Llanwynno.

early 1860's. After then the continuous growth came to an end.[1] There were still years when the flagging of production could be ascribed to trade crises or to industrial disputes; but there were deeper causes at work. The iron industry of the area was declining, and the amount of coal worked in the parish of Aberdare for use in the ironworks of the valley fell from about 245,000 tons in 1863 to about 67,000 tons in 1874. More important, the lead in the steam-coal trade was passing from the Aberdare valley to a region which had hitherto been less intensively developed—the Rhondda valleys.

'A wild and mountainous region where nature seemed to reign in stern and unbroken silence. Not a human being besides myself appeared to be treading these solitudes, nor was there a human habitation to be seen.' Such was a traveller's impression of the Rhondda in 1836.[2] Even ten years later, when sinkings were proceeding apace in the neighbouring Aberdare valley, the Rhondda was still 'this solitudinous and happy valley', the 'gem of South Wales'; its river not yet an unlovely murk but 'one of the joyous mountain streams that excite the ardour of the fly-fisher'.[3]

The picture conveyed by these descriptions was not, however, the whole truth. Although the iron industry had never established itself in the Rhondda, the coal trade had made a much earlier start here than at Aberdare. Coal had been worked in the Rhondda for an outside market since the beginning of the nineteenth century. It was from the Dinas colliery at the entrance to the Rhondda Fawr valley that Walter Coffin had dominated the coal trade of Cardiff in the

[1] According to R. Hunt, *Mineral Statistics*, the coal output of the Aberdare valley in 1869 was 2·2 million tons; this included the output of the parish of Aberdare, the output of the Navigation colliery, and part of the output of Deep Duffryn entered under Llanwynno parish. The Powell Duffryn Company, owning ten of the thirty collieries in the valley, raised 738,000 tons; the two collieries of Messrs. Nixon, Taylor, and Cory at Mountain Ash yielded 263,000 tons.

[2] Thomas Roscoe, *Wanderings through South Wales* (Birmingham, 1836), part 33, p. 244.

[3] C. F. Cliffe, *The Book of South Wales* (1847), pp. 83, 85, 122.

1820's, and in 1840 he was still second in importance only to Thomas Powell. On his entry into the Rhondda coal trade Coffin had constructed a tramroad which gave him a link to the Glamorganshire Canal, and this tramroad to Dinas remained the chief highway for the valley for over thirty years. During this period his successors were few and insignificant; typical of the cluster of small levels was that of Crawshay at Eirw (worked to supply a small ironworks at Treforest) which employed only thirty men and boys in 1841.[1] Even the output of Coffin, the giant of the valley, still remained comparatively small, his shipments on the Glamorganshire Canal in 1840 amounting to 50,913 tons.[2]

In the 1840's the pace began to quicken. George Insole, a Cardiff coal-shipper who had already opened a house-coal colliery at Maes-bach in the Taff valley, extended his activities into the Rhondda in 1844. At first he worked only small levels, but in 1847 he sank the Cymmer pit, to which he added the New Cymmer pit, opened in 1855.[3] John Calvert sank the Newbridge pit in 1845, and four years later began a second colliery on land he had leased at Gyfeillon. The boom year of 1845 had also seen the establishment of collieries at Ynys-hir and Troed-y-rhiw, the first by Shepperd and Evans, the second by Leonard Hadley, a Caerleon flour-miller.[4]

At first sight it seems difficult to reconcile these operations, and others of lesser importance that accompanied them, with the description of pastoral beauty given by Cliffe in 1847. A closer study of the location of these collieries dispels this difficulty. In its upper reaches the Rhondda consists of two valleys, the Rhondda Fawr and the Rhondda Fach, which meet at Porth. The valley from here down to Pontypridd, where the River Rhondda flows into the Taff, constitutes the Lower Rhondda. All the collieries which were opened before 1850 were concentrated, in the main, in this lower end of the

[1] *Children's Employment*, p. 525.
[2] Ibid., p. 636. [3] *MG*, 2 Aug. 1856.
[4] A full account of the development of the Rhondda is given in the unpublished thesis of E. D. Lewis cited above.

valley. Dinas and Cymmer, it is true, were situated at the entrance of the Rhondda Fawr, while Troed-y-rhiw and Ynys-hir were at the foot of the Rhondda Fach; but much the greater part of these valleys was still unworked, still the habitation of sheep and shepherds. It was these valleys that Cliffe was portraying in such rapturous terms.

The development that was taking place in the Rhondda in the 1840's offered no real parallel to the activity shown in the Aberdare valley at the same time, as it rested on the reputation the Rhondda had acquired for a different type of coal. The Dinas colliery had never worked the lower steam-coal series, but had concentrated on the overlying seams, seams which—owing to denudation and other geological influences —were generally not to be found in the Aberdare valley. These coals, from the Nos. 1, 2, and 3 Rhondda seams, were house and coking coals of the highest quality. 'They constitute', so a report stated, 'the trade of the Valley for the supply of Coals to the manufactories at New Bridge and the shipping at Cardiff. The lower Seam [No. 3], in particular ... supplies several hundreds of tons per day to Cardiff, and is much esteemed for domestic purposes, as well as for the excellent Coke which it yields.'[1] The markets for this coal were coastal; in 1830 Coffin testified before a Select Committee that he sent almost his entire output to Ireland.[2]

It was the reputation that the No. 3 Rhondda seam, 'Coffin's coal', had acquired which lured the speculators of the 1840's into the valley. The development of the Rhondda during these years was thus a continuation of the old pattern of the Welsh coal trade seeking its outlet in the slowly expanding channels of coastal traffic. This expansion, as was usual, both produced and was encouraged by the provision of improved facilities for transport. The Taff Vale Railway, as completed in 1841, had included a short branch in the Rhondda to con-

[1] CCL Bute MSS. VII. 11. Report on the Coal Seams under three farms in Lower Rhondda, by W. P. Struvé.
[2] Evidence of W. Coffin, *Select Committee on Coal Trade*, P.P. 1830, viii.

nect with the Dinas tramroad (Coffin was the Vice-Chairman of the Railway Company's Board) and by 1849 extensions had been made as far as Dinas colliery in the Rhondda Fawr and Ynys-hir colliery in the Rhondda Fach.[1]

The quality, reputation, and shortage[2] of Coffin's No. 3 coal are sufficient to account for the increased activity in the Rhondda at this time. There were no attempts to extend operations to the steam coals, even though such attempts might have been expected in view of the growing success of this trade in the Aberdare valley. Several reasons, however, explain the delay in the search for similar seams in the Rhondda. The iron industry had not developed in the region and hence the transport facilities were poor, the knowledge of the coal resources of the region less complete, and there was an absence of families like the Waynes who could branch from one industrial activity into another. Added to this there was a widespread conviction that the coals lay too deep for practical working. The twin Rhondda valleys are almost exactly in the centre of the coal basin; the steepness of the dip at the northern and, more especially, the southern outcrops suggested that these central coals lay at inaccessible depths.[3] They would, indeed, have done so had the dip continued unbroken. The basic synclinal pattern is, however, interrupted by a great anticlinal fold running from east to west. This Pontypridd–Maesteg Anticline traverses the greater part of the coalfield near the southern outcrop[4] forming a ridge within the basin and throwing up the coal measures towards the surface. The existence of this anticline was not unknown

[1] *MG*, 25 Aug. 1849.
[2] Vide E. D. Lewis, op. cit., p. 75. 'In the early 'forties, as the Letter Books of the firm of Insole's, coal shipper at Cardiff, conclusively prove, there was a definite shortage of this coal.' The authors have been unable to trace the present location of these Letter Books.
[3] The dip from the northern outcrop is generally about 1 in 12, and this easy dip usually persists well into the centre of the coalfield; from the southern outcrop it is often as much as 1 in 2 and rarely less than 1 in 4.
[4] Running north of Risca and south of Pontypridd and reaching Swansea Bay between Port Talbot and Swansea.

before 1850, but its precise consequences could not be gauged and the depth at which the coals could be expected to be found was still highly uncertain. It was this reasonable uncertainty, and not an ignorant belief that the coal lay at fantastic depths, that held back development in the Rhondda. It was not enough that the coal should be within reach of contemporary practice; it was also necessary that it could be won at a cost which would enable it to compete with the produce of the Aberdare valley.

These uncertainties apart, the initial winning of the coal was inevitably beset with unusual hazards. The twin valleys of the upper Rhondda boasted no roads; the railway extended only to the collieries working the proven house-coal seams at the lower end of the valley. Somehow cumbersome sinking machinery had to be transported into the area, the men provided for, and the capital found. In face of all this the offer of the Taff Vale Railway directors to present £500 to anyone who would sink for coal at the upper end of the Rhondda to a depth of 120 yards below the river bed was no great incentive. Altogether, it was not a project to attract the normal capitalist coal-owner. The risks were unusually great and the reward unlikely to equal, let alone surpass, that which could be obtained from working the steam coal of the Aberdare valley, where it was still possible to lease mineral tracts. It called for a capitalist with wider interests and it found him in the person of the Marquis of Bute (and later in the Bute Trustees, for the second Marquis died in 1848 leaving an infant son to succeed him). The Bute Estate included lands in the Rhondda from which a large potential revenue might be obtained once the mineral value was established; it also included a dock at Cardiff to which any Rhondda coals would be sent. It was primarily with these interests in mind, and only very secondarily with a view to the direct profits from working coal, that the Bute Trustees determined to win the Rhondda steam coals.

Acting on the advice of W. S. Clark, his mineral agent in Glamorgan, the Marquis of Bute had bought Cwmsaerbren farm, at the top of the Rhondda Fawr, from William Davies in 1846.[1] It was here that the sinking of the trial pit was started on 16 October 1851.[2] The Upper Four Feet seam was eventually reached at a depth of 125 yards. While the Taff Vale Railway was reacting to this by extending its line up the valley, a second shaft was sunk between 1853 and 1855 to serve as an upcast. On 21 December 1855 the first train of Rhondda steam coal was sent to Cardiff.[3]

This was rightly heralded as a triumph and a portent, but there was no swift rush to win the steam coals. The mineral lands of both the Rhondda Fawr and the Rhondda Fach were quickly bought or leased by such landowners and speculators as the Bute Trustees and Crawshay Bailey, but there were few sinkings. Not until 1858 was another colliery, the Tyla-coch, sunk to the steam measures, and by 1865 only three undertakings in the Rhondda Fawr—including the original Bute Merthyr at Cwmsaerbren—had won the steam coals. In the Rhondda Fach only the Ferndale colliery had been opened to win the steam coal.[4] This was not the full extent of colliery activity in these valleys during the ten years, as sixteen further enterprises had been started to work the upper coals, particularly the No. 3 Rhondda, wherever they could be found. The slighter interest displayed in the steam-coal measures, even after their accessibility had been demonstrated, suggests that development was still retarded by the belief that they could be worked more advantageously in the Aberdare valley. W. S. Clark, even though he had advised the purchase of Cwmsaerbren, had appreciated this difficulty. He stated that his surveys led him to believe that the Upper Four Feet seam might be found only at a depth of 150 yards beneath the valley floor, and added: 'Not that the depth I have stated involves any particular difficulties in working but simply

[1] The purchase was agreed in 1845, but not finally completed until 5 Nov. 1846. At that time £5,000 of the purchase money was outstanding as an agreed balance at 4 per cent. NLW Bute MSS., Box 70. Letter Book 1845–6.
[2] See Diaries of W. S. Clark.   [3] *MG*, 29 Dec. 1855.
[4] E. D. Lewis, op. cit., pp. 127, 138.

that these seams of coal cannot be worked so beneficially so long as the same seams of coal can be had nearer to the Crop or surface at a less outlay of Capital and working charges.'[1] In 1864 the production of coal in the Rhondda was still little more than half a million tons—made up, for the most part, of house or coking coals.[2] By the mid-sixties, however, the shallower Aberdare seams were being fully worked and hence, with the demand for steam coal rising, more serious attention began to be directed to the Rhondda, where the steam coal had already been proved and transport facilities provided. The deeper pits of the Rhondda, and the larger outputs associated with them, needed greater capital resources, but by the mid-sixties, too, capital was becoming more readily available. By 1874 the output of the Rhondda was already over two million tons, and the increase was overwhelmingly attributable to the extended winning of the steam coals. In the ten years ending in 1875 sixteen new collieries were opened to these measures in the Rhondda Fawr, and four in the Rhondda Fach.[3] Yet despite the substantial contribution they had already made to the output of the valley they were mostly still in the process of being opened out. In the next decade the annual production of the valley was to rise by a further $3\frac{1}{2}$ million tons, an increase arising mainly not from new collieries but from the extension of those already in being. In the Rhondda area, unlike that of Aberdare, the period between 1840 and 1875 marked only the prelude to the full exploitation of the coal resources.

[1] CCL Bute MSS. VII. 27. Report on Cwmsaerbren Farm, 1845. A mining engineer representing the vendor believed that the Four Feet seam would be found only 20 yards below the valley floor. Clark disagreed, and accordingly wanted the purchase price to be reduced from £11,000 to £9,000. Wm. Davies would not consent to this; not surprisingly, for besides the potential profits or royalties, the farm —as Clark pointed out—commanded the top of the valley and would yield a high way-leave income when this was opened out.
[2] E. D. Lewis, op. cit., pp. 129–30.　　　　　　　[3] Ibid., p. 127.

V

LANDOWNERS AND COAL-OWNERS

THE period of active participation by the landowners in the development of the coal industry had already passed by the middle of the nineteenth century. Thenceforward the role of the majority of the landowners was bounded by the clauses enumerated in their mineral leases. But if the field was thus narrowed it was still important; the pace of the exploitation of the area was partly dependent on the terms upon which leases were granted. The strong impression which emerges from an examination of a considerable number of mineral leases in South Wales is that the lessees were not encumbered with undue restrictions.[1]

It is, however, difficult to generalize beyond this, because one of the most marked features of the mineral lease was its extreme flexibility. The bare framework, it is true, was fairly uniform. The minerals were granted for a term of years in return for the payment of stipulated royalties levied on every ton of coal (or other mineral) that was raised. There was a way-leave charge—also on a tonnage basis—for the carriage over or beneath the property of coal that had been worked from the estates of other landowners; and there was a dead, or certain, rent to ensure the landowner a basic minimum rental no matter how little coal was worked. All the elements that made up the mineral lease were, however, capable of widespread variation.

As sinkings became deeper and as the amounts of capital necessary to work a property became more substantial, the prime essential for the lessee came to be security of tenure. Without this the lessees were unlikely to be induced to lay out

---

[1] There are numerous mineral leases in the following manuscript collections: Nevill, Bute, Vivian, Penrice and Margam, Dunraven, Ewenny, Haverfordwest (Williams and Williams).

the capital needed to develop the estates.[1] This was recognized in most of the leases granted in South Wales during this period, the general term being between forty and sixty years. It is not difficult, however, to find exceptions. When the Bute Trustees, for example, let a single seam of coal (the Brithdir seam) lying under only 24 acres in the Bargoed–Rhymney valley to Benjamin Wood of Staffordshire in 1874 the term was for only twenty-one years.[2] There were, however, usually special reasons for such departures; the area involved was small, or it lay close to the surface, or—as in the example above—it was an isolated taking which could be most conveniently worked from an existing colliery.

The level of the royalty was hardly less important. For steam coal the royalty usually varied from $6d.$ a ton for large coal and $3d.$ a ton for small, to $10d.$ for large and $5d.$ for small, although extreme instances could be found on either side of this range. On house coal the rate was generally higher as this coal was normally obtained from the uppermost seams and could thus be worked with a smaller outlay of capital. A lessee in 1873, for example, offered a royalty on the No. 3 seam and above (the house-coal seams) of one-tenth of the selling price of the coal delivered into wagons at the colliery, and on the seams below the No. 3 (the steam coals) of one-twelfth of the selling price.[3] The way-leave charge, both surface and underground, showed a similar variation, ranging from $\frac{1}{4}d.$ to $2d.$ a ton, although the most general charge was $1d.$

The theoretical basis of these variations was, so Sir Lowthian Bell told a Royal Commission later, 'the difference in cost between the cost of production and placing in the common market of the most favourably situated mine and that which is most expensive to work, and which yet can be

---

[1] Benjamin Jones, who leased the Gors-goch colliery in Carmarthenshire from the Bishop of St. David's, complained that an attempt of his to form a company had been unsuccessful because of the short lease. As a result of this complaint he was granted a new lease in 1867. Lucas MSS, No. 134.

[2] NLW Bute MSS., Box 106.

[3] Dunraven MSS. 390. Bundle marked 'Aberkerdin', W. T. Lewis to Henry Randall, 20 Nov. 1873.

worked at a profit'.[1] But in practice there was little justification for applying a Ricardian rent theory to the payments to mineral-owners. The extended duration of the mineral lease was in itself enough to nullify such conceptions, while—unlike land—the same coal could not be worked over and over again. The royalty was simply a charge by the property owner for the removal of an irreplaceable asset from his property, and its variations appear to have arisen as much from *ad hoc* causes as from theoretical principles.

The length of the mining leases, for example, often meant that in a developing district the less favourably placed mines, which were started later, paid as high a royalty as better situated collieries which had been opened earlier, when the prospects of the district were less assured. Theoretical calculations, too, were apt to be upset where the relative bargaining strength of lessor and lessee was ill-balanced. It was early pointed out, moreover, that one of the factors telling against the successful participation of joint-stock companies in coal-mining was the tendency for the basic importance of the mineral lease to be too little appreciated by directors with little experience in the industry who found this to be one of the first problems that confronted them.[2] More generally, the level of the royalty was likely to be substantially determined by the state of the trade at the time it was negotiated. During the boom of 1872–4, for example, many leases were accepted at imprudent levels of royalty. One Monmouthshire coal-owner, who had taken two leases in 1873, complained to the Royal Commission on Royalties that his royalty of 1*s.* was excessive in comparison with those of his neighbours at 8*d.* and 9*d.*[3] Others were more prudent. F. S. Dering, in negotiating a lease for the Welsh Main Coal Company in

---

[1] *Royal Commission on Mining Royalties. First Report*, P.P. 1890 (C 6195), xxxvi, app. A, iv.
[2] *MJ*, 6 Jan. 1849. Letter from Jos. Richardson, Neath, on Mining Companies in Wales.
[3] Evidence of J. Barnes, *Royal Commission on Mining Royalties*, 1890–1 (C 6331), xli.

1873, told the Dunraven agent that 'in the event of the coal owner's profit being reduced to something like what it was four years ago you must allow your (proposed) royalty would be untenable'.[1] In this instance the solution suggested by the lessee was a royalty on a sliding scale based on the selling price of coal at the pit-head. A sliding scale for royalties, however, became widespread in South Wales only during the boom of the 1870's when it proved a useful means of reconciling the excessive demands of the lessors, based on the unusually high prices that were current, with the fears of the lessees as to the future trend of prices. Where the sliding scale was adopted, however, the lessor generally insisted upon the insertion of a minimum royalty clause.[2]

The dead, or certain, rent was nearly always calculated on the basis of the acreage of the mineral taking, most frequently at a charge of between £1 and £2 an acre. The dead rent was levied to secure a minimum income to the landowner regardless of the quantity worked, and thus served to deter coal-owners from leasing large tracts and leaving them undeveloped. There were, however, several considerations which prevented the lessee from viewing the imposition of a dead rent as an undue hardship. In the first place the invariable practice was for the dead rent to merge into the royalty payments. The lessee thus had every incentive to aim at an output large enough for his royalty payments to exceed his dead-rent commitment, and his expectation was that this would be the normal situation. As collieries became deeper, moreover, landowners were generally willing to accept a nominal or reduced dead rent in the early part of the lease while the pits were being sunk and the property opened out. When Eliza Stepney, for example, leased a coal property in Carmarthenshire to Benjamin Jones it was agreed that the dead rent should be £20 for the first year, £30 for the second, £70 for

[1] Dunraven MSS. Bundle marked 'Welsh Main Coal Co.' F. B. Dering to Henry Randall, 24 Nov. 1873.
[2] See, e.g., Dunraven MSS. Ibid., F. B. Dering to H. Randall, 29 Dec. 1873; W. T. Lewis to H. Randall, 20 Nov. 1873.

the third, and £100 thereafter.[1] The dead rent, too, was generally coupled with an average clause—usually of from three to five years—which allowed the 'shorts' (the extent to which the royalty on the quantity worked fell short of the dead rent) to be set against royalty payments in excess of the dead rent in ensuing years.

The normal form of lease also included many provisions which were favourable to the coal-owner. Coal used for the colliery engines and furnaces, for example, was generally free from royalty payments, as was that allowed to the colliery workmen. Sometimes a limit was placed on the amount of coal which was allowed free of royalty for these purposes; most of the Bute Estate leases restricted the workmen's coal to 14 cwt. a month, and many other landowners limited the engine and workmen's coal to 5 or 10 per cent. of the total output.[2] At least one important concession was preserved for the coal-owners rather by the absence of any clause forbidding it than by its explicit approval by the landowners. There was no stipulation as to the order in which the seams were to be worked, with the result that the coal-owners exploited the most profitable seams first.[3] More important were the conditions under which the lease could be surrendered or determined before it had expired, as these were the conditions which enabled the lessee who could not carry on to divest himself of his lease. In the early part of the period many leases still permitted surrender only when the seams had become exhausted or unprofitable, but it gradually became the practice to make surrender permissible at twelve months' notice. To ensure that the lessee should make a substantial contribution to the development of the property, however, the right of surrender was often withheld during

[1] Cardiff MSS., 2 Mar. 1857.
[2] See NLW Bute MSS., Boxes 106 and 143; Cardiff MSS., 1 Jan. 1839, 5 Dec. 1877.
[3] This freedom involved waste. There were fewer technical difficulties if the top seams were worked first, and the lower ones afterwards, but this order was not followed if the lower seams were immediately more profitable. The result was that sometimes the upper seams became unworkable.

the first few years, or until a shaft had been sunk to an agreed seam or depth.

Welsh coal-owners, too, generally enjoyed liberal rights of assignment. The permission of the lessor was required before the lease could be assigned to another party, but this was not to be 'unreasonably withheld'. Ease of assignment was of particular importance when limited companies were being formed on a widespread scale since nearly all of these were floated to purchase an existing lease or colliery. The landowners occasionally withheld their permission to the assignment until they had inserted minor revisions in their own favour,[1] but there is no evidence that difficulties over assignment were an impediment to the development of the coalfield.

Whatever the merits of the leases, there were inevitably occasions when the relationship between the two contracting parties was far from smooth. In particular, the coal-owner frequently found his obligations under his lease to be oppressive: bad trade, technical difficulties, strikes, inundations, explosions, could all lead him to seek concessions from the landlord. The reception he received naturally varied with the personalities involved. Many, like Henry Randall, the agent for the Dunraven estate, refused applications for actual reductions in royalty or dead rent in times of slack trade, preferring to afford assistance by deferring their payment.[2] Even those who were reluctant to grant concessions to meet temporary changes in trade conditions, however, could be induced to extend assistance on other grounds, both transient and permanent. The payment of the agreed dead rent at Dinas colliery, for example, was deferred for five years on account of the difficulties experienced in winning the steam coals.[3] In 1868 the Glyn Neath Steam Coal Company pleaded that it wished to work on a scale too large to be accommodated at

[1] See, e.g., Dunraven MSS. 390. Manuscripts relating to 'Blaen Rhondda Colliery'. F. W. Harris to Henry Randall, 13 July 1872.
[2] Ibid., Manuscripts relating to 'Dunraven Adare Colliery'. C. W. Masterman to Henry Randall, 9 Aug. 1876; Lucas MSS. 78.
[3] Dunraven MSS. Correspondence with Coffin and Co.

Swansea docks but that the extra cost of sending its coal to Cardiff would put it at a disadvantage with its better placed Aberdare competitors. The company also pointed out that, while the Admiralty trials had shown its coal to be inferior to that of Aberdare, its cost of working was higher. These arguments satisfied the mineral agent and the royalty was reduced from 8*d*. to 6*d*. a ton for a period of fifteen years.[1]

The protracted nature of the negotiations for leases, especially where the minerals concerned belonged to more than one landowner,[2] was a further source of dispute. Clashes were all the more likely to develop because operations were often commenced before the final agreement was reached; once a brief agreement to lease, embodying an outline of the main terms, had been drawn up the lessee was usually allowed to take possession. The papers of the Dunraven agent indicate that these delays gave rise to sharp differences between lessor and lessee. Only rarely, however, did they give rise to legal proceedings. This was not merely because most agreements and leases included an arbitration clause; it was also because the lessor was usually in a superior bargaining position, in that once the lessee had started operations he could not extricate himself without loss, while the developments he had made added to the value of his landlord's property. As one tenant, who had been working a mineral estate for eight years, ruefully informed the landlord's solicitor, the landowner's terms for the final lease were accepted 'simply because we could not help ourselves'.[3]

---

[1] Dunraven MSS. 422. Royalty Accounts. Glyn Neath Steam Coal and Iron Co. Ltd.

[2] When an enterprise was started to work minerals under lands belonging to several owners the location of the pits was a matter of prime importance to the landlords. The pit enhanced the value of the property on which it was sunk—the landlord received way-leave payments for coal brought to bank on his land, but worked on adjoining properties; he gained, too, if the lease was surrendered. Usually the landowner whose land was most largely taken could insist on the pits being sunk on his land even where this was not technically the most suitable situation.

[3] Penrice and Margam MSS., No. 9354. James Brogden and Sons, Tondu Iron and Coal Works, to Wm. Llewellyn, 17 June 1870.

It is impossible to obtain comprehensive figures of the incomes derived by the landowners from the exploitation of the mineral resources of the district. The largest single element in the income that accrued to them derived from the royalty payments. On the output of some 16 million tons that was achieved in the coalfield by the mid-seventies the income from royalties on coal alone, on the basis of a low average of 6*d.* and with an allowance of 10 per cent. for royalty-free coal, was of the order of £360,000. The distribution of this was dominated by a few large landowners, the Bute Estate alone yielding a royalty income of over £50,000 by the year 1875— and even then about half of the 27,000 acres of mineral land still remained unlet.[1] In 1848–9 the income from mineral royalties on the Bute estates had been £10,765; in the years 1848–53, after the new Dowlais lease had been signed, it averaged £24,068; in the years 1871–5 it averaged £55,969.[2] The greatest royalty payments came from the iron companies established on the estate—at Rhymney, Dowlais, Aberdare, and Gadlys—but the growth by 1875 derived largely from the development of the Bute estates in the Rhondda valley.

Royalties, moreover, were not the only benefit that fell to the landowners when their mineral estates were exploited. The value of the surface land, apart from that taken for colliery purposes, also increased as colliery villages sprang up and as roads and railways were constructed. At the ports the rise in the value of property was even more marked and those who benefited most from this were also great mineral landlords: the Marquis of Bute at Cardiff, the Morgans, of Tredegar Park, at Newport, and the Duke of Beaufort at Swansea. A report of 1894 indicates the magnitude of this increase at Cardiff. Lord Bute's gross income from ground rents for working-men's cottages and tradesmen's premises in Cardiff rose from £214 in 1830 to £26,289 in 1893.[3]

[1] Evidence of W. T. Lewis, *Minutes of Evidence on the Barry Dock and Railway Bill*, 1884. The property was at the head of the Rhondda valley and in the Merthyr, Aberdare, and Rhymney valleys.
[2] CCL Bute MSS. X; Cardiff MSS. 4. 937.   [3] CCL Bute MSS. XI. 20.

Finally, the industrialization of the area afforded a return to those of the landed classes who invested in the development. This participation usually took the form of assisting the improvement of the transport facilities of the area. Charles Morgan of Tredegar Park, for example, provided river wharves at Newport and was a substantial shareholder in the Newport docks which were built on his land. The Earl of Jersey lent £20,000 to the Briton Ferry Dock Company;[1] the Duke of Beaufort was active, though often with baneful results, in the various Swansea dock schemes; and Lord Windsor gave assistance to the Penarth dock and railway undertaking. Above all, the Bute family, besides incurring an impressive expenditure in building Cardiff docks from their own resources, also promoted and partly financed the Rhymney Railway to serve as one of the feeder lines for this enterprise. In addition, the names of the landowners, great and small, are frequently encountered amongst the shareholders of the railway and dock companies which served the district. Their interest in transportation projects arose only partly because these seemed attractive investment opportunities in themselves; often it was of greater importance that these improvements were vital to the development of their property at the port or in the coalfield. A landowner was more likely to find a lessee, and on better terms, if a railway ran over or near his property and if a sufficient sea outlet were near at hand. It was from indirect results of this kind that the great increase in the Bute income arose, as the return on the capital invested in the Bute docks at Cardiff, despite their initial construction having been an enterprise of considerable hazard, averaged only 4·7 per cent. in the thirteen years from 1858 to 1870.[2]

[1] *MG*, 30 June 1860.
[2] A higher return might have been expected as the Bute mineral leases contained a clause requiring that all coal intended for shipment should be sent to the Bute docks, or pay dues as if it had been so sent. As it was, the new capital expenditure on the docks during these years normally exceeded the annual income.

Even so, the Bute example was far from typical, and the general contribution of the landowners to the transport undertakings was almost certainly surpassed by that made by the coal-owners themselves in this field. Elsewhere the services the landowners rendered were slight. They granted leases on terms which did not impede the growth of the industry; the clauses they inserted for good and efficient working played some part in raising technical standards; and some landowners attempted to ensure that their lessees were sound and substantial men. The mainly negative nature of these functions, however, was indicative of the basically passive part played by the landowners in the development of the coal industry during these years.[1] Normally assured of a certain income from their ownership of the minerals lying beneath their lands, they were content to leave the hazards to others.

The active agents in the coalfield were the men who leased the minerals, the coal-owners. At no time during this period, however, can the coal-owners be said to have formed a homogeneous social group. They differed greatly in the scale of their operations. At one extreme was Thomas Powell, owning over a dozen collieries in two counties, a substantial shareholder in the Taff Vale Railway, in the Monmouthshire Canal and Railway, and in the docks at Penarth and Newport, and a timber merchant and shipowner. Surpassed by none in the coal export trade, his name was a household word wherever steam coal was used. At the other extreme were the numerous small owners, employing fewer workmen than Powell had collieries, and themselves scarcely distinguishable from the colliers they employed.[2] The distribution throughout this range, moreover, was widespread. Some owners failed to progress through misfortune or lack of personal ability. Many

[1] Sometimes landowners sank trial pits on their estates, as higher royalties could be charged once the coal had been proved.
[2] In 1863 Philip Thomas, for example, proprietor of a colliery near Llansamlet, was fined £5 for permitting his daughter to work underground. *CG*, 23 May 1863.

others were quite content to operate one or two successful collieries. It was only the few who were most able, active, enterprising, and fortunate who tended to add colliery to colliery; and amongst even these Thomas Powell was unique. Before 1840 he had already become, through his activities in Monmouthshire and at Gelli-gaer, the greatest single figure in the trade in bituminous coal. He later achieved a similar supremacy in the steam-coal trade of the Aberdare valley even though he was in his mid-sixties and heavily handicapped by deafness when he began to build up this entirely fresh business. It was characteristic that the day before his death, in 1863 when he was eighty-three years old, he had been at work in his Newport office.[1]

An industry which offered such scope to men with widely diverging capital resources was naturally built up by coal-owners whose social origins showed a similar diversity. For every grocer amongst them there was a lawyer; every shipper who turned coal-owner had his counterpart who had been a merchant. There were owners of humble origin, like David Williams of Ynyscynon who had worked with his father as a sawyer at the Aber-nant ironworks before starting, as a working collier, his career in the coal industry. William Thomas, too, of Brynawel, was one of the youthful underground workers whom the Children's Employment Commissioners reported on in 1842,[2] while George Elliot was fond of boasting that he had started off at the age of nine as a pit-laddie in Northumberland. Thomas Powell himself was proud of being a 'self-made man'. 'My friends were not born before me', he said, 'I had nobody who ever gave me anything; I began the world with very little. I have been now 48 years in the coal trade, and I must have made very bad use of my time if I had not made a little.'[3] Such origins contrasted sharply with those

[1] *Cardiff Times*, 27 Mar. 1863.
[2] *MG*, 13 Sept. 1851; *Aberdare Times*, 7 Mar. 1863; *Cardiff Times*, 14 Mar. 1903.
[3] Evidence of Thomas Powell, *Select Committee on Rating of Mines*, P.P. 1857 (241, sess. 2), xi.

of men like Colonel Owen of Landshipping colliery in Pembrokeshire, who was a son-in-law of Sir Charles Morgan of Tredegar Park, and of men like Reginald Blewitt of Llantarnam Abbey, an extensive landowner who had been educated at Rugby and who was the member for the Monmouth boroughs when he embarked upon the coal trade.[1]

A source of recruitment for owners that stood out during this period was the growing class of mining engineers and colliery managers. In an industry in which expert technical knowledge was becoming increasingly important there were frequent opportunities for these men to rise from the position of salaried officers either to a partnership in the same concern or to ownership of a new venture. The men who rose from the ranks of the working colliers usually served as salaried officials before becoming owners; George Elliot spent some time as a mining engineer in Northumberland, while William Thomas of Brynawel was colliery clerk, surveyor, and manager before he was made a partner in the enterprises that he had superintended. Another example of engineer becoming owner was Archibald Hood who, himself the son of a Scottish colliery official, found time to study after his fourteen-hour day as a surface engineman in order to become a mining engineer. At the age of twenty-two his training and ability had already won him the post of chief mineral agent to the important Scottish iron firm of Dunlop and Wilson. This situation enabled him to make the acquaintance of men of some capital to partner him in various colliery enterprises and he consolidated his position by marrying the eldest daughter of William Walker, a pioneer of the South Ayrshire coal trade. Hood was thus already an established coal-owner in Scotland when in 1860 he came south to investigate the growing coalfield of South Wales. He came in his capacity of mining engineer on behalf of other parties, but stayed to become the managing partner of the Glamorgan Coal Company.

[1] David Williams, *John Frost* (Cardiff, 1939), p. 87; T. Nicholas, *Annals and Antiquities of the Counties and County Families of Wales* (1872), vol. ii.

W. T. Lewis (later Lord Merthyr) was a mining engineer and agent for the Bute estates before he became a colliery proprietor in his own right, while Edward Jones had been a manager at one of Crawshay Bailey's collieries before he joined W. B. Partridge in colliery enterprises near Pontypool.[1]

Insufficient evidence survives for a reconstruction of the biographical details of most of the coal-owners and generalization about them can only be tentative. The majority, however, seem to have been Nonconformist in religion. Joseph Tregelles Price, of the Neath Abbey collieries, was a Quaker whose family came to South Wales from Cornwall at the end of the eighteenth century, but he seems to have been the only representative of the Society of Friends in the industry.[2] More typical were Samuel Thomas of Ysgubor-wen, a Congregationalist;[3] David Davis of Blaen-gwawr, who was a manager and liberal supporter of the Wesleyan Training School at Aberdare;[4] David Davies of the Ocean collieries, who was a Calvinistic Methodist; and Walter Coffin, of Dinas, a Unitarian.[5] The predominance of Nonconformists, however, provides in this instance no basis for generalizations about the relation between religious beliefs and entrepreneurial activity. It arose more directly from the simple preponderance of Welshmen among the ranks of the coal-owners. Certainly it is not difficult to find many important exceptions. The Waynes who sank the first pit to serve the steam-coal trade from the Aberdare valley were members of the Established Church and gave generous aid in the building of St. Mary's, Aberdare.[6] Others of the same denomination were Edward Jones, Thomas Powell, and Sir Thomas Phillips, a zealous churchman who

[1] *Cardiff Times*, 1 Nov. 1902, 14 Mar. 1903; *Western Mail*, 5 Sept. 1903; *South Wales Coal Annual* (1914), article on 'Glamorgan Coal Company Ltd. and Lysberg Ltd.'.
[2] T. M. Rees, *The Quakers in Wales* (Carmarthen, 1925), p. 58.
[3] See *D. A. Thomas, Viscount Rhondda*, by his daughter and others (1921).
[4] *CG*, 26 May 1866; *Aberdare Times*, 26 May 1866.
[5] Ivor Thomas, *Top Sawyer* (1938), pp. 3, 15; Caroline E. Williams, *A Welsh Family from the beginning of the eighteenth century* (1885), pp. 68–72, 146–8.
[6] *Aberdare Times*, 12 Nov. 1864.

was the principal founder and one of the most active directors of the Welsh Committee for the Education of the Poor.

The coal-owners of this generation were consciously pioneers, with all the merits and defects of the type. Their presence in a speculative industry, moreover, suggests a touch of adventurousness, while the best amongst them showed initiative and perseverance in gaining new markets. Their faults were largely the faults of their virtues. Industrious themselves, they tended to drive others; thrustful, they resented opposition; thrifty, they could become avaricious. These traits could make their attitude to their workmen high-handed and unsympathetic. The sentiment which William Crawshay expressed on the occasion of a strike in 1853 was one which was shared by most of the coal-owners of the district: 'I was and am', Crawshay told his men, 'thoroughly determined that they [the works] shall stop if I am not to be Master and the Sole Arbiter of what wages I can afford to give.'[1] Nevertheless, their relations with their men were usually best when they resided in the district and had direct personal contact, and their inflexibility towards their workmen was often tempered by a paternalistic outlook.[2]

It was easy, too, for the drive they applied to their business to harden into ruthlessness and for their enterprise to overstep the bounds of morality. When Thomas Joseph went bankrupt in 1858, for example, his father-in-law, David Davis of Blaen-gwawr, paid off the creditors and took over Joseph's three collieries. The understanding was that the collieries would be returned when the money (plus interest) paid out by Davis on Joseph's behalf had been recovered from the profits. Thomas Joseph, however, claimed that his father-in-

---

[1] Merthyr of Senghenydd MSS., No. 383. Printed letter from William Crawshay to Thomas Stephens, chairman of the men's protest meeting.

[2] William Crawshay, for example, rebuked his son Robert for having the works doctor to attend on him and accompany him fishing. 'Have your own medical man if you like, as many other weak men on this point have had and still have, but I cannot again, in my conscience, let 10,000 men be neglected for the Fancy of one other.' Crawshay MSS., Box V, Bundle 33. W. Crawshay to R. T. Crawshay, 1 Oct. 1862.

law neglected these collieries, took wagons and stores from them to use as his own undertakings, and became increasingly reluctant to let the collieries pass out of his possession. In the event, Joseph regained his property only after an acrimonious lawsuit.[1] There was, too, especially when a landowner had no qualified mineral agent, a strong temptation for a coal-owner to commit coal trespass, since without close inspection this was not easy to discover. Many minor trespasses were, indeed, committed quite innocently but, occasionally, the offence was more deliberate. Both Thomas Powell and Thomas Prothero encroached on the Tredegar property in this way. Powell had leased, from J. H. Moggridge and Lord Dynefor, coal under two pieces of land which were separated by Sir Charles Morgan's property at Place Bedwellty. He wished to raise the coal from both these properties at his Buttery Hatch pit on Moggridge's ground, and for this purpose applied to Sir Charles in 1834 for a way-leave. The terms he was offered, however, he refused as being exorbitant, yet he proceeded to work as if a way-leave had been agreed. When the trespass was discovered in 1840, Powell put forward the unlikely plea that he had accepted the way-leave terms and had kept full accounts with the intention of paying Sir Charles the amount due to him. Powell lost his case and paid substantial damages.[2] Thomas Prothero, the other main figure in the Newport trade in the 1840's, had also trespassed on Sir Charles's land from his Woodfield colliery, the offence being the more reprehensible in that, at the time it was committed, he had actually been engaged by Sir Charles as an agent.

The coal-owners of this period were almost wholly first generation men whose primary concern was the establishment of their firms. Their non-business activities, although often extensive, were thus usually centred upon their own particular locality. They played, for instance, no prominent part in the national politics of the time, except when their business interests were directly involved. The imposition of an

[1] Dowlais MSS., Deeds 463, 475.   [2] *Merlin*, 10 Apr. 1841.

export tax on coal in 1842 spurred them into activity, as did the struggle to secure a preference in supplying naval contracts, but rarely did a coal-owner seek or secure election to Parliament. The industrialists from South Wales who, from time to time, sat at Westminster during this period usually had their main interest in either the iron or the copper industry: Sir John Guest of Dowlais, Richard Fothergill of the Aberdare Ironworks, Crawshay Bailey of Nant-y-glo and Blaina, and Henry Hussey Vivian (later Lord Swansea) of the Swansea Copper Works. Many other Welsh ironmasters secured seats in Wales or elsewhere—nine were returned in the election of 1841 alone—but Walter Coffin of Dinas seems to have been the only coal-owner as such to enter Parliament from South Wales during these years.[1] In 1852 Coffin, whose father had been a tanner at Bridgend, successfully contested the Cardiff Boroughs against the Rt. Hon. John Nicholl, who was supported by the powerful Bute interest. As a parliamentarian Coffin was undistinguished, but he was notable in that he was the first of a long line of Welsh Nonconformist Liberal members of Parliament.

The coal-owners who engaged in public affairs were more prominent in local matters where their activities were widespread and numerous. Those who were interested in politics were often influential and energetic members of the local party associations, usually being found amongst the Liberal supporters. It was David Williams of Ynyscynon, for example, who proposed H. A. Bruce (later Lord Aberdare) at the Merthyr hustings during the election of 1859, while David Davis, Maesyffynnon, the President of the Aberdare Liberal Association, was reported to have introduced Henry Richard, the 'Member for Wales', to Merthyr in 1868.[2] The owners

[1] For 1841 see *Merlin*, 17 July 1841. George Elliot, managing director of the Powell Duffryn Company, became the member for North Durham in 1868 but should perhaps be counted as a north country coal-owner. David Davies, Llandinam, chief proprietor of the Ocean Coal Company, was elected member for the Cardigan Boroughs in 1874. He had, however, acquired his influence mainly as a railway builder.

[2] *Cardiff Times*, 6 Mar. 1863, 15 Nov. 1884.

participated more directly in local government. Joseph Latch, maltster and coal-owner, was, for example, the first mayor of Newport under the Act of 1835, while Thomas Powell was one of the first six aldermen. In Cardiff, too, Walter Coffin of Dinas colliery was the first to fill the position of mayor under the new Act. In a lawsuit which arose at Neath in 1873 between Evans and Bevan, colliery proprietors, and Messrs. Bankart and Son, copper-smelters and coal-owners, David Bevan, mayor and alderman of Neath, stated that he had made considerable friendly concessions to Bankart as they had been fellow town councillors.[1] Edward Jones and Thomas Beynon at Newport, Richard and John Cory at Cardiff, and Frank Ash Yeo at Swansea were others who served as councillors, aldermen, and mayors in the boroughs of the district. Everywhere, too, coal-owners were to be found serving as Poor Law Guardians, magistrates and, after 1870, on the Local School Boards, while they were also strongly represented on the Newport, Swansea, and Llanelly harbour commissions and the various local gas and water undertakings.

Many gave not only of their time but of their purse. The chapels were often the chief beneficiaries of their philanthropy, it being said, for example, of David Davis, Maesyffynnon, that 'there is not a single religious institution in the neighbourhood but is deeply indebted to him for support, and his acts of private charity exceeded his public benefactions'.[2] Less typical, but of considerable significance, were those few who displayed an interest and regard for Welsh educational and cultural causes that found its vent both in personal activity and financial assistance. The enthusiasm and vigorous support of such men as the Davis's of Ferndale and David Davies of the Ocean Coal Company for the idea of a University College at Aberystwyth were hardly less important to that institution than were the funds they provided. Moreover, although many

[1] *CG.* 25 July 1873.
[2] *Cardiff Times*, 15 Nov. 1884.

lent their patronage to the various eisteddfodau, local as well as national, at least two—William Thomas of Brynawel and David Williams of Ynyscynon—were active as competitors. David Williams, indeed, not only reached high eminence as a poet under the bardic title of Alaw Goch, but as Treasurer to the Council did much to infuse the National Eisteddfod with vitality. 'His zeal, energy and openhandedness in the assistance rendered by him to free and liberal education, our literary institutions and Eisteddfodau, both local and national, have become proverbial, and were it possible to lose the name of David Williams, Ynyscynon, still the name of Alaw Goch will be as a household word in Morganwg.'[1]

It could be argued that many of these activities of the coal-owners had a more or less direct connexion with their business interests. As large ratepayers it was prudent that they should be represented on the Boards of Guardians and local councils; their dependence on shipping facilities made essential their participation as harbour commissioners; and their educational and religious philanthropy probably improved their relations with their workmen. It would be false, however, to look to calculated self-interest as their only motive in these matters. They were the natural leaders of the society in which they lived and regarded their participation as a public duty rather than as a private gain. They, as was said of one of them on his death in 1902, 'belonged to the old school of colliery proprietors who came into daily personal contact with their men—a type unfortunately rapidly becoming extinct'.[2]

[1] *Aberdare Times*, 7 Mar. 1863, 8 Apr. 1865; *Cardiff Times*, 14 Mar. 1903.
[2] *Western Mail*, 5 Sept. 1903.

VI

THE STRUCTURE OF INDUSTRY AND CAPITAL FORMATION

THE three- or four-fold increase in Welsh coal output that took place during this period was naturally not without its impact upon the structure of the industry. In some ways, however, this impact was less radical than might have been expected. Thus the size of the unit—the individual colliery—underwent a significant expansion rather than a revolution, as much of the extra production was obtained by the multiplication of new units rather than by the extension of older undertakings. In 1840 an output of over 50,000 tons a year was unusual. In 1874 an examination of the output returns for 103 collieries producing altogether nearly 5 million tons, almost one-third of the total output of the coalfield, gives the following result:[1]

Size	No. of collieries	Output of group (000's of tons)	Percentage of total output
Over 100,000 tons	13	1,930	38·6
50,000–100,000 tons	26	1,840	36·8
20,000–50,000 tons	28	1,003	20·1
Under 20,000 tons	36	220	4·4

Several features emerge. In the first place the range of output was still very wide. At one extreme was the Aber-nant colliery producing over 260,000 tons a year; at the other the

[1] R. Hunt, *Mineral Statistics*, 1874. The collieries were those lying in the parishes of Aberdare, Llanwynno, Ystradyfodwg, and Gelli-gaer, i.e. the Aberdare and Rhondda valleys and part of the area between the Taff and Rhymney valleys. The sample probably has some bias towards the larger unit since this was the area that had undergone the greatest development since 1840.

tiny Mynachdy level with an output of only 134 tons. The small collieries still predominated so far as numbers were concerned but they had ceased—in terms of contribution to the total output—to be the characteristic unit of the industry. The large colliery, with an output of around 500 tons a day, was still appreciably smaller than its counterpart in the north of England, but was both growing and becoming more usual. On the basis of this sample, something like three-quarters of the total output now came from collieries producing over 50,000 tons a year. The exception of 1840 had come to be rather less than the average of 1875.

In some respects the change in the size of the firm had been even less startling than that in the size of the unit. If the iron and copper firms are excluded, the normal holding by each firm in 1875 was, as it had been in 1840, one or two collieries only. Whereas at the earlier date, however, Thomas Powell and Thomas Prothero stood out alone amongst the sale-coal owners as significant departures from this pattern, the number of exceptions had, by the later date, multiplied.[1]

	1874: *Number of collieries held by individual firms*												
No. of collieries	1	2	3	4	5	6	7	8	9	10	11	12
No. of firms .	183	40	17	5	3	4	2	1	—	—	—	1

This meant that firms owning only one or two units accounted for 263 collieries while 144 units belonged to firms which each controlled three or more collieries.

The degree of concentration is, however, underestimated when stated only in terms of the numbers of collieries owned by each firm. It seems reasonable to assume that the collieries of the larger firms were generally bigger than those of their rivals, but this can be tested only for those firms which were members of the 1873 Coal Owners' Association.[2] Although these constituted a large enough sample of the industry—

[1] Based on the lists of collieries in the Mines Inspectors' Reports for 1874.
[2] W. G. Dalziel, op. cit., gives the figures of coal output of the member firms.

accounting for over 70 per cent. of the total output of the coalfield in 1873—they were not altogether representative. In particular they comprised a much greater proportion of the larger than of the smaller firms. This bias can be eliminated by removing the great iron concerns which between them produced some 5¼ million tons.[1] The distribution of the remaining 6¾ million tons that was produced by the purely coal-selling members of the Association illustrates that the industry was already coming to be dominated by the larger firm.

---

4 firms each producing over ½ million tons accounted for 2,535,000 tons or 37·5 per cent.

14 firms each producing 100,000–500,000 tons accounted for 2,040,000 tons or 30·2 per cent.

20 firms each producing 50,000–100,000 tons accounted for 1,445,000 tons or 21·4 per cent.

28 firms each producing under 50,000 tons accounted for 738,000 tons or 10·9 per cent.

This picture of the broad pattern of the industry is in some ways misleading. In particular, it disguises the different development that took place during this period between the house- and the steam-coal trades. If a general breakdown between these two sectors were possible it would certainly reveal that the larger colliery and the bigger firm were much more typical of the steam-coal industry. Even a partial analysis is suggestive. In the forty-nine collieries in the parishes of Llanwynno and Gelli-gaer where the two types of collieries are distinguished, the ten steam-coal collieries produced an average of (in round figures) 68,000 tons each; the thirty-nine house-coal collieries averaged 26,000 tons each. In the Owners'

[1] As the iron companies were producing coal for sale to remove them completely is to ignore an important element in the coal trade. It is not possible, however, to ascertain how much of its output each firm sold. If all their output is included, then firms producing over 500,000 tons accounted for 48·5 per cent. of the output of the Association. Their inclusion also affects the assessment of the degree of concentration measured by the number of collieries controlled by each firm, as nearly all the iron companies owned a large number of collieries. If all their collieries are included, then firms with three or more collieries accounted for 359 collieries.

Association returns three of the four sale-coal firms that produced over ½ million tons (Powell Duffryn, Ocean, and Ferndale) dealt almost entirely in the steam-coal market and the fourth, the Glamorgan Coal Company, largely so; while most of the companies in the group with an output between 100,000 and 500,000 tons were also steam-coal producers. There were sound reasons for this. The steam-coal collieries were generally a post-1840 development when collieries were being opened on a larger scale; the seams they were exploiting lay deeper than the house-coal seams and so necessitated larger scale working to cover the higher capital cost of operation; and the wider market that was open to steam coal—where the order was often for a ship's cargo—encouraged a more intensive development than did the house-coal trade, where the order was more likely to be in terms of a wagon load. And much of what was true of the house-coal industry applied also to the anthracite industry which in 1875 had still failed to break out of its traditional narrow specialized market.

The essential prerequisite for both the growth of output and the changes in the structure of industry was a supply of capital. Towards the end of this period changes in legislation were enabling some part of this need to be met from the organized capital market by the flotation of limited companies. It was not, however, till the great coal boom of the early seventies that this source reached significant proportions; for most of the period the industry continued to depend on unorganized individual initiative. The revolutionary expansion of the market that had taken place with the realization of the steam-raising powers of Welsh coal had, however, provided a strong incentive for such activity. Since the typical investor put his abilities as well as his money into the industry—the capitalist was also the entrepreneur—the most pertinent questions seem to be who were the investors? and whence did they come?

Unlike those who had earlier built up the iron and copper

industries in South Wales, the men who, after 1840, turned their energy and resources towards coal were mainly drawn from within the coalfield itself. Partly this was because local knowledge was at a premium in the coal industry. More substantially, it was simply because of the later blossoming of the industry: the men who developed it were themselves largely a by-product of the changes wrought by the earlier activities of the London and Bristol merchants who had become the ironmasters of Wales. It was the industrialization that had already taken place in the district by 1840 that had produced the group of solicitors, mining engineers, shopkeepers, and others with small capital resources which they wished to employ. The iron industry was beyond their grasp; when new iron companies were started—as several were in the anthracite coalfield in the 1840's—they almost invariably raised their capital from outside Wales. It was the ability of the coal industry at this time to absorb small resources without the necessity for their mobilization through a complex capital market that was the essential factor allowing much of the new capital to be provided from within the coalfield.

In contrast to the iron trade, the unit in the coal industry in 1840 was still small and the fixed costs involved in beginning in a modest fashion demanded no great wealth. This was particularly true where the coal could be worked by level, but even when a shaft was necessary mineral development had no need to wait on the provision of capital from outside. A report on a coal district near Llanelly in 1836 estimated that the cost of sinking a shaft for 90 fathoms was only £1,400 with a further £2,000 for the engines and pumps. It was thought that another shaft of 70 fathoms in a neighbouring district would cost £1,000 and £2,500 for the engines and pumps.[1] These estimates do not cover all the fixed capital items—omitting, for example, the cost of opening up headings and the surface and underground railways—but they serve none the less as indicators of the magnitudes involved.

[1] Nevill MSS., No. 18.

The instance of Walter Coffin, one of the more substantial coal-owners of this time, may put the matter more concretely. Robert Beaumont reported in 1846 that Coffin's pit which was 80 yards deep, bricked for 60 yards, and at which 70 colliers were employed, may have cost—together with the machinery and airways—as much as £7,000. The terms of the report indicated that this was clearly large for the time.[1] One Monmouthshire coal-owner asserted in 1843 that the average cost of opening a colliery was £14,000, but the occasion for this remark—a conference between the owners and the men at the time of a general stoppage in Monmouthshire—was one that gave him every incentive to exaggerate the figure.[2]

It is true that the working capital required was relatively heavy in proportion to the fixed capital, reflecting the unmechanized nature of the basic processes and the consequent high ratio of labour cost. In absolute terms, however, it was not large. The total working costs of delivering the coal from the Gelli-gaer, Llancaeach and Tophill collieries into barges at Cardiff in 1841 were put by a reliable authority at 6s. 6d. a ton and this was probably representative.[3] This on the (for the time) sizeable output of 30,000 tons a year would amount to £9,750. On the normal basis of trading by three months bills this suggests a sum of from £2,500 to £3,000. And that for the prudent. It was, moreover, often possible to reduce the need of working capital by letting out the colliery or parts of it to small contractors. This course was followed, for example, by Samuel Thomas at Ysgubor-wen. Hugh Powell, one of these contractors, stated that he had incurred the expense of driving 9 or 10 yards through rock at a cost of £3. 10s. to £4 a yard and a further 19 yards through a fault in the coal at a cost of 18s. a yard.[4] But whether such expedients were adopted or not it was certainly possible to enter the coal industry on a moderate scale with less than £10,000 and often

[1] CCL Bute MSS. VII. 46.
[2] *MG*, 1 Apr. 1843.
[3] CCL Bute MSS. VII. 44.
[4] *MG*, 24 Mar. 1860.

—if the working were by level, the output small and the individual venturesome—with much less.[1]

The force of the incentive to invest is much more difficult to gauge. Even in the few instances for which the total profits are known it is almost impossible to relate these to the capital employed. However, in the colliery for which it was indicated above that the cost of sinking the shaft and providing machinery had been estimated at £3,400, some £7,289 was spent on opening the pit by the end of 1839. In the eleven years from 1840 to 1850 the total profit (in the sense of excess of receipts over working costs) was £29,590 or an average of £2,690 a year.[2] It seems highly unlikely that this could have represented a return of less than 20 per cent. on all the capital employed. It is perhaps of small moment that all this is highly tenuous. The potential investor was likely to be tempted as much by the solid certainty that a few coal-owners—like Thomas Powell, Walter Coffin, and Thomas Prothero—were emerging as men of substance as by the dubious reliability of calculations made in advance. The calculations could always be confounded by unforeseen changes in the character and condition of the seams. There was always this element of gamble about investment in the coal trade.

Whether real or imaginary, the attractions were sufficient to entice many minor local capitalists into the business. The success of some of these was such that they—or their successors—came to rank among the giants of the industry. Thomas Powell, whose entry was of an earlier date and who was already an outstanding figure by 1840—had started as a timber merchant in Newport. At his death his steam-coal collieries alone were sold to the Powell Duffryn Company for £365,000. David Davis, a draper of Merthyr and Aberdare, entered the coal trade in 1842 when he leased the tiny Rhigos

---

[1] For example, David Williams, a collier, sold his one-third share in Rhiw sarn colliery, Llantrisant, in 1864 for £128. CCL Assignment, 24 Dec. 1864.

[2] Nevill MSS. XLVIII. The annual profit ranged from £5,334 in the boom year of 1845 to £1,408 in 1843. In one year—1842—there was a loss of £1,117.

level from Lord Bute,[1] branched into the Aberdare valley in the following year when its steam coals were winning recognition,[2] and finally followed the tide into the Rhondda to work the vast Ferndale taking. Samuel Thomas, whose son became Lord Rhondda, was a grocer at Merthyr before he opened the Ysgubor-wen pit with his brother-in-law, Thomas Joseph, in 1849 and so laid the foundations of the great Cambrian combine.[3] But spectacular success came only to the few; many more were content with modest conquests or failed altogether. In the nature of things the bulk of these have left no trace at all or are encountered only as a name in a lease or deed. The evidence of these leases, deeds, and newspapers, however, makes it possible to assert with confidence that the small capitalists within the coalfield played a vital part in the development of the industry. People like Phelps, the Monmouthshire solicitor whose colliery transactions brought him to the bankruptcy court but who returned to try again;[4] or David Williams the small farmer who was one of the first to realize and exploit the potentialities of the Aberdare district;[5] or Latch and Cope who added colliery enterprises to their business as maltsters and brewers at Newport;[6] or the Bryn Colliery Company whose members were all drawn from the Llanelly district and included two clergymen, three shopkeepers, a tallow chandler, a mineral surveyor, and a victualler.[7] Such examples could be multiplied indefinitely for it was the activity of innumerable men of this stature that was largely responsible for the steady expansion of the Welsh coal industry during this period.

There was still enough scope left for the inflow of capital and enterprise from outside the district. John Nixon, a north of England mining engineer, had already been impressed with

[1] NLW Bute MSS., Box 141, Parcel 5.
[2] Maybery Papers. David Davis to Maybery and Williams, 20 Sept. 1843.
[3] *D. A. Thomas, Viscount Rhondda*, by his daughter and others (1921), pp. 3–4. *MG*, 24 Mar. 1860.
[4] *Merlin*, 7 Aug. 1847.   [5] Ewenny MSS., Doc. No. 374.
[6] *Merlin*, 9 Jan. 1846.   [7] Nevill MSS., Deeds, No. 51.

the qualities of Welsh steam coal, and been engaged in winning a market for it in France, before he joined with two Bristol merchants and David Williams, the farmer of Ynyscynon, to work the Werfa minerals.[1] Later he bought the Deep Duffryn colliery from David Williams and J. H. Insole[2] and sank the pits at Navigation and Merthyr Vale. In these later enterprises he was associated with William Cory, one of the largest of the London coal merchants, and Hugh Taylor, a prominent coal-owner of the north and M.P. for Lynmouth.[3] The north of England coal trade also supplied Carr Bros. and Co., who traded first at Newport and then worked three collieries in the Aberdare valley before their failure in the crisis of 1857.[4] A later but no less thrustful figure from the same district was George (later Sir George) Elliot, the Northumberland pit-boy, turned mining engineer, turned coal-owner, who came to South Wales to value Thomas Powell's extensive steam collieries and proceeded to form the Powell Duffryn Steam Coal Company to buy and work them. These three all had their main activities in the Aberdare valley. By 1860, when Archibald Hood, a Scottish mining engineer, came into the coalfield, the Aberdare minerals had been largely leased and attention was being turned to the Rhondda valley to meet the still rising demand for steam coals. Hood, who had come to report on the unpromising Wern Colliery for G. M. Innes and Archibald Campbell of Liverpool, recognized this, and induced Innes and Campbell to back him in working coal at Gilfach Goch in the Ely valley and, more important, at Llwynypia in the Rhondda.[5] The last notable inflow from outside Wales during this period was provided by a group—Burnyeat, Brown and Company—of merchants and manufacturers from Liverpool and Whitehaven who in 1874 leased the Abergorci property in the

[1] NLW Bute MSS., Box 106.
[2] P.R.O. Company Records. Nixons Navigation Co. Ltd.
[3] NLW Bute MSS., Box 128. [4] Ibid., Box 28.
[5] NLW First Account Book of Glamorgan Colliery, Llwynypia; *South Wales Coal Annual*, 1914.

CAPITAL FORMATION

Rhondda valley and bought the Lletty Shenkin colliery in the Aberdare valley.[1] These were the main persons who brought their enterprise and capital into the Welsh coal industry from outside during this period. The group was small and, although several of the undertakings were large, external entrepreneurial capital clearly never dominated the coal industry at this time as it had earlier dominated the iron industry.

The dependence upon individual capitalists moving into South Wales was also limited by the spread of banking. Hitherto the area had relied on small, private banks; these were now supplemented by the establishment of joint-stock banks, which not only increased the facilities available by the wider resources upon which they were able to draw, but also extended the application of banking services in the geographical sense. The smaller and older concerns were generally situated in the agricultural regions bordering the coalfield—Chepstow, Carmarthen, and Brecon; the location of the branches of the joint-stock concerns was more consciously determined with a view to catering also for the needs of the industrial communities. In the mid-forties, for example, the West of England and South Wales Bank had branches at Cardiff, Merthyr, and Newport; the National Provincial at Cardiff, Bridgend, and Swansea; the Glamorgan Banking Company at Neath and Swansea; the Monmouthshire and Glamorgan Bank at Newport, Pontypool, and Tredegar; while the private Brecon Old Bank had extended to include Merthyr and Llanelly as well as several agricultural districts

[1] NLW Bute MSS., Box 106. The members of the company were William Burnyeat, Whitehaven, ship-owner; Alexander McKibbon, Liverpool, produce broker; George Bentinck, Middlesex, M.P.; Joseph Brown, William Steward, John Moore, and Samuel Sherwen, Whitehaven, ironmasters; William Dickinson, Workington, ironmaster; William Reile, Liverpool, engineer; William Dalzelle, Whitehaven, tobacco manufacturer; Thomas Dalzelle, Liverpool, ships' stores dealer; J. H. Dodgson, Liverpool, draper; George Jackson, Whitehaven, tobacco manufacturer; and J. Hargrave, Liverpool, ship-owner. The external capital that was attracted by the formation of limited liability companies is dealt with later in this chapter.

in South Wales.[1] By 1864 there were nine private banking firms in South Wales (one of which—the Brecon Old Bank—had seven branches), and four joint-stock banks with fifty-nine branches, and, although most of these branches were outside the district, they were an indication of the wider area upon which South Wales could draw.[2] This growth was not uninterrupted; the Monmouthshire and Glamorgan Bank, for instance, was forced in the forties to close its branches at Swansea and Cardiff and, in 1851, to the alarm of the district, this Bank failed altogether with liabilities of £800,000, bringing down with it the Newport Old Bank.[3] Despite such setbacks, however, it was during this period that industrial South Wales acquired a more or less adequate banking system.

There were several ways in which the banks played some part in the development of the coal industry. They were a source of short-term loans; in particular, by discounting trade bills, they reduced the amount of working capital required. 'I had some conversation with A. Hill', one of the proprietors of the Brecon Old Bank wrote in 1841, 'and I find that the West of England discount R. and A. Hill's Notes payable at Bristol. I told A. Hill that this system would not suit us, but that we would Discount their Trade Bills for his pays.'[4] This was doubtless the normal way of business. David Davies of the Ocean Coal Company did, indeed, boast that he had never discounted any of his bills at the bank but he clearly regarded himself to be in this—as in so many other respects—exceptional.[5] Such limited and cautious bank assistance did not satisfy men who were conscious of large opportunities foregone because of small resources. Their need was for easy credit; and the sentiments of the coal-owner who

[1] *MG*, 14 Feb. 1846; *Cambrian*, 22 Feb. 1845; *Merlin*, 29 Dec. 1848.
[2] *Return of all Banks existing on 1 June 1864*, P.P. 1865 (15), xxx.
[3] *MJ*, 31 May 1845; *Merlin*, 11 Oct. 1851.
[4] Maybery Papers, 11 Feb. 1841. J. Parry de Winton to J. Jones. Richard and Anthony Hill were the owners of the Plymouth Iron Works at Merthyr.
[5] Llandinam MSS. 282. Annual Report of North and South Wales Bank, Jan. 1879.

CAPITAL FORMATION

protested at the inadequacy of the banking facilities at Swansea must have been often echoed. There were, in 1847, only two banks at Swansea: the Glamorgan Bank which 'was accommodating as far as is prudent and compatible with its means' but which had too small a capital; and the Bank of England branch which was not a bank 'for tradesmen and others of limited capital, who cannot always comply with its stringent regulations'.[1]

The extent to which the banks were willing to provide more liberal aid in the form of semi-permanent funds varied both with the circumstances of the times and the prudence of the banker. In 1841, at least, the Brecon Bank discouraged this practice and also decided 'not to discount promissory notes, or, what is quite as bad, discount the Bills of the Pool Colliery Co. and other Companies and drawn by one partner on another and renewed *ad infinitum*, for we cannot suffer these companies to trade with our capital, and it is quite enough in these times to give the full command of . . . our Capital by discounting their trade bills at long date'.[2]

None the less most of the banks from time to time probably extended more than short-term credit to the industry. The Brecon Bank itself found the more stringent policy necessary in 1841 because of large advances it had made in the past; the attitude of 'we must not suffer Accounts to be permanently overdrawn' was clearly a reversal of the policy pursued in the good years immediately before.[3] In 1845, after the failure of the Monmouthshire Coal and Iron Company to which it had advanced £16,000, the Monmouthshire and Glamorgan Bank was forced to take over the Victoria Ironworks as security.[4] More spectacular was the way in which the Bank of England over-stepped the bounds of prudence by advancing £270,000

[1] *MJ*, 18 Sept. 1847.
[2] Maybery Papers, 6 Feb. 1841. J. Parry de Winton to J. Jones.
[3] Ibid.
[4] *MJ*, 25 Jan. 1845. One shareholder strongly condemned the bank for its over-active interest in industrial concerns: '. . . accommodation, almost unprecedented, has been afforded to men of no property, and as little character . . . .' *MJ*, 31 May 1845.

to the English Copper Miners Company, four of whose directors were also directors of the Bank.[1] Between 1851 and 1853 the Cefn and Garth collieries and ironworks were mortgaged to the Royal British Bank for £58,000.[2] These firms were mainly engaged in the iron industry, although all also participated in the coal trade; the records survive because these were the most striking instances. There is enough evidence, however, to suggest that—although it was usually on a smaller scale—the banks occasionally became similarly involved with coal companies. In the examinations before the Bristol bankruptcy court that followed the failure of the Newport Bank of Williams and Sons it emerged that this bank, with a total capital of £30,000, had advanced £70,000 during the previous six years to the colliery business of Allfrey Brothers, who were also large brewers at Newport.[3] After the failure of Messrs. T. and D. Price, coal proprietors at Abertillery, the banking firm of Bailey, Gratrex and Co. tendered proof of debts for £56,000, only £20,000 of which were covered by securities.[4]

If these were exceptions to the cautious practices that prevailed in English banking, they were large enough and numerous enough to warrant notice. But even where the banks themselves withdrew, they still played some part in providing the longer-term funds of the industry.[5] The Brecon Old Bank, for instance, in 1841 hoped to find through the Clerical Insurance Company a rich client to take a mortgage of the

---

[1] Penrice and Margam MSS. 9266–7, 9315; *MJ*, 19 Feb., 1 July, 25 Nov. 1848. When the Bank was forced for a time to take over the company, William Crawshay complained of having to compete with the low prices set by the Bank, which could print its own notes to pay the workmen. If the Bank was to be free to sell iron he wished to be free to print notes. *MJ*, 9 Dec. 1848.
[2] Penrice and Margam MSS. 8972–6.
[3] *Merlin*, 16 July 1851. [4] *MG*, 9 Aug. 1862.
[5] There was always a tendency for short-term loans to become semi-permanent. The Glamorgan Banking Co. having allowed Penrose and Evans of the Eaglesbush colliery to overdraw their current account by £3,600 were obliged to take a mortgage on the property to cover this sum and any further sums that might so accumulate. CCL Glamorgan MSS., 27 May 1852.

CAPITAL FORMATION 147

Clydach Iron Works.[1] The earlier importance of the mineral lease as a security for raising funds by mortgage[2] had, indeed, lost little of its force. Penrose and Evans, for instance, raised capital on the security of their leases of the Eskyn and Eaglesbush collieries in the Vale of Neath from William Fox of Wiltshire in 1844, from Rees Williams and John Rowlands in 1849, from the Glamorgan Banking Company in 1852, and from John Rowlands and John Thomas in 1855.[3] On the basis of the evidence examined, it seems to have been less usual to meet the needs for capital expansion by taking in new partners. Although only occasional instances have been found, supplemented by a few advertisements for partners, the practice was, however, probably more frequent than this suggests.[4]

Evidence is equally elusive as to the extent to which the capital required for growth was secured by the ploughing back of profits. This must, however, have been considerable. Thomas Powell, one suspects, was a prime example of this. There is certainly no indication that he squandered his colliery profits in ostentatious living or social ambition, while his holdings in banking, railway, and dock companies were undertaken to further the interests of his coal enterprises and financed from colliery proceeds rather than the other way about. Samuel Thomas of Ysgubor-wen and David Davis of Ferndale would be parallel cases. A more concrete example is that of the Ocean Coal Company. From its commencement in 1865 to 1875 the total profits of this firm reached £493,000, but much less than half, £204,000, had been distributed as dividends. The bulk of the remainder had been ploughed back by transference to capital account (£27,000), or as payments of the calls on new shares created to open further collieries (£182,000) or in the form of a reserve balance (£52,000). A decade later all but £120,000 of the total paid up capital of £465,000 had been raised from profits. These increases in

[1] Maybery Papers, 11 Feb. 1841.   [2] A. H. John, op. cit., pp. 42-44.
[3] CCL Glamorgan MSS., 26 Dec. 1844, 27 May 1852, 7 July 1853, 7 July 1855.   [4] NLW Bute MSS., Box 28. Tyla-coch Colliery Deeds.

capital were matched by the expansion in physical assets. The output of the company in 1885 was over one million tons; it owned six collieries on which £286,000 had already been spent and one of which was still being opened out, and its other assets included such items as 494 cottages, 711 railway wagons, and 3,400 trams.[1]

The number of companies that endeavoured to raise their capital through the public issue of shares before the legislation limiting liability was passed was small. The extra risks attached to mining magnified the normal hazards of unlimited liability, while the experience of this type of firm was not encouraging. The failure of the two grandiose north of England enterprises—the Durham Coal Company and the Northern Coal Mining Company—at the end of the thirties was not easily forgotten,[2] and the memory of investors was jogged by the experience of Cameron's Coal Company in the next decade. This company was founded in 1845 to work the coal under the property of 1,300 acres belonging to Col. Cameron at Loughor, between Llanelly and Swansea. Its story is a record of imprudence that rapidly degenerated into disaster. Despite the early commendations of the press and a favourable Admiralty report on the coals, the project was from the outset hopeless. The company undertook to pay Cameron nearly £150,000 for his property; this, with the other fixed capital expenses—including a substantial sum for parliamentary and promotion expenses and an ominously modest outlay on the actual colliery working—made a total of nearly £180,000. One Welsh mining engineer considered that to pay even 5 per cent. on this outlay would require an output of something like 300,000 tons a year. But the shareholders had never paused—in the roseate days of 1845—to consider how such quantities were to be raised from their insignificant levels and adits, nor to ponder where it was all to be sold. The actual

[1] Llandinam Papers, 101, 104; A. Stanley Davies Docs., 32, 36, 39.
[2] R. L. Galloway, *Annals of Coal Mining* (1904), p. 11.

CAPITAL FORMATION

performance of the company was at best rather less than 20,000 tons a year. This level of output made it impossible not only to give a return on capital, but even to cover the working costs. An exorbitant dead-rent of £2,000 a year (paid to Cameron) alone put 2s. a ton on the cost of this production; the transport of the coal over considerable distances by carts before the projected railway could be built cost a further 4s. 6d. a ton; while heavy administrative expenses at Swansea and London were equally crushing. It was estimated that the cost of getting the coal to Swansea was at least 10s. 6d. a ton when similar coal was selling for 7s. The realities of the situation were disguised from the willing shareholders for a time by the payment of handsome dividends out of capital. Even after 1848, when the bubble burst, the extravagance of its agreements with Cameron led the company to try several reorganizations before, in 1851, it was finally recognized that the delay in winding up could only increase, rather than reduce, the liabilities. The enterprise was profitable only to the Cameron family; to all others it was only a warning.[1]

The Acts of 1855 and 1856 facilitating the adoption of general limited liability came just at the time when Welsh coal-mining was beginning to pass out of the stage where adequate finance could be provided from the resources of individuals or small partnerships. The advantages of the limited liability company in enabling large amounts of capital to be assembled, while permitting the individual shareholder to limit his risk to his investment, were thus becoming increasingly relevant to South Wales. The need for capital was growing as deeper winnings were made, demanding larger scale working and often involving a long period of waiting before the coal was reached. The industry, moreover, was inevitably a risky one especially when new areas, where the presence and formation of seams were uncertain, were being opened up. The risks were enhanced by the recurrent danger of a setback from inundation or explosion or by the possibility

[1] There are numerous references to this company in *MJ*, 1845-51.

that a venture undertaken when trade was prosperous and prices high might come to fruition some years later when, for a time, profit expectations had radically changed. Consequently, the limitation of financial risk for the investor was an invaluable aid in attracting the larger amounts of capital required. Ventures such as that undertaken by the Newport Abercarn Black Vein Steam Coal Company, Limited, for example, would have strained the resources of even the wealthiest individual or partnership. The company was formed in 1872 to acquire and work the Celynen estate of 1,200 acres adjoining the Abercarn colliery of the Ebbw Vale Company. Its nominal capital of £150,000 in ordinary shares was later increased by the issue of a further £40,000 in debentures, taken up by the shareholders, to continue the financing of the three pits being sunk and the erection of cottages. It was not until 1876 that the winding engines were started and the first coal raised.[1]

The movement to take advantage of the new legislation, however, started slowly and on a much smaller scale. The first limited company to be formed for coal-mining in South Wales was the Rhydydefed Colliery Company, provisionally registered on 14 November 1855,[2] which leased about 300 to 400 acres of land near Swansea from George Byng Morris (the younger son of Sir John Morris, the founder of Morriston). This company, together with the Penclawdd Company, was later registered afresh under the 1856 Act. The table on page 151 shows the growth of registrations in the ensuing years.

By no criterion, except that of being harbingers of future developments, could the early companies be considered important. Formed mainly to exploit mines in the western sector of the coalfield, where output was expanding least, their capitalization was small and their life was short. Out of the nine companies registered before the end of 1859 only three

[1] *CG*, 1 Dec. 1876.
[2] *Returns of Joint Stock Companies formed under the Act of last year*, P.P. 1856 (60), lv.

were still in operation in 1864, a record which seemed unlikely to encourage imitation.[1] None the less, after the beginning of 1864 the pace quickened and companies conceived on a more substantial basis began to enter the industry. Of the nine flotations of that year, for example, three were of considerable magnitude. The South Wales Colliery Company had been formed to purchase John Russell's Cwmtillery colliery and was the first important limited company connected with the Monmouthshire coal industry. It had a

Limited Companies in South Wales, registered between 1856 and 1875[2]

Year	No. of companies	Total nominal capital	Year	No. of companies	Total nominal capital
		£			£
1856	2	45,000	1866	8	310,000
1857	3	68,500	1867	3	131,000
1858	2	60,000	1868	4	136,000
1859	2	116,200	1869	2	70,000
1860	3	62,500	1870	3	105,000
1861	6	213,000	1871	7	275,000
1862	6	147,100	1872	13	1,057,300
1863	6	330,000	1873	29	3,185,000
1864	9	948,000	1874	27	2,210,000
1865	14	770,500	1875	9	551,000

nominal capital of £200,000 and by the end of 1864 had acquired 1,558 acres of freehold and leasehold mineral land.[3] The United Merthyr Colliery Company, formed to purchase the Cwmneol and Fforchaman collieries, which adjoined each other near Aberdare, leased a mineral estate of 1,200 acres and had a nominal capital of £120,000. The most important, however, was the Powell Duffryn Steam Coal Company, which purchased the steam-coal collieries of Thomas Powell in the Aberdare and Rhymney valleys and which, with a

[1] *Returns of Joint Stock Companies* . . , *P.P.* 1864 (452), lviii.
[2] Based on Returns of Joint Stock Companies formed. Limited companies known to be primarily concerned with iron manufacture have been excluded.
[3] *CG*, 12 Mar., 24 Dec. 1864.

nominal capital of £500,000, stood out as a colossus among the sale-coal collieries.

This first substantial wave of company promotion, a product of a period of high demand for Welsh coal, came to an end with the financial crisis of 1866. The ensuing years of dull trade, and the memory of 'Black Friday', were not conducive to company promotion; not until the boom years of 1872–4 were companies again registered in any significant numbers. These later companies were usually planned for winning on a larger scale. Whilst the average nominal capital of the thirty companies registered by the end of 1863 had been nearly £35,000, the average for the sixty-nine companies registered in the boom years of 1872–4 was almost £95,000. The feverish optimism had, however, been abating with the steady fall in coal prices in 1874, while the long strike of the early months of 1875 acted as a further brake on promotions. From the beginning of December 1874 until the following November only three companies were registered, but the sliding scale agreement, with its prospects of industrial peace, restored confidence a little and six more companies were registered at the end of 1875.

The importance of the limited company in coal-mining was considerably accentuated by the ironworks companies, themselves great coal-producers. By 1875 nearly all the Welsh iron firms, with the significant exceptions of Dowlais and Cyfarthfa, had been converted into limited companies. At this date something approaching one-half of the coal-production of South Wales was controlled by limited companies. The size of this fraction, however, was substantially swollen by these great iron companies, those of Ebbw Vale, Tredegar, Rhymney, and Blaenavon alone producing nearly 3 million tons of coal. Amongst the sale-coal companies it was only the larger firms that produced over 100,000 tons annually, the Powell Duffryn Company, mining about one million tons, standing alone. But even if the ironworks are omitted a little over one-quarter of the sale-coal collieries in South Wales were owned

CAPITAL FORMATION

by limited companies in 1874.[1] On any basis the new form of organization had achieved significance, though not predominance, by the end of this period. It is important, however, to remember that this significance had mainly arisen from the large number of registrations made between 1872 and 1874. Until the years immediately before 1875 the limited companies had played a comparatively minor role in the industry.

All the indications are that this development was accompanied by an inflow of capital into the industry from outside South Wales. The companies were, for example, usually promoted by London firms and the directorates drawn from people with no previous connexion with the coalfield. The first company, the Rhydydefed Colliery Company, was in this typical of many later ones. Promoted by James Chatterton, baronet and major-general, living at Limerick, and Thomas Tatham, merchant, insurance broker and underwriter, of London, its provisional directorate included Lord Alfred Paget, M.P., two colonels, a London wine merchant, Tatham himself, and three other Metropolitan names.[2] The same preponderance of outside capitalists is found in the lists of shareholders. The majority of the twenty-two shareholders in the Rhydydefed Colliery Company lived in the London district, nine of them bearing the name of Tatham. Other companies drew upon a wider field. By the time it was agreed to wind up the Bute Merthyr Steam Coal Association in 1859 the ten shareholders included a London merchant, a clerk from Southampton, a Glasgow wine merchant, a London housekeeper, a Parisian banker, and a civil engineer in the East Indies. Of the main shareholders of the Cardiff and Swansea Steam Coal Company, nineteen living in Wales and Monmouthshire held 3,580 shares, twelve from England held

[1] W. G. Dalziel, *The Monmouthshire and South Wales Coal Owners' Association*, 1895, pp. 10–11. This gives the output of member firms in 1873. The output of the individual firms in the Association in 1875 is given in South Wales Coal Owners' Mss. Association Minutes, vol. ii, p. 19. The collieries and their owners throughout the coalfield are listed in MIR for 1874.

[2] *Returns of Joint Stock Companies formed under the Act of last year*, 1856.

1,500 shares, four living in Scotland held 3,530 shares (Thomas Coats of Paisley taking 3,000 of these), and one Irish shareholder held 100 shares. Occasionally the holdings were more concentrated in one area. In the Great Western Colliery Company, Benjamin Ashton, a Manchester cotton manufacturer, at first held 2,035 out of 3,088 shares taken up, but by 1874 the capital was largely held in Bristol and the head office was moved from London to Bristol in that year. Bristol men, too, figured prominently among the shareholders in the Hirwaun Coal and Iron Company.

To a lesser extent, the new facilities also served to mobilize capital within the coalfield. Companies with a local directorate, though the exception, were to be found. Members of the Board of the Dylais Coal and Iron Company were drawn mainly from Glamorgan and Brecknockshire, while three of the directors of the Ynysawdre Coal, Coke and Brick Company were John Cory, Ebenezer Lewis, a coal-owner of Bridgend, and Thomas Beynon. Thomas Beynon, a colliery proprietor and coal-shipper of Newport, was also managing director of the Newport Abercarn Black Vein Steam Coal Company, in which his brother-in-law, John Cory, coal proprietor and shipper of Cardiff, was a fellow director. Local men, too, sometimes became directors of companies which took over collieries which they had previously owned. John Wightman became managing director of the company which took over his Blaendare colliery in 1865 and Thomas Joseph similarly remained as managing director when he sold his collieries to the Dunraven United Collieries Company. Nevertheless when the Swansea and Neath Colliery Company was formed in 1873 to work a mineral property of 2,000 acres purchased from H. H. Vivian, M.P., the fact that the local office was located at Swansea and that three of the directors were Swansea men could excite comment as an unusual feature likely to prove a source of strength to the company.

It was equally unusual for a company to be dominated by Welsh shareholders. There were exceptions. Nearly all the capital for the Bargoed Coal Company, for instance, was provided by Brecknockshire people (including the de Winton family of the Brecon Old Bank) and the registered office of the company was at Brecon. Although 1,100 shares in the Dunraven United Collieries Company were in the hands of distant holders—including Bryan Donkin, the noted engineer, who took 85 shares—this company, too, attracted an unusual number of local investors. Besides Thomas Joseph, half of whose 4,000 shares came to him as vendor, the shareholders included F. Carlyle, a Merthyr draper and tea dealer (44); E. Purchase, a farmer (60), and W. R. Smith, an attorney (120), both of Merthyr; J. D. Thomas, high bailiff, Swansea (120); L. V. Sherley, solicitor, Cardiff (40); William Davies, colliery proprietor, Bridgend (100); and a motley collection of local innkeepers, clerks, drapers, engineers, and others.

In general, however, the new form of organization set out to mobilize capital from beyond the coalfield and many were the devices adopted to attract the investor. When, as was usual, existing collieries were taken over it was stressed that the undertaking was not speculative or doubtful, but merely needed more capital for fuller development. To support this, reports on the property by mining engineers of repute were obtained. The vendor, too, had to show his faith in the enterprise. Thomas Joseph, for example, not only became managing director of the Dunraven United Collieries Company but also took £50,000 of the purchase money in shares of the company and guaranteed a minimum dividend of 10 per cent. on paid-up capital for the first five years. This guarantee of dividend to cover the period while the property was being developed was a widespread practice, sometimes part of the purchase money being invested in Consols or deposited with a bank to provide security for the honouring of the agreement.[1] Another variant of the same device was typified by the

[1] For example, when Richards and Company, Ltd. was formed Richards and Power, the vendors, guaranteed a dividend of 10 per cent. for five years, secured by £10,000 left with the company and by £15,000 of debentures deposited with the Bank of England. *CG*, 9 Oct. 1874.

undertaking of H. H. Vivian, M.P., to refrain for five years from selling the 2,000 fully paid up shares he received from the sale of his estates to the Swansea and Neath Colliery Company.[1] Promises, too, that calls on shares would be made only in limited amounts and at not too frequent intervals were a standard practice. Finally, there was the lure of a high prospective profit, often over 20 per cent., this rate being part of the blandishments of a prospectus but also reflecting the deeply rooted belief, prevalent in the industry, that something well over 10 per cent. was a fair return on capital in normal times.

Not all the money that flowed in as a result of these enticements added to the capital of the industry. So far, for example, as a company was merely taking over an old undertaking it was only allowing existing capital to be realized and replaced. Promotion expenses often took up—and frequently were meant to take up—large sums, to which the costs of winding-up had often to be added. Above all, the numerous failures meant that only a fraction of the nominal capital of the limited companies ever reached Wales. An examination of the fate of fifty-three out of the sixty-four companies formed between 1856 and the end of 1867 shows that three were abortive, ten had failed by 1864, a further thirty-one had failed before the end of 1870, and two more failed in 1874.[2] Only seven of these fifty-three companies were still in existence at the end of 1875.

In some respects, this proportion of failures seems unexpectedly high. Most companies were formed to acquire already existing levels or pits where the seams had been proved and business connexions established. Thus the element of risk was much reduced where, for example, the Cardiff and Swansea Smokeless Steam Coal Company took over three

---

[1] *CG*, 28 Nov. 1873.

[2] Information derived from a sample study of the records of companies at Bush House and the P.R.O.; *Return . . . of all Joint Stock Companies wound up . . . since August, 1862, P.P.* 1868–9 (104), lvi; advertisements in the *CG*.

well-developed collieries and arranged from the outset that the sales should be entrusted to the well-established coal-shipping firms of Cory Bros. of Cardiff, and Cory, Yeo and Co. of Swansea. Most of the failures, therefore, can hardly be explained by 'wild-cat' promotion or the grossest forms of fraud. None the less, the risks that remained were still formidable and were not reduced by the usual practice of leaving control in the hands of directors who had little knowledge of the district or even of the industry. The directors were usually drawn from the ranks of the titled or from those who were already directors of railway, shipping, or banking companies, men, often, who could be attracted by gifts of qualification shares, such as the 25 shares given to Sir Edwin Pearson of Wimbledon, director of the Caerphilly Colliery Company.[1] Moreover, company promotion was perilously easy and properties could be purchased without involving any large immediate need of cash. The Bettws Llantwit Company, for example, formed in 1873, bought for £45,000 a mineral lease held by one Boyle from Lord Dunraven. Boyle was to receive £7,000 in cash on the execution of the agreement and £5,000 in cash when the company took possession. £9,000 was to remain on mortgage for five years at 6 per cent., £14,000 was to be paid in 6 per cent. shares, and the balance of £10,000 was to be paid only when the Nine Feet seam was struck under the property. Boyle had received only the first £12,000 by the time the company was winding up in 1876.[2] Another company bought three collieries for £285,000 without making any immediate cash payment, the vendors accepting paid-up shares and 6 per cent. debentures redeemable at three, four, and five years.

This practice had its dangers as well as its attractions. It often meant that the proportion of actual risk-bearing capital was too low and saddled the company with the burden of excessive interest charges and capital repayments. This was all the more likely since most companies were formed during

[1] *CG*, 2 Mar. 1877. [2] Ibid., 24 Nov. 1876.

periods of good trade, which both tempted the promoters to buy and encouraged the colliery owners to sell out, at valuations which reflected the current spirit of optimism. Marshall, the owner of the Van colliery near Cardiff, had informed Filton, a former advertisement and election agent, that he would pay Filton £5,000 if he brought out a company to take the colliery for £30,000. But when the Glamorgan Iron and Coal Company was formed in 1865, through Moore and Delatoir of Cheapside, Marshall received £48,976 for this colliery.[1] In the iron industry, Wickens bought the Aberaman Iron Works and mineral estate from Crawshay Bailey for £250,000 and resold them to a company formed a few months later for £350,000,[2] and there were doubtless similar instances amongst the coal companies formed at this time.

If a period of good trade was sufficient—even where there was no actual fraud—to encourage the formation of companies on an unsound basis, bad trade was usually enough to bring them down. Particularly swift was the collapse of most of the eight companies formed in 1866, one proving abortive and four others being wound up in the next year or so. The collapse of Overend, Gurney and Co. at the end of 1866 made the following year particularly difficult, but any recession subjected the companies to strong stresses. Even where the company was not very young, the temptation to declare high dividends in good years made the presence of adequate reserves unlikely; calls on shares were hard to realize when the money market was disturbed; and the commitments to vendors for interest and capital payments became especially onerous. No doubt there was some deliberate fraud, but ignorance and misjudgement in the boom years when companies were generally founded is enough to explain many of the failures. This is the more likely in that the local knowledge, important for the success of a coal-mining enterprise, was

---

[1] *CG*, 8 Dec. 1866. The company was wound up in 1867.
[2] In the event a dispute over the acreage involved prevented this transaction from being completed. *MG*, 15 July, 19 Aug. 1864, 23 June 1865.

often only largely represented in a company in the person of the vendor, whose chief interest was to sell his property at a high valuation.

It would, however, be wrong to over-emphasize the extent to which the company mortality rate reduced the amount of external capital drawn into the district after the passage of the limited liability Acts. Not all the companies that failed in business failed to bring capital into the industry; some spent considerable sums in developing their property before they fell. More important, the companies that survived during these years included several of the most substantial. Prominent amongst these were several companies founded by small groups who, without making any appeal to a wide circle of investors, wished to limit their own risks. All the shares in the Glamorgan Coal Company, for instance, were taken up by the seven members who signed the memorandum of association in 1862, and the Bargoed Coal Company which had only 40 shares of £500 each similarly resembled the partnership type of organization.

It was on this basis that the largest of the Welsh sale-coal companies, the Powell Duffryn Company, was established in 1864. An account of the formation and development of this company will serve not only to illustrate the way in which the limited companies could bring external capital into the industry, but also to underline the weaknesses of many of the other flotations of these years. Thomas Powell died on 24 March 1863 and by the terms of his Will—which was stolen but recovered by a policeman disguised in woman's clothing in circumstances that would have rivalled any Victorian melodrama—his property passed to his three sons. Of these, Thomas Powell junior soon gave up his interest in the steam-coal collieries, confining his attention to the Llantwit house-coal pits, while Walter and Henry Powell were reluctant to carry on business on so large a scale. A valuation of the steam-coal property was prepared for the brothers by three eminent mining engineers—George Elliot, T. E. Forster, and William

Armstrong—during the course of which investigation Elliot became so impressed that he determined to form a company to work the property. Accordingly, he arranged to buy the steam-coal collieries from Henry and Walter Powell for £365,000 and a limited company was registered on 28 July 1864, under the name of the Powell Duffryn Steam Coal Company, to acquire and work the Lower, Middle, and Upper Duffryn, Aber-nant-y-groes, Aber-gwawr, and Cwm-dare collieries in the Aberdare valley, together with the New Tredegar colliery in the Rhymney valley. The company bought the business at the same price as Elliot had agreed to pay the Powell brothers, so there was no extravagant burden for promotion expenses.

The nominal capital of £500,000 was divided into 100 £5,000 shares, all of which were taken by nine subscribers: George Elliot, S. E. Bodlen, Thomas Brassey, P. G. Heyworth, J. R. McClean, Alexander Ogilvie, Richard Potter, J. Swift, and W. Wagstaffe. George Elliot assumed the general supervision of the collieries at a salary of £1,000 a year. The subscribers were almost certainly familiar with one another through ties of business or friendship. There was a close connexion, for example, between Richard Potter of Stonehouse, Gloucestershire (the father of Beatrice Webb), Peter Heyworth of Liverpool, and Thomas Brassey, the railway contractor. Richard Potter, who, appropriately enough, had made his money in the timber trade during the Crimean War, was married to a Heyworth and was indebted to his friend 'Tom' Brassey for the advice that gifts in the right quarter would solve his difficulty in securing payment for timber supplied to the French government.[1]

Once formed, the company soon added to its holding mainly by buying adjoining coal areas. It is worthy of note, however, that these purchases were made in years of poor trade and financed by the partners themselves. The Ynyscynon and Treaman collieries which had been worked by David Williams

[1] Beatrice Webb, *My Apprenticeship* (re-issue 1929), chap. i.

until his death and which adjoined the company's Aber-gwawr pits, were bought in 1865 for £8,750.[1] A year later the Fforchaman and Cwmneol collieries, near Aberdare, were bought from the United Merthyr Collieries Company for £80,000,[2] and in 1867 the Aberaman estate, including a colliery and ironworks, was purchased from Crawshay Bailey for £123,000.[3] To help finance these purchases the capital of the company was increased in 1866 to £600,000 by the issue of 1,000 £100 preference shares carrying interest at $12\frac{1}{2}$ per cent., and taken up by the partners in proportion to their original holding. No doubt these properties were acquired on reasonable terms; trade was languishing, the United Merthyr Company was winding up, the ageing Crawshay Bailey was anxious to sell, and David Williams's property came on to the market after his death. None the less, only a company with large resources, considering the future rather than the immediate present, could have taken advantage of the low prices of these years.

This company had been founded after a searching valuation made by some of the most eminent mining engineers of the day, one of whom—George Elliot—had bought the property on this basis; its operations were conducted by a man—George Elliot—of the highest repute in the industry; and it had a sound capital structure backed by men of considerable substance. Despite all this the company came close to dissolution in the deep depression of 1868-9, a forcible illustration of the risks of company promotion in the coal industry at this time. The company alleged that a subsequent examination of the ledgers had shown that the yearly cost of working the collieries had been under-stated at the time of

---

[1] *CG*, 29 July 1865. These collieries, which had been unprofitable for some time, were bought mainly to assist the drainage of the other collieries of the company. [2] Ibid., 14 July 1866

[3] Ibid., 16 Feb. 1867. This was the estate that, in the better trading conditions of 1864, Crawshay Bailey had agreed to sell for £250,000. The Powell Duffryn Company was chiefly interested in the excellent steam-coal measures under the estate. The company tried unsuccessfully to sell the ironworks which were ultimately closed, the site being used for the engineering work and the wagon locomotive repairs of the company.

the purchase by over £11,000. This belated discovery was clearly not unconnected with the strains induced by the adverse change in the state of trade and the substantial sums that the partners had had to raise in a tight money market, largely to pay the instalments of the purchase money.[1] The company thus pressed for either the contract to be rescinded or the purchase price to be abated by £72,000. The eagerness with which the company for a time pressed for the rescinding of the contract showed how deeply even so apparently sound-based an enterprise was affected by the depression of the late sixties. At first, in 1869, the Vice-Chancellor ruled in favour of rescinding the contract, but ultimately it was decided at the Court of Appeal in Chancery that the contract should stand and that the purchase price should be reduced by £52,020.[2]

In general, however, it is the essential strength and solidity of a company like Powell Duffryn that is the most lasting impression. When the Rhymney Railway Bill was under the consideration of a Parliamentary committee in 1867 the secretary of Powell Duffryn could claim that the company was raising 800,000 tons of steam coal a year and shipping 600,000 tons from Cardiff.[3] By the close of our period the output of the company had risen to one million tons. If the history of limited liability over the previous twenty years had been littered with numerous failures it had nevertheless produced its surviving giants.

[1] Between 1866 and 1869 £2,500 per share, or a total of £250,000, was called up as well as the full £10,000 for the preference shares.
[2] *CG*, 12 Nov. 1869, 4 June 1875.
[3] Ibid., 13 Apr. 1867.

VII

COMMERCIAL ORGANIZATION

THE most marked feature of the commercial organization of the coal trade during this period was its diversity. One of the sources of this variation was that several markets were being exploited. The sales structure was at its simplest in those, usually very small, collieries that catered only for country sales, collieries such as that of William Thomas of Llantrisant parish who, in 1842, was rated on a daily output of fifteen sacks of 2 cwt. each.[1] Here the buyer—usually a farmer or small merchant—would send his cart to the colliery, buying the coal at a pit-head price. The system practised at the Dowlais works before that company entered the general coal market was somewhat similar; two coal-yards were maintained from which local sales were made to the householders of Dowlais and Merthyr.

A few further refinements were added for the conduct of the coastal trade. In this case the coal-owner usually sold either to the master of one of the numerous vessels that plied in this trade or received a direct order from a customer in the west of England, Ireland, or mid-Wales, in which event it was usually the buyer that chartered the vessel.[2] By 1840 the direct order had already become more normal than sales to captains, and this tendency gathered strength with the passage of time. The practice of selling to the captains of ships had grown because coal provided an ideal back freight for vessels bringing copper ore from Cornwall or provisions from Bristol or Ireland. It tended to decline as merchants at the distributing ports in Ireland and the west country grew sufficiently in

---

[1] Notes re Glamorgan County Rating Enquiry, 1842. Compiled by J. E. Bicheno, J.P., p. 178. [2] NLW Bute MSS., Box 141, Parcel 5.

stature to place their own orders, and as gas and steam packet companies emerged which were able from their size and obliged by their particular needs to deal direct. The coal-owner's risk was thus normally restricted to putting the coal on board at the shipping port. 'You know our rule is not to contract for delivery but only to put the coals on board', was the reply of R. J. Nevill to one of his customers,[1] although the rule was always likely to be broken where it was necessary to win a new market or retain an important order.

There were other minor variations on the general pattern. Some coal proprietors—like Thomas Powell—owned their own coastal vessels and so cut out one middleman, the ship's master, for part of their sales. Some owners, too, employed their own agents in the main markets. George Insole and Co., for example, engaged in 1845 one Armitage who was 'to carry out their instructions, promote their interest and extend their connexion to the utmost of his ability' in Ireland for the ensuing three years in return for a salary of £120 a year and 20 tons of coal.[2] Others sold all or most of their output to coal-shipping firms who undertook its sale and shipment. When R. J. Blewitt, the parliamentary member for the Monmouth boroughs, opened a pit at Cwmbrân he did not ship his own coal 'but delivered it at a fixed price to Messrs. Ann Rees and Co., in whose sales I had no interest or concern whatsoever'.[3] Similarly the Aberdare Coal Company at first disposed of all its coal to the London coal merchants, Edward Wood and Co., doubtless because this was the most direct method of gaining a foothold in the market, but in 1839 it applied for a wharf at the Bute Dock from which it could conduct its own sales.[4] This method, however, had not won general acceptance in South Wales in 1840; this, indeed, was one of the reasons Lord Bute gave for not selling the coal from his Glamorgan estates as he did in the north of England.

[1] Nevill MSS. 8. Nevill Brown to Thomas Gillespie, 15 Nov. 1834.
[2] *MG*, 27 July 1850.   [3] *Merlin*, 20 Feb. 1841.
[4] NLW Bute MSS., Box 141, Parcel 5. E. M. Williams to W. H. Smyth, 7 Nov. 1839.

In the north, he said, 'there is one ingredient . . . that I look upon as a *sine qua non*—that is, that we carry on the business through a Fitter—that is to say a Shipping Merchant upon a *del credere* commission—which is, the Owners pay a higher rate of Commission and have no risk of bad debts. I have never yet been able to find a merchant who would fit my coals at Neath upon a *del credere* Commission, and until then I will have nothing to do with any Coal Trade.'[1]

The reluctance of the coal-owners in the coastal trade to ship much of their coal on their own account largely derived from the freightage risk that this involved and the limitations of their knowledge of and connexions in the various markets. These risks were much greater in the overseas than in the coastal trade; one method of meeting them was to conduct a higher proportion of the foreign than of the coastal coal trade by selling to shippers and merchants who bought at an f.o.b. price and assumed responsibility for the transport and ultimate sale of the coal. Many of the largest buyers, however, —the steamship companies and the home and foreign railways—obtained their supplies by inviting tenders. Here the contract usually called for an f.o.b. price, the buyer arranging the shipping or, if a home railway company, providing the wagons and asking for a price delivered into wagons at the pit-head or some suitable junction. These conditions gave the coal-owner every incentive to tender direct without the intervention of any third party. Occasionally, however, these companies appointed some shipper or merchant to buy on their behalf or—as was the common practice with naval contracts—the tender asked for prices to be quoted for delivery to some home or overseas port. In such sales, to avoid the freight risk, the coal-owner would probably quote an f.o.b. price to a coal-exporter from whom he hoped to secure the order.

To fulfil these functions there grew up at all the main ports

[1] NLW Bute MSS., Box 70, Letter Book, vol. 7. Bute to Capt. Steel, 9 Jan. 1841.

a group of firms who specialized in the business of coal-shipping. Typical of these were Cory Bros. of Cardiff, whose father had been a ship's chandler at the port; Beynons of Newport, and Livingstone, Richards, and Almond at Swansea, as well as those London merchants, such as Edward Wood and William Cory, who conducted a large business in South Wales. These firms not only tendered for the large coal contracts but also secured orders from their agents overseas and chartered the vessels for their fulfilment. The coal they required for these purposes they secured partly by *ad hoc* purchases, at f.o.b. prices, from the coal-owners. This method alone, however, particularly for long contracts for which they had submitted tenders, left them too much at the mercy of price fluctuations. Greater security was obtained by contracting with various coal-owners for a given quantity of coal spread over a lengthy period. Sometimes this took the form of undertaking to dispose—on a commission basis—of the entire output of a colliery. In 1857, for example, William Cory undertook the sale of Waynes's Aberdare coal for ten years in return for £300 a year, 1*d*. a ton on all coal shipped and postage, stationery, and travelling expenses.[1] From this it was no great step for these firms to move back into direct participation in the coal-owning business. William Cory was a principal partner in the firm of Nixon, Taylor, and Cory who owned the Navigation, Deep Duffryn, and Merthyr Vale collieries, some of the most extensive on the coalfield. Thomas Beynon was a director and large shareholder of the Newport Abercarn Black Vein Steam Coal Company Ltd. John and Richard Cory were the proprietors of the Pentre and Church collieries in the Rhondda valley, while Thomas Cory and F. A. Yeo, coal-merchants of Swansea, owned the Resolven colliery in the Neath valley. When, in 1873, Yeo and the Corys sold the three last-named collieries to a limited company, in which they remained substantial shareholders, part of the agreement was that for at least seven years the only agents for the sale

[1] *MG*, 5 Feb. 1859.

of the company's coal were to be Cory Bros. of Cardiff and Cory and Yeo of Swansea. For this service these firms were to receive a commission of 5 per cent. on all sales.[1] The middleman's profit of the shippers and merchants derived from the special knowledge they possessed of freight rates and foreign markets and also from the service they provided to the coal-owners with whom they dealt by securing a more or less regular outlet for part of their production. Inevitably there were criticisms that these services were dearly bought. 'Despite the increased demand for coal', was one contemporary comment, 'the price is still receding and in many instances sold at such a low figure that it is a question whether it compensates the proprietors, as the greatest part is sold through brokers and agents, who take off the principal part of the profit; and the competition is so great among these people that they will sell the coal at a very low rate . . . as they calculate their profits on the chartering of vessels to convey the coal which they sell.'[2]

This over-stated the importance of the middleman. In the judgement of a well-informed authority in 1874 'a large proportion of the steam coal raised in this district is consumed on the various lines of English and Continental mail steamers, the contracts for which are almost invariably made direct between the coal owners and the steam companies. The general export trade is carried on by means of sales, also made direct between the producers and buyers abroad, and to some considerable extent through the agency of merchants or "middlemen".'[3] Nor was it always at the expense of the coal-owners that the middleman made his profit. The agent of the Dowlais Iron Company explained that he could sometimes sell odd cargoes through brokers if he could allow them 2d. per ton 'which would in all cases be covered by an extra price beyond our present selling price'. He did not at all

[1] P.R.O. Company Records. Cardiff and Swansea Smokeless Steam Coal Co. Ltd. [2] *MG*, 28 May 1859.
[3] T. Forster Brown, 'The South Wales Coalfield', *SWIE*, vol. ix.

relish this practice—which meant in effect that the broker was making an extra profit at the expense of the foreign buyer who had entrusted an order to him—but thought that it was the only way of getting orders that were going to other coal-owners.[1]

Throughout this period the greater part of the Welsh coal output was probably sold without the intervention of middlemen. Besides the trade they secured through tenders and as a result of direct inquiries, many of the coal-owners maintained agents—on a salary and commission basis—at ports such as Liverpool and London. Advertisements from people offering their services in this capacity were a common feature in the local press. Connexions overseas also had to be built up. The practice of the Troedyrhiw Coal Company may serve to illustrate one common method of achieving this. Matthew Cope, the senior partner, was in many ways typical of the pioneer coal-owner; uncultivated in his manner and miserly with his money. It is not surprising to discover that his action in dispatching his son to France for a year to complete his education was not altogether prompted by his faith in the value of a liberal education. These were the days when the travelling salesman formed an important part of the commercial structure of the coal industry and his son's knowledge of foreign languages was—after he had served for a few years as a clerk at half-a-crown a week—put to the service of the firm by travelling to France, Spain, Italy, and Sicily, as well as Cornwall and Ireland, in search of orders. 'Of course', the son wrote later, 'I had not the field to myself by a long way. All the other South Wales collieries had their travellers out.'[2] Similarly, when in 1861 the Dowlais Company contemplated starting in the house-coal trade their Cardiff agent warned them that to do so they would have to organize a connexion in Ireland and the west of England 'which I believe can only

---

[1] Dowlais MSS. Cardiff Agency Letters. S. Howard to Dowlais Iron Co., 19 Mar. 1862.

[2] 'Reminiscences of Matthew Cope', *Western Mail*, Mar.–May 1928.

be done by getting an apt and steady man to go slowly, carefully and, it may be, repeatedly over the ground'.[1]

The key figure in the trade, however, was the owner or his salaried agent at the shipping port. He it was who decided or advised upon general sales policy and was the medium through which many sales were effected. 'When I was young', one coal-owner later recalled, 'the business that is now done in the Exchange was mostly done on the pavement. We walked up and down in front of our offices and there we did our deals with our clients or customers.'[2] The routine duties were no less vital. Urgent amongst these was the need to ensure by the rigorous exclusion of shale and clod that the coal was not being shipped in a dirty condition. It was on this that the reputation of the coal in the market largely depended. 'The people who have got their names up, have watched with an extreme interest the filling of that coal to see that it was free from impurity', the trustee of the Dowlais Iron Company was informed when Dowlais first determined on an extensive coal sale.[3] And thenceforward the Cardiff agent of the company was constantly returning to this theme, perpetually impressing on the collieries the urgency of ensuring that the coal was sent away clean. 'I fear that if such a company were to break off with us on account of quality', he wrote when a complaint on this score was received from the New York and Philadelphia Steam Ship Company, 'it would be very likely to ruin our trade in Liverpool.'[4] The government and many of the important steam shipping lines kept their own inspector at the port to examine the coal as it was shipped; if these rejected cargoes because of dirty or soft coal it became difficult to sell to any steamship company. Complaints from the government inspector were particularly serious: 'If we get

[1] Dowlais MSS. Cardiff Agency Letters. S. Howard to Dowlais Iron Co., 28 Aug. 1861.
[2] 'Reminiscences of Matthew Cope', loc cit.
[3] Dowlais MSS. Cardiff Agency Letters. S. Howard to G. T. Clark, 24 Aug. 1859.
[4] Ibid., S. Howard to Dowlais Iron Co., 5 Dec. 1865.

struck off the Government list I think it would affect our price to the extent of 1s. a ton on all coal sales.'[1]

The pressure from buyers was always apt to be more severe when trade was slack. At such times the more unscrupulous buyer not only took the natural advantage of his stronger position as against the seller to insist on a higher and more uniform quality than could be exacted when trade was brisk, but also resorted to fastidious complaints as a means of freeing himself from contracts that failed to reflect his superior market position. 'If the contract should happen to go against them very much they would have the advantage common to all buyers of coal—that of objecting to the quality and refusing to go on with the contract', although the writer—the Dowlais agent—added that respectable firms did not 'descend to that sort of shift'.[2] The agent, however, was convinced from his frequent personal inspections of the wagons that the complaints against Dowlais shipments were often well founded. At one stage, indeed, he felt obliged to hire a man to stand at the hatchway to remove clod and 'what he throws out remains alongside the ship for all our competitors to point out'.[3] To rectify this he sought to impress upon his own company the care taken by their competitors: 'I am informed that at the Ferndale pit they only lift one tram at a time but that they have four screens so as to give plenty of time to well examine and clear the coal from anything which may have been neglected underground.'[4]

The need to avoid delays to the colliery wagons was another function that demanded the vigilance of the agent. The prices quoted for contracts were based on estimates of the pit-head costs and the costs of transporting the coal to the port or other place of delivery. Most of these transport costs, such as the railway charges, were more or less fixed and predictable, but the costs of the wagons figured as an important variable. They were expensive and the number that was required to deal with a given annual output depended largely

[1] Dowlais MSS. Cardiff Agency Letters. S. Howard to Dowlais Iron Co., 24 Oct. 1868.
[2] Ibid., 1 Apr. 1865.   [3] Ibid., 16 May 1867.   [4] Ibid., 20 Mar. 1868.

COMMERCIAL ORGANIZATION 171

on the number of round trips that were made by each wagon during a year. Their efficient use also avoided demurrage payments and maintained custom by giving prompt delivery. 'The cost of delivery here depends on the rapidity with which our wagons could be worked',[1] but the attainment of this speedy turn-round was greatly complicated by the irregularity of the trade; an irregularity which was much more marked for the individual firms than for the district as a whole. The swift swings between slackness and high pressure, together with the inevitable occasional delays at both ends, made it impossible to maintain a steady flow between colliery and port. But care and attention and frequent badgering of port and railway authorities could do much to ensure that wagons were sent where they were needed and to reduce delays in loading at the ports and stoppages through lack of wagons at the pits. It was also possible to insure against these difficulties to some extent. Dowlais did so by contracts to sell part of its output at the pit-head into wagons provided by the buyers and also by keeping stocks loaded into wagons during periods of inactivity for ready disposal by its agent.[2]

There was, too, a tendency for buyers to express their wants more rigorously. 'If I could get it', wrote one customer to the agent of the Rhigos colliery in 1841, 'I do not wish to have a nob in the Cargo larger than a man's fist but to be rubbly, the size of eggs, and free from dead small.'[3] In the most important market, that for steam coal, it was the exclusion of small coal that was most insistently demanded. At first this demand was met by the introduction of the system of hand-picking the large steam coal. Nevill claimed that since he had 'made it a rule to ship them by hand', he had completely removed the complaints that his steam coal contained small.[4] Later it

[1] Dowlais MSS. Cardiff Agency Letters. S. Howard to Dowlais Iron Co., 16 Jan. 1862
[2] Ibid., 23 July 1861, 12 Mai. 1863, 21 Sept. 1863, and Sect. D., William Jenkins, cashier, to G. T. Clark, 15 Nov. 1861.
[3] NLW Bute MSS., Box 141, Parcel 5. B. Richards to W. Thomas, 1841.
[4] Nevill MSS. 8. R. J. Nevill to Dublin and London Steam Marine Co., 7 Feb. 1834.

became more usual to separate the small by passing the coal over screens, about 13 feet long by 7 feet wide, the bars of which were on the average 1⅛ inches apart. This was always done at the pit-head and the coal was then known as 'colliery-screened large' but it was usually repeated at the port, the coal being known as 'single-screened' or 'double-screened' at the time of shipment depending on whether one or both the screens at the shipping shoot were open.[1] Double-screened coal always commanded a higher price, but it is doubtful if this was ever a source of profit to the coal-owner and it could be a source of considerable loss. The custom was to charge an extra 6d. a ton for double-screened coal but the Dowlais agent mentioned at least one example where 11½ per cent. of the coal sent down, or the equivalent of 10d. a ton, had been removed by the process.[2] The practice was one that was forced upon the coal-owners by the competitive nature of the trade and the demands of their customers.

It was also in part the product of the competition for trade between the various ports in the district; any attraction that was offered to buyers and shippers at one port tended to be reproduced, if possible, at the others. This inter-port rivalry was a constant element in the sales competition of the district. Among the bases of this competition were the relative facilities that the different ports offered for shipping. Llanelly, for example, with its difficult approach and inadequate provision for large vessels, was able to hold its own in the 1830's when its chief rivals—Neath and Swansea—suffered from similar disabilities. 'I do not wish', Nevill wrote, 'to engage to load vessels afloat nor do I think you will find this absolutely necessary for vessels always take the Ground at Swansea and Neath and the layerage is much better here.'[3] But as the average size of the vessels in the trade grew and as other ports made improvements, Llanelly, despite its own efforts in this

---

[1] T. Forster Brown, 'The South Wales Coalfield', *SWIE*, vol. ix.
[2] Dowlais Papers. Cardiff Agency Letters. S. Howard to Dowlais Iron Co., 3 July 1863.
[3] Nevill MSS. 8. R. J. Nevill to Samuel Rhode, 23 Nov. 1833.

direction, found its relative position to be severely declining. On the other hand, superior port facilities made a vital contribution to the meteoric rise of Cardiff as a coal port at this time. Trade could also be attracted by a low level of port charges. It was, for instance, said of Neath in 1843 that its low tolls had done much to make it a favoured harbour of ships' captains and coal-buyers.[1] And the offer of low tolls was reinforced by the custom of granting gratuities to captains. Speed of dispatch offered another ground for rivalry. The advertisements that around 1840 were commonly inserted in the local press by coal-owners to attract the captains of coastal vessels rarely failed to mention that the turn-round would be swift. The usual coal charter in 1840 provided for loading 'in regular turn'; if there were delays 'small vessels will not engage for coasting voyages but at a considerable advance in freight'.[2] By 1875 this system of regular 'turns' had become obsolete 'having given place to the introduction into nearly all forms of contract of a scale of lay days varying according to the size of the ship; about eight days (Sundays excepted) being the basis for ships of 400 tons, extending at the rate of one day for each 100 tons of cargo in excess. Special conditions are, of course, made applicable to steamers, ranging (for a carrying capacity of 1,000 tons) from 24 to 50 hours. In all cases protecting clauses are inserted providing against delays from strikes, accidents and other unavoidable causes.'[3] The change in system had increased the need to give quick dispatch; even apart from the spur of demurrage, shippers still gave preference to ports that offered a quick turn-round.

---

[1] NJ.W Bute MSS., Box 141, Parcel 5. Lionel Brough to Thomas Collingdon, 14 Jan. 1843. The writer went on to express fears that this advantage would be lost if the proposed harbour improvements resulted in a raising of the tolls; but it was not the absolute level of charges but their level in relation to the facilities offered and to charges and facilities elsewhere that was important.
[2] Nevill MSS. 8. Nevill Brown to William Langdon, 15 Nov. 1833.
[3] T. Forster Brown, 'The South Wales Coalfield', *SWIE*, vol. ix.

The coal trade, by whatever mechanism it was carried on, was almost always extremely competitive. Occasionally the coal-owners in different regions came together to agree on a price level, but these agreements were neither sufficiently permanent nor sufficiently binding to go far towards stifling competition. There were times, too, when the co-operation of owners was confined to a particular sale or contract. Thus in 1833, when Welsh participation in government contracts was still limited to a few coal-owners in the west, R. J. Nevill of Llanelly informed his London agent that he had agreed with his chief rivals 'not to tender ourselves for the Contract which is to be made next week nor to receive a lower price than 8*s*. a ton free on board for whatever coals we may supply to parties by whom the Contract may be taken'.[1]

Action on a grander scale had been taken as early as 1830 by the shippers of house coal at Newport who had agreed to restrict output to bolster prices. This arrangement enjoyed an intermittent existence for the next twenty years. That it, or a similar organization, was in effective operation between 1836 and 1839 emerges from the evidence of Lewis Thomas, colliery owner, in a coal trespass case a few years later, and from the remark of the Tredegar agent in 1837 that a coal area he had just let could not be worked immediately because the lessees adhered to the monopoly arrangement and could not expand their output until the current agreement ended.[2] Two years later a new agreement was reported, the main proprietors undertaking to sell their coal to the Newport Coal Company, which was to conduct the sale of coal from Newport. At the same time the price was raised to 10*s*. a ton.[3] For a time the Newport Coal Company became the largest seller of coal from Newport, but within a year the break-up of the combination was heralded by the re-emergence of Thomas Powell, one

[1] Nevill MSS. 8. R. J. Nevill to S. Rhode, 11 May 1833.
[2] *Merlin*, 10 Apr. 1841.
[3] *MG*, 2 Feb. 1839.

of the outstanding figures in the trade, as an independent shipper.[1]

The years from 1837 to 1839 were years of thriving trade and buoyant prices; the apparent effectiveness of the Newport cartel during these years probably arose because there was little need to impose hampering restrictions on its members. The less favourable outlook of 1840 placed a greater strain on their loyalty and, in the competition to supply a more cautious demand, the trade again dissolved into individual selling. As the depression deepened, however, and as prices crumbled, negotiations were reopened through the member for the Monmouth boroughs, R. J. Blewitt, to re-establish united action. In July 1841 a new agreement was reached under which the quantities that each was to bring to market were controlled, the price being advanced by 1s. to 9s. 6d. a ton.[2] After a six months trial this arrangement was extended for a further three years, a dinner at which the principal coal-owners and shippers at the port were present being held to celebrate the event. The High Sheriff of the County, Samuel Homfray of the Tredegar iron- and coal-works, a son-in-law of Sir Charles Morgan, and R. J. Blewitt were appointed arbitrators under the scheme.[3] This combination must have continued, or been revived after it was due to expire in 1845, since it was reported in 1849 that it was to be disbanded in May of that year, although not without hopes that a new agreement would again be effected.[4] It is difficult to conceive, however, that any cartel at Newport in the 1840's could have achieved much success in raising prices. At this time Newport was ceasing to be the main seller of house coals from the Welsh coalfield as the shipments from Cardiff, the outlet for the expanding production from the house-coal seams of the Rhondda valley, increased in volume. It is unlikely that the market for this type of coal expanded sufficiently to absorb

[1] *MG*, 16 Feb. 1839, 11 Jan. 1840.
[2] Ibid., 31 July 1841; *Merlin*, 10, 17 July 1841.
[3] *Merlin*, 15 Jan. 1842; *MG*, 15 Jan. 1842.
[4] *Merlin*, 5 May 1849; *MG*, 10, 17 Mar., 5 May 1849.

easily this extra production, so only the most stringent restriction of output by the Newport producers would have enabled them to maintain prices.

The attempt made over the course of two decades to control prices and output in the Newport house-coal trade was much the most determined effort in this direction that took place in the industry during this period. It was a frequent occurrence for the coal-sellers at a particular port to meet informally to fix a price or agree upon an advance or reduction,[1] but these measures represented only very minor efforts to control the course of prices. They were embodied in no definite agreements, involved no restriction of output, and carried with them no machinery for their enforcement. The limit of their effect was probably to hurry on a price advance that would have come in any event or to postpone slightly the general acceptance of a fall in price.

The obstacles to a more rigid control were formidable. The existence of the other British coalfields, particularly that of Northumberland and Durham in the most important market for steam coals, greatly restricted the range within which the Welsh producers could act alone. There could, moreover, be no effective price control without a restriction of output, but in a rapidly developing coalfield where many producers were still in the expansionary stage, it would have been difficult to secure agreement for a quota system. The problem was complicated, too, by the relatively modest size of the average unit, especially in the house-coal industry; by the large number of individual producers in the coalfield; and by the unrestricted freedom of entry into the industry—conditions the reverse of those under which employers' combinations are expected to flourish.

Moreover, even where coals were of the same broad type—steam or house or anthracite—they varied considerably in their reputation in the market. The interests of the different producers were thus not identical. In the early stages of a

[1] See, e.g., *Cambrian*, 17 Jan. 1846; *MG*, 16 Oct. 1863.

revival in trade the sellers with the best coal, or the coal best established in the market, would find 'such a rush for their coal' that it was hard for them to determine which customers to supply and which to turn over to their neighbours. These producers were naturally the first to press on others the need for an advance in prices but it was not necessarily to the advantage of all to follow their lead immediately. As the Dowlais agent pointed out on one such occasion, '*our* connection is not so large . . . we have lost some of our best customers through stiffness in price . . . and yet it is now sought to define the terms on which alone we should be at liberty to regain such customers'.[1] If output was not controlled the mere setting of a fixed price for, say, steam coals at Cardiff was unlikely to be effective. It carried with it the implicit assumption that all the steam coals sold at the port were of the same quality and standing. Since this similarity did not exist the setting of a fixed price would simply have directed demand first towards the coals of the best repute. Finally, it was difficult to contrive machinery that would ensure that any agreement was operated in good faith, and without such machinery any combination stood little chance of survival.

These considerations were a powerful bar to the negotiation of effective selling arrangements.[2] Moreover, in so far as the secular expansion in demand helped to maintain prices, the need for a combination for this purpose was less strongly felt.

[1] Dowlais MSS. Cardiff Agency Letter Books. S. Howard to Dowlais Iron Company, 6 Aug. 1863.

[2] George Elliot did, indeed, inform the *Select Committee on Dearness of Coal* in 1873 that an agreement for the maintenance of high prices in the steam-coal trade was quite feasible. He had in mind, however, not a combination of independent producers but their amalgamation into a single company. Although the steam-coal trade, more than the other branches, was tending to be dominated by a comparatively small number of firms working larger units, it is difficult to imagine that the plan was practicable. Apart from the difficulty of securing agreement on the valuation of the different undertakings, the area of exploitation of the steam coals was at that time being greatly extended. Even as Elliot was speaking pits were being sunk in the Rhondda valleys that were to double the Welsh steam-coal output in the next decade.

Apart from the intermittent combinations at Newport no association of owners based on the control of prices, or even including this amongst its functions, emerged during this period. The nearest approach to such a body arose out of the strike of 1871 when a Sale of Coal committee was set up with representatives of all those owners who had resisted the demands of the men. This met daily with the object of resisting the expected onslaught on coal prices by buyers and middlemen urging that the market could not take the extra supplies. For a time all local negotiations for the fourteen companies (owning twenty-eight pits in the Aberdare and Rhondda valleys and controlling an output of $2\frac{1}{4}$ million tons) were conducted centrally through their Secretary. This was, however, only a temporary expedient and the main function of the committee, which continued to operate for a year or so, was to compile weekly statistics of shipping arrivals and colliery capacities, and so provide a better basis for the exercise of the judgement of its individual members.[1] Each company thus maintained its full sovereignty; none was faced with the awkward questions that the Dowlais agent had once asked his employers when a more formal arrangement was under discussion: 'How far would it behove a seller to suffer for an ideal? Would you, for instance, stop one of your pits if it were called for?'[2]

The most potent force leading to the growth of closer association between employers was, as will be seen later, the need to present a united front to their workmen. Unity over price-control schemes rarely appeared and never endured. Much of the social history of the period becomes more intelligible when this prevalence of keen competition, and its effect in inducing employers to resist changes which might enhance costs of production, are remembered.

[1] A. Dalziel, *The Colliers' Strike in South Wales* (1872), pp. 171-2; Minute Book of David Davies and Co., 4 Nov. 1871. (Made available by courtesy of Mr. Ralph Thomas, the Secretary of the Ocean Coal Co.)
[2] Dowlais MSS. Cardiff Agency Letter Books. S. Howard to Dowlais Iron Co., 6 Aug. 1863.

VIII

SAFETY

'IT is a life of great danger both for man and child: a collier is never safe after he is swung off to be let down the pit.'[1] Thus a collier summed up his working conditions in 1841. A generation later a mines inspector could write of his report that 'this account of death, contusions, fractures, amputations, and other surgical operations, altogether sounds like the description of military movements in the field rather than the ordinary report of industrious and peaceful pursuits'.[2] Nevertheless, while coal-mining inevitably remained a dangerous pursuit, considerable progress was made, during the years between 1840 and 1875, in the struggle to reduce the loss of life to a minimum.

Not a great deal was achieved before 1850. A sign of the alarm that accidents were causing, and of the hope that it might be possible to reduce their frequency, was the appointment of a Select Committee of the House of Commons to investigate this problem. In its report,[3] issued in 1835, this Committee made no decisive recommendations, hoping that the collection of information itself would prove valuable. It suggested that ventilation should be adequate; that miners should receive a better education and that management should be placed in the hands of competent officials able to enforce an effective discipline—themes that were to recur in the decades to come. But no witness from the South Wales coalfield had given evidence before this Committee and its suggestions, in South Wales at least, bore little immediate fruit. A partial beginning of safety legislation came with the Act of 1842,[4] which followed the first report of the Children's

[1] *Children's Employment Commission. First Report*, P.P. 1842, xv, p. 135.
[2] MIR Report of Lionel Brough for 1864.
[3] *Report from Select Committee on Accidents in Mines*, P.P. 1835 (603), v.
[4] 5 and 6 Vict., c. 99.

Employment Commission, with its disquieting revelations of the conditions of employment of children and young persons in mines. The clause prohibiting anyone under fifteen years old from being in charge of winding-engines was clearly a safety measure, while the exclusion of boys under ten from underground work removed from the mines children who were too young to appreciate their danger. But the subsequent reports of Seymour Tremenheere, the sole inspector who was appointed to enforce this Act, dealt, not with safety or the condition of the underground workings, but with the general social and moral conditions of the mining population. Clear public recognition that an attempt should be made to lessen the dangers of mining by legislative control came only with the Coal Mines Act of 1850.[1]

Before 1850 no systematic record of accidents was kept, nor were those connected with the industry willing to give information about their number and nature. A lack of concern about accidents, before complacence was shaken by catastrophic explosions, is suggested by the casual procedure for inquests. 'When a man dies the viewer looks at the body and sends to the coroner; and, unless a case of suspicion is made out to the coroner, he does not come, but sends an order to the constable to bury; and frequently the coroner does not attend until there are five or six cases to clear off.'[2] Inquest verdicts were not likely to ascribe blame, as it was difficult to get unbiased evidence and an impartial decision when both witnesses and members of the jury might be workers in the same pit, reluctant to condemn their own employer or one of their fellows. At Dinas colliery, for example, the overman had taken down the manager's son, a young boy, to help in the examination of the headings and stalls before work began, and it was in a stall examined by this boy that an explosion occurred, leading to the loss of

[1] 13 and 14 Vict., c. 100.
[2] *Children's Employment*, p. 550. Evidence of Henry George, innkeeper, Blackwood.

twelve lives. The coroner strongly condemned the conduct of the overman but left it to the jury to decide about a committal on a charge of manslaughter. 'The jury intimated that such a charge would receive no countenance from them' and returned a verdict of 'Accidental Death'.[1]

A similar indifference prevailed to the insidious undermining of health caused by working conditions which were, if not dangerous, 'extremely unwholesome'. 'The principal seam at present in work for the supply of the export trade of Newport', it was remarked in 1841, 'is a red-ash coal, in which fire-damp is not found. The absence of fire-damp in this vein (the Mynyddislwyn) has operated very prejudicially throughout the district, by creating a confidence in the minds of the parties engaged, that whatever the state of the ventilation may be, no explosion of fire-damp can possibly occur; consequently the ventilation of the collieries is much neglected.' Colliers, although sometimes compelled to stop work because their candles would not remain alight, continued at work as long as possible 'but the small quantity of air necessary barely to maintain combustion must be a very unhealthy atmosphere for respiration'.[2] In such pits, it was noted, 'many men suffer from the asthma' by the age of thirty-five or forty, and their life, or their working life, was shortened.

A sign that this feeling of indifference was coming to an end was the growing belief during the 1840's that further state control of mining conditions was essential. Whilst this nation-wide change in public opinion was, perhaps, caused mainly by events in the north of England, nevertheless a series of accidents of grave magnitude in South Wales occasioned a similar change there. In 1844 shortly after the explosion, already referred to, at Dinas colliery, Rhondda, forty lives were lost in an inundation at Landshipping colliery, Pembrokeshire. Commenting on this, the press called for the appointment of government inspectors to examine mines and

[1] *MJ*, 13 Jan. 1844.
[2] *Children's Employment Commission. First Report*, 1842, p. 75.

the qualifications of managers.[1] The same feeling of disquiet was evident in 1845 when Penrose and Evans, lessees of Eaglesbush colliery—really two collieries, Eaglesbush and Eskyn—applied to the magistrates at Neath Petty Sessions for summonses against some of their workmen who had left work without giving the required notice. This colliery had an unenviable reputation for fire-damp accidents and the magistrates dismissed the application, feeling that 'as the works were notoriously deficient in ventilation it would be hard to compel any men to labour in them and thereby to expose them to great peril'. That the magistrates generally shared these qualms is shown by their decision at Quarter Sessions to request the Secretary of State to send a surveyor to the colliery to examine it, particularly as the owners had not fulfilled their promise to make a survey themselves. Not only should workmen, who could not protect themselves, be protected, but also the ratepayers of Neath Union should be guarded against the cost of supporting the injured and bereft, as neither the owners nor the men had any accident fund.[2] Later in 1845 there was an explosion at Thomas Powell's Duffryn colliery when twenty-eight people, including two nine-year-old boys, lost their lives. A special jury was summoned including some members prominent in the coal industry, particularly Matthew and Thomas Wayne of Gadlys, Henry Kirkhouse, Cyfarthfa mineral agent, John Nixon of Werfa, and David Williams of Ynyscynon. The membership of this jury was another indication of the growing concern, but while the jury criticized the ventilation, which allowed gas to seep into the tramroads from old workings, they did not criticize the use of naked lights, even though Nixon expressed his belief that this would be the first of a series of accidents in the Aberdare valley.[3] Many of the victims of the

[1] *MG*, 6 Jan., 24 Feb. 1844.   [2] Ibid., 5 July 1845.
[3] Ibid., 8 Aug. 1845. Thomas Powell rejected the offer of a subscription after this accident and made an allowance to the five women who were widowed by it of 9s. a week, with a house and supply of coal for each. After a shaft accident at Llantwit in 1849 Powell also placed the sufferers and their families 'on his list of pensioners'. *MG*, 26 May 1849.

explosion at Risca in 1846, when thirty-five men were killed, were men who had come to the district from Somersetshire and Gloucestershire, the local workers being reputed to dislike the colliery as they thought an accident likely.[1] In 1848 twenty men lost their lives in an explosion at the Eskyn (Eaglesbush) colliery, where there was a reliance on natural ventilation only, the use of a furnace having been discontinued. At the inquest it was stated that forty or fifty men had been burnt by explosions in the last four years and that the men had recently complained of the state of the pit. The verdict of 'Accidental Death' was badly received in the district, local opinion being that it should have been one of manslaughter against Penrose and Evans.[2] A year later Nixon's prophetic foreboding about the Aberdare valley received justification when fifty-two perished in an explosion at Lletty Shenkin. The verdict at the inquest, which was attended by Kenyon Blackwell on behalf of the government, was 'Accidental Death', with a rider that the old workings should be separately ventilated and never be connected with the colliery air intake. As Lletty Shenkin was not below the general standard of ventilation of other collieries in the district no other verdict would have seemed just. Colliers' meetings took place after this accident and it was decided that five men be deputed from each pit to inspect the colliery workings and report on them. The main complaints arising out of these inspections, which all coal-owners who were approached permitted, were that sometimes the air-ways were of an inefficient size and that gas was allowed to accumulate in abandoned workings.[3]

This growing perturbation, reflected in the press, the decision of the Glamorgan magistrates, and in local opinion in parts of the South Wales coalfield, led to the belief that, however repugnant the idea was to the coal-owners, more drastic government intervention, on lines similar to those prevailing

[1] *MG*, 16, 23 Jan. 1846.   [2] Ibid., 8, 22 Apr. 1848.
[3] Ibid., 18, 25 Aug., 29 Sept. 1849.

in Belgium and France, was required to lessen this recurrent sacrifice of human lives. Joshua Richardson wrote that 'the force of public opinion, it is alleged, is quite adequate to induce the owners of mines to adopt those improvements which are imperatively required. Experience, however, has proved that such a remedy, in a great many instances, is quite inoperative, and that something more compulsive is necessary.'[1] Richardson's book was occasioned by the signs that new legislation was envisaged and was written to allay, by diffusing information, the opposition 'interference' was sure to provoke. He was merely reiterating the conclusions drawn by Sir Henry de la Bèche and Dr. Lyon Playfair, who had earlier been requested by the government to inquire into the causes of accidents in coal-mines, and who had recommended the appointment of government inspectors and the compulsory use of safety lamps in all fiery collieries. After inquiries had been made into individual colliery disasters, and firedamp explosions generally had been investigated by a Select Committee of the House of Lords in 1849, the following year saw an Act passed 'to provide for the Inspection of Coal Mines in Great Britain'.[2] This Act, tentative at first and limited to five years, was epoch making. Not only did it involve government control of underground mining, a wholly male and preponderantly adult occupation, but it also both laid the foundation for the development of a safety code and, as accidents could not be wholly prevented, ultimately led logically to the introduction of workmen's compensation.

By the Act of 1850 owners were compelled both to keep accurate plans of their collieries and to notify the Home Secretary of all fatal accidents, while coroners were required to give two days' notice of inquests. Four inspectors were appointed for the whole of Britain with the legal right to enter any colliery and to notify owners of any defects revealed by

[1] J. Richardson, *The Prevention of Accidents in Mines* (Neath, 1848), v Preface.   [2] 13 and 14 Vict., c. 100.

their inspection. If necessary, the inspector could serve the owner with a formal notice that his colliery was 'dangerous and defective' and report this to the Home Secretary. Inspection began in November 1850. Kenyon Blackwell, who had been one of the two commissioners appointed by the Home Secretary in 1849 to make a preliminary survey of the state of the mines, was the first inspector for the South Western district, which included the South Wales area. But Blackwell resigned on 17 August 1851, thus serving for too short a time for his period of office to be in any way significant, and after this, for a few months, South Wales was virtually without an inspector as the acceptance by Joseph Dickinson of the responsibility for the South Western in addition to his own district could be little more than a temporary formality. The real beginning of mines inspection in South Wales came when Herbert Francis Mackworth took up his duties as inspector for the South Western district on 12 November 1851. Mackworth, after receiving a scientific education at King's College, London, had been employed as an engineer making railway tunnels and had subsequently spent two years in superintending collieries for Thomas Powell.[1] About twenty-seven years of age when first appointed inspector, his district included the whole South Wales coalfield until 1855 and then Monmouthshire until his death in 1858. His reports to the Home Office give a good indication of the difficulties he encountered and of mining conditions as he found them, although no doubt the collieries where conditions were least satisfactory and accidents most frequent figure disproportionately largely in any inspector's reports.

There were many reasons why it was unlikely that the Act of 1850 and the work of a single inspector would make much immediate impression on the problem of safety in South Wales. The South Western district was a large one, comprising some adjacent English counties in addition to South

[1] *MJ*, 3 Jan. 1852; evidence of Mackworth, *Select Committee on Coal Mines*, *P.P.* 1852 (509), v.

Wales and Monmouthshire, and to have inspected all the collieries in his district only once, Mackworth said, would have taken between four and five years.[1] A large district was not wholly a disadvantage, however, as it gave an inspector a wider experience and greater scope for generalizing the practice of the best-regulated collieries. In any event, as a later inspector remarked, the inspector was 'always in his district ready to inquire into the cause of accidents, to listen and attend to any complaints made by the colliers, and to give his assistance and advice to the managers'.[2] The inspector could concentrate his attention on the more dangerous collieries, and it was expected, too, that the moral force of any advice he gave would be strengthened by his presence at inquests, where he could draw attention to any neglect of his cautions.

Safety was more difficult to achieve in regions where output was increasing swiftly. This was most marked in the parish of Aberdare where production increased from 477,208 tons in 1850 to 1,575,856 tons in 1860, this increase being achieved partly by opening new mines or by deepening old ones to new seams, both enhancing the danger from gas. In the interests of rapid output owners were tempted to sacrifice safety considerations and to postpone necessary repairs, while the severity of competition meant that a selling price sufficiently remunerative to provide easy finance for safety improvements could not always be attained. The standpoint of the inspector, not placing considerations of monetary costs of production on a higher plane than those of safety and free from the preoccupation of satisfying the insistent claims of an ever-expanding market, stood out in opposition to this attitude, but not always successfully.

The rapid growth of some regions also involved an influx into the industry of workers not used to its risks—though even those starting a collier's life from childhood became so inured to risk that caution sometimes was forgotten—and, above all,

---

[1] *Select Committee on Accidents, First Report*, P.P. 1852–3 (691), xx, p. 38.
[2] MIR Report of Thomas Evans for 1861, p. 127.

it aggravated the difficulty of finding a sufficient number of competent overmen. Mackworth noted that, while some owners had put their mines in charge of competent engineers, most overmen were ignorant. The dangerous state of Lletty Shenkin colliery in 1849, for example, had been attributed to the lack of competence of the overman. After a period under a highly qualified engineer the management was then taken over by John Johns, an illiterate man of little experience, 'quite incompetent to be entrusted with the charge of 180 lives in one of the most dangerous collieries of England'.[1] Johns did not know the printed rules of the colliery, and his giving orders conflicting with these—ordering a collier to work away a pillar of coal, using a naked light close to a fall from which gas was escaping—led to an explosion in which three men were killed and fifteen burnt. Samuel Dobson, principal manager of the Duffryn collieries, also remarked, in 1854, on the great deficiency of overmen in South Wales; he had several who could not read or write.[2] Dobson had found the introduction of men from the north of England unsatisfactory as a remedy because they took a long time to become reconciled to Welsh habits and methods of mining, and, not speaking Welsh, could not command the sympathies of the workmen as local overmen could.

The overmen (and firemen too), Mackworth found, were usually fewer in numbers than in comparable mines in the north of England, and were often withdrawn from supervision while they put up doors or enlarged air-courses. Yet the overmen, as Mackworth's successor remarked, 'are the thews and sinews of coal mining; on them the routine and steady progress of day and night operations entirely depend'.[3] Most of the accidents Mackworth investigated were, he considered, 'attributable to the neglect or recklessness of the proprietors or managers of mines, whilst they generally con-

[1] MIR Mackworth's Report for 1853, p. 180.
[2] Evidence of Dobson, *Select Committee on Accidents in Coal Mines, Third Report, P.P.* 1854 (277), ix.
[3] MIR Lionel Brough's Report for 1863, p. 111.

tent themselves with attributing the same faults to the men'.[1] Yet, while the constant facing of danger did breed indifference, skilled and adequate supervision could make reckless men more careful. In an attempt to avert the disasters which arose when experience was the only technical school, Mackworth, choosing Aberdare as the danger spot where knowledge was most needed, started lectures there which were well attended and helped to form an overmen's association which held monthly meetings there. Mackworth also lectured in other parts of the coalfield, but his hope that a mining school would be established in Swansea was not realized. Even when, partly at his instigation, the first centre in the south for the instruction of working colliers was established at Bristol in 1856 it was never well supported. The problem remained, and in the reports of Mackworth's successors there were recurrent references to the need for more competent overmen, particularly in the smaller collieries. At Cyfyng colliery near Swansea, for example, where an explosion caused the loss of six lives in 1858, the overman was a working collier who was paid 10s. a month beyond his normal wages to see that everything was right underground.[2] In 1863 two colliers were drowned while working in Tre-gob colliery, near Llanelly, which was sunk a few yards to the coal near the outcrop to work some pillars of coal left from earlier workings. 'This, like many other of the small collieries in the district,' the inspector commented, 'is left in charge of a working man, altogether unfit to perform the duties required.'[3]

Efforts to reduce the death roll in the South Wales coalfield were also retarded by the prevalence of fiery seams and unsafe roofs. In the Aberdare valley the Upper Four Feet seam was particularly dangerous, being liable to sudden 'blowers' or excessive discharges of gas which normal ventilation could not sufficiently dilute, and here alone, between 1845 and 1852, in four explosions at the collieries of Upper Duffryn, Lletty

[1] MIR Mackworth's Report for 1854, p. 113.
[2] MIR Thomas Evans's Report for 1858, p. 109.
[3] MIR Thomas Evans's Report for 1863, p. 145.

Shenkin, and Middle Duffryn 159 lives had been lost.[1] The natural dangers of the mines in this valley aroused the apprehensions of Mackworth, as did similar dangers at Bryn-du, Morfa, Risca, and Ton-du in other districts. Not only were some of the mines technically difficult to ventilate but also there was genuine uncertainty about which method of ventilation was the best to adopt. Greater safety waited on the gradual solving by engineers of the problems of efficient ventilation and the slow waning of the objections to the use of the mechanical ventilator.

Where the safety lamp had been adopted it was used in a way the inventors had never intended. 'In nine cases out of ten the safety lamp is not used to work by, but as a test for the presence of fire damp.'[2] It was mainly used by the fireman who, in the best conducted collieries, went round the working places before work started, foulness of the air being indicated by the appearance of an elongated cap on the flame of the lamp. If conditions appeared safe, working was then carried out with candles or open lamps. But the margin separating safety from danger was slender and the test was a delicate one. Also, even if carefully performed, it was no safeguard against conditions altering if, say, there was a 'blower', or if a ventilating door was accidentally left open. However, spurred on by Mackworth's advice and learning from bitter experience, owners were beginning to work the more dangerous collieries exclusively with locked safety lamps. But good safety lamp discipline could not be acquired overnight and, as the locking devices were not necessarily efficient, the collier was constantly tempted to take the top off his lamp to get more light. Also, the custom throughout nearly all South Wales was for the collier to buy his own lamp, just as he paid for his candles, and light and cheapness might be considered before safety.

While ventilation in fiery mines was adequate for health if not for safety, in non-fiery mines it was still 'lamentably

[1] MIR Mackworth's Report for 1855, p. 136.
[2] MIR Mackworth's Report for July–Dec. 1852, p. 159.

neglected', resulting in conditions so injurious to health that the collier's working life might be shortened by ten years. At Pantyforest colliery, owned by the Beaufort Company, for example, where natural ventilation was considered adequate, the direction of the air current varied with the outside temperature, 'a most barbarous state of things'.[1] 'Few persons', Mackworth wrote, 'who have not visited the extremities of the non-fiery mines of this country are aware of the foul and poisonous atmosphere in which the miner is condemned to work. I say condemned, because starvation or the parish are often the alternatives. Some managers tell me that the miner becomes acclimatized; but the registers of death prove the contrary.'[2]

Another constantly recurring danger was that arising from falls of coal and stone from the roofs and sides of working places and of travelling ways—a danger which was present to a much more marked degree in South Wales than in any other coalfield. 'We have treacherous roofs,' an inspector later wrote, 'roofs that to look up at, and to try with a pick, sledge, or any other tool, sound like thick cast iron, or like rock of vast depth, yet they are often so complete with concealed slips or "backs", "bell moulds", joints and "grimes" that perhaps a minute after trying or sounding, a fall, without the slightest warning in the world, will take place, and then those planes and surfaces of structural division are clearly enough seen, many of them as smooth and as polished as plate glass.'[3] Falls, consequently, were almost a weekly occurrence, causing over a period of any length more destruction of life than the occasional calamitous explosion. Skilled and careful propping was the main safeguard against falls, and the extent to which this propping of the working places was left to the discretion of the collier in South Wales occasioned much criticism. Colliers

[1] MIR Mackworth's Report for 1857, p. 92.
[2] MIR Mackworth's Report for 1854, p. 117.
[3] MIR Lionel Brough's Report for 1867, p. 89. In 1866 Brough had told the South Wales Institute of Engineers that 'they had the worst roofs in the world in South Wales'.

were paid, not for the amount of timber they put in their stalls, but for the coal cut and, in their anxiety to make a profitable day's work, they became too absorbed in their hewing. Their sitting or lying position, too, did not help them to notice the roof, so that timbering was apt to be neglected—a neglect which usually became more marked near the dinner hour or just before men were leaving their work. Mackworth, and his successors, recommended that a change-over should be made to the method which prevailed in Northumberland and Durham, where much of the propping was done or supervized by skilled deputies. This recommendation was without avail, however, opinion in Wales remaining firmly convinced that the Welsh method was the most appropriate one for local conditions. Not only was there a great difference in the nature of the roofs in South Wales compared with those in the north of England, but also deputy propping was associated with the two-shift system of the north whereas in Wales the single shift prevailed. Thus, while Mackworth had anticipated that the success of inspection in reducing the danger from falls was likely to be slight, in practice its success proved to be negligible.

No 'swift and mighty triumph over death' was probable, then, in a coalfield which presented such natural difficulties, but the limited powers of the mines inspector made the possibility of such a triumph even more remote. The inquiries preceding the Act of 1850 had pointed out that the inspection of mines would prove to be much more complicated than that of factories. The immense variety in conditions from colliery to colliery; the lack of certainty about the fittest remedies; the probability that inspectors, however competent, would encounter many colliery officials with knowledge and experience equal or superior to their own; the belief that inspection would be ineffectual without some degree of willing co-operation from the industry; all these considerations favoured starting with an inspectorate whose powers were mainly advisory.

Mackworth's advice met with a mixed reception. In 1853 he could speak with satisfaction of 'the improvement I have seen in a great many collieries where I have made suggestions which have been carried out'.[1] At some collieries his advice was welcomed for humane reasons and as a means of avoiding the economic loss accidents caused, sometimes by damaging the structure of the mine and always by interrupting work, as the men withdrew from the pit after a fatal accident, sometimes remaining out until after the funeral. But at many collieries, on visiting them a second time, Mackworth found that his suggestions, or the promises made to him, had not been carried out. The widespread attitude of indifference was typified by John Evans, the principal manager of Dowlais, who denounced inspection as a 'mere burlesque', saying that after accidents at Dowlais Mackworth had not recommended any improvements, merely concentrating on trying to secure verdicts of manslaughter at the subsequent inquests. This wildly inaccurate account led Mackworth to comment that Evans, like many others, was professedly anxious for amelioration while in reality ignoring his responsibilities and the evils of the mines.[2] Because of this apathy often little or nothing had been done, even after four or five years of inspection, to secure safer working conditions. Many collieries, despite the Act of 1850, were still without plans of present or previous workings, this neglect increasing the danger from flooding through breaking into waterlogged old workings. In the Tredegar collieries the men were still permitted to brush out fire-damp with their jackets, while at Risca, notwithstanding the loss of life explosions had caused, naked lights were still used. The management of Thomas Powell's Gelligaer colliery was 'lamentably defective', there being no rules for safe working and no examination of the working places by a fireman before the men entered; the manager, who had

[1] Evidence of Mackworth, *First Report from Select Committee on Accidents in Coal Mines*, P.P. 1852–3 (691), xx.
[2] *Select Committee on Accidents in Mines. Third Report*, P.P. 1854 (277), ix, p. 5; MIR Mackworth's Report for 1854, p. 114.

not been informed of any of Mackworth's recommendations, said that the men 'looked after their own safety'. At Lletty Shenkin the overman had resigned when the owners would not allow him to keep open airways he considered essential for safety.[1] The notice, served on David Williams, that his Aberaman colliery was 'dangerous and defective' provides a final illustration both of what Mackworth tried to achieve and of his feeling of failure.[2] The works were not under the direction of a qualified mining engineer, nor were the lives of the workmen safe in the hands of an overman who was a heavy drinker. The current of air was defective or entirely lacking in most working places and there was no attempt, as there should have been, to see that only locked safety lamps were used. No adequate printed rules, enforced by fines, were read out to the men; the propping was not in the hands of experienced miners; the walls of the shaft were unbricked and dangerous and there were no covers to the cages. 'The accidents in your own and neighbouring collieries seem equally without any effect on the management of your works.' A sense of defeat is conveyed by Mackworth's remark, made to the Society of Arts in 1855, that he had once been sanguine enough to believe that owners could be induced to adopt safety measures by persuasion alone.[3]

The effectiveness of the Act was further lessened because, if accidents occurred at collieries where the advice of the inspector had been disregarded, no judicial consequences followed. The complaisance of the 'worse than useless' juries, who returned repeated verdicts of 'Accidental Death' whatever the evidence, meant that the criminal laws relating to death caused by the neglect of others were 'wholly inoperative'. Workmen, too, were reluctant to give evidence impugning the efficiency of colliery owners and officials, and when men did overcome this reluctance, as at the inquest after the

[1] MIR Mackworth's Report for 1855, pp. 110–12.
[2] Ibid., p. 139.
[3] See report of Mackworth's lecture, *MJ*, 7 Apr. 1855.

Cymmer disaster of 1856, it was alleged that they did not easily find work afterwards.[1] On the rare occasions when a coroner's jury did return a verdict of 'Manslaughter' no conviction was secured at the subsequent trial owing to the difficulty of determining exactly where the responsibility for any section of the management lay. At the inquest after the explosion at Lletty Shenkin in 1853 a verdict of 'Manslaughter' was returned against David Simms, the resident trustee for the owners, who had omitted to inform the overman, Johns, of the inspector's criticisms of the conduct of the colliery. But Simms claimed at his trial that he was in charge of only the surface and not of the underground work and he was accordingly acquitted, the judge ruling that he could not be held criminally responsible. Two years later, after a disastrous explosion at Cymmer, the judge at Swansea assizes gave the same reason for his decision that the manager, Jabez Thomas, was 'not guilty' of 'Manslaughter'.[2]

In the five years 1851–5 there were 738 deaths from accidents in coal-mines reported in South Wales and Monmouthshire. Of these 173 were caused by explosions, 300 by falls of roof and sides, 143 by accidents in shafts, 98 by miscellaneous causes, and 24 by surface accidents.[3] There were two particularly tragic features of this death roll. While boys between ten and fifteen years old comprised only about one-ninth of the employees they accounted for more than one-fifth of the deaths from accident. The work of the youngest boys was minding ventilating doors, but many of them ran along with the hauliers to open doors for them; indeed in the following decade the overmen in the Aberdare district said that the hauliers 'would not work without having the boys to travel with them'.[4] It was easy for boys to miss their footing as they ran past the horse and trams to get to the next door in time

[1] MIR Mackworth's Report for 1856, p. 124.
[2] MIR Mackworth's Report for 1854, p. 128; Thomas Evans's Report for 1856, p. 142.
[3] MIR Mackworth's Report for 1855, pp. 143 et seq.
[4] MIR Thomas Wales's Report for 1865, p. 121.

to open it for the haulier. At a young age the boys became hauliers themselves and then, as the horses usually pulled the trams without shafts, they had to assist in holding back the load, yet attempts to control the ponderous iron trams taxed even the strength of men. Accordingly death of young workers from 'crush of trams' was all too frequent an occurrence.

Accidents were all the more tragic because of the poverty they could cause. Benefit societies were widespread but their funds rarely provided support for more than a few weeks. Even where there had been gross neglect by the management, all considerations—the cost of litigation, the difficulty of getting a solicitor, the inevitable influence proprietors had over juries—were ranged against any effort to recover compensation. The poverty caused by the major disasters was alleviated by the relief funds launched on the wave of public sympathy they aroused, and to these funds the coal-owners subscribed not ungenerously. Out of the £971. 10s. 3d. expended from a relief fund in the first three years after the explosion in 1852 at Middle Duffryn, to help the 29 widows and 69 children left by the 65 men who lost their lives, Thomas Powell, the owner, had contributed £616. 13s. 3d.[1] After the calamitous explosion at Insole's Cymmer colliery in 1856, the first in Wales to cause the loss of over 100 lives, a public subscription was raised and among the many donations from coal-owners were £500 from George Insole and £100 from Thomas Powell.[2] But there were innumerable accidents on a smaller scale which failed to attract this public attention. Here an attempt would usually be made to find light work at the colliery for the maimed, and the widow might have 'her house and coal found for her', at least, perhaps, until the children grew up. 'In the case of the death of a collier', a coal-owner from the Swansea valley told a committee in 1857, 'there is generally great sympathy felt for his family, and the proprietors of works find occupation for

[1] MIR Mackworth's Report for 1855, p. 116.
[2] *MG*, 26 July 1856.

the children; they take an interest in them and get them brought up as colliers.'[1] But the small allowances paid from sporadic relief funds and a general solicitude for those affected by accidents were an unsatisfactory substitute for systematic compensation, and they could have averted dependence on poor relief for but a fraction of those bereft or injured.

Thus, although Mackworth had been merely recommending measures which were generally agreed to be necessary by those primarily interested in greater safety, the first few years of inspection were marked by little solid achievement. Generally accidents remained most frequent not so much in mines where they were inevitable through fiery seams and treacherous roofs but in mines where the apathy of the management meant that precautions were inadequate and where the lack of proper discipline and skilled supervision meant that 'the men looked after their own safety'. While the inspectorate remained a tentative novelty with mainly advisory powers its victories were less obvious than its defeats. Some could think, with *The Economist*, that, as perfect inspection was impracticable, once the industry had been fully investigated, those in it could be told 'to make their own bargains, and to blame only themselves if they go down a pit with worthless gear, or work in a pit which an ignorant or greedy proprietor will not so ventilate as to secure it from an explosion'.[2] Others, however, could believe that the remedy was to increase the number of inspectors and to give them greater powers.

The Mines Act of 1855[3] was passed after two Select Committees on Accidents had reported in 1853 and 1854. Also in 1854 the coal-owners had acceded to the request to hold meetings of representatives in London to discuss the question

[1] Evidence of John James, *Select Committee on Rating of Mines*, P.P. 1857 (241, sess. 2), xi.
[2] *The Economist*, 12 Aug. 1854.
[3] 18 and 19 Vict., c. 108. An Act to amend the law for the Inspection of Coal Mines in Great Britain. This Act was to remain in force for five years.

of safety.[1] The outcome of these meetings, where the inspectors had been given an opportunity to put forward their views, was that the coal-owners, while still apprehensive about 'interference' which might lessen the responsibility of managers, agreed that it was desirable to establish safety rules which would have the force of law. Consequently the new Act, which came into force in 1856, required that each colliery should establish printed rules, a copy of which was to be displayed at the colliery and a copy handed to each workman. There were seven 'general' rules, applicable to every colliery. These stipulated that ventilation should be adequate for safety under normal conditions, that every working shaft was to be securely lined if the natural strata were not safe and that all shafts out of use were to be fenced.[2] The other general rules dealt mainly with winding—that there should be a means of signalling in the shaft and that the engines used for winding should have a proper brake and an indicator to show the position of the cage in the shaft. Besides these general rules, each colliery was to have its own 'special' rules, framed to cover the safety requirements arising out of local conditions. The owner had to submit these special rules to the Secretary of State for his approval—in practice this meant to the inspector, and Mackworth claimed that he had shown restraint in proposing amendments 'to avoid the risk of failure whilst the formation of rules was in agitation throughout the district'.[3] Disputes over proposed amendments were to be decided by an arbitrator who was to be selected from a list of names submitted by the coal-owner. Offences under the Act had to be tried within three months of the commission of the offence before not less than two Justices of the Peace. The penalties for non-compliance with the rules were, for all workmen and

[1] *Select Committee on Accidents in Coal Mines. Third Report*, 1854, pp. 59 et seq. Only J. Richardson and S. Dobson from South Wales attended most meetings, while Thomas Powell (jun.), John Nixon, and W. P. Struvé attended some meetings.
[2] This last requirement had, from 1840 at least, been a standard clause in all Bute leases.   [3] MIR Mackworth's Report for 1855, p. 117.

officials, a fine not exceeding £2 or not more than three months' imprisonment and, for owners or principal agents, a fine not exceeding £5. Once an owner had been notified in writing of a defect in his colliery he was liable to a further penalty of £1 a day while the fault remained unremedied and during this period any workman could leave without becoming liable to proceedings for quitting work without notice. To assist the enforcement of the Act the number of inspectors was increased to twelve, Thomas Evans being appointed inspector for South Wales, now made a separate district, while Mackworth continued to inspect mines in Monmouthshire and in parts of Brecknockshire and Glamorgan.

Special rules for each colliery were slowly drawn up and approved, although even six months after the passing of the Act there were still thirty-six coal-owners in the South Wales district who had not established them, and even by May 1857 agreed special rules had not been drawn up at John Russell's Cwmtillery colliery. The arbitration clause did not work well because owners could nominate proprietors who were themselves reluctant to devise rules which were acceptable to the inspector. Some owners, too, tried to introduce commercial rules—that a workman be fined for absenting himself without reason; that no payment be made for any tram containing more than 6 lb. of refuse when brought to bank—hoping thereby to give the impression that they had equal force with the safety code.[1]

The Act of 1855, however, had no provision debarring justices associated with collieries from sitting when offences under the Act were being tried. This caused little difficulty in the Merthyr district, where there was a stipendiary magistrate, but it weakened the effect of the Act in Monmouthshire, where the coal-owner magistrates proved to be advocates rather than judges. On 3 July 1856 ten persons were killed in an explosion at Cruttwell and Levick's Old Coal Pit, Coalbrookvale, and in addition the fireman, Hopkin Lewis, sacrificed his life in a

[1] MIR Mackworth's Report for 1855, pp. 118–21.

despairing rescue attempt. Mackworth attributed the accident to inadequate ventilation and the lack of examination of the working places. There was an explosion at Crawshay Bailey's Cwmnant-ddu colliery when a collier tried to brush or waft out fire-damp. At Rhymney collieries, after an explosion, Mackworth found fire-damp still present, with no means being adopted to remove it, no danger signals, and with naked lights being used near it. The manager declined either to remove the men, or to work the district with locked safety lamps, as the special rules required. Yet the magistrates at Tredegar Petty Sessions refused to hear these cases of the violation of the Act. Two of the magistrates concerned were G. P. Hubbuck, the principal manager of Rhymney works, and the coal-owner Frederick Levick.[1] After a man had been killed by a piece of stone falling down the shaft of the Abercarn colliery the magistrates—G. P. Hubbuck, Thomas Brown, owner of the Abersychan collieries, and Capt. H. G. Marsh, owner of the Rock colliery—refused to accept the evidence that the shaft was in a loose state and imposed the derisory fine of 1s. because there was no cover to the cage. When William Needham, colliery agent supervising Pantyforest colliery owned by the Beaufort Company, was tried before four magistrates, a collier stated in evidence that there was no current of air in the level where he worked. The colliery had no furnace or fan to assist ventilation, yet the Bench dismissed the case, being of the opinion that 'the colliery was under ordinary circumstances sufficiently ventilated'. Three of the magistrates, Levick, Hubbuck, and Brown, were themselves under notice from the inspector for violation of the Act.[2] Indeed these violations were on such a scale that proceedings could be taken against only a few of the owners guilty of them. An Act which should have raised safety from something merely morally desirable to a matter of legislative justice was thus, in Monmouthshire at least, 'seriously obstructed and

---

[1] MIR Mackworth's Report for 1856, pp. 111–12.
[2] MIR Mackworth's Report for 1857, p. 92.

retarded'. The example set by the coal-owner magistrates weakened the influence of the new rules and made Mackworth despair of going to court when he found violations of the rules elsewhere.

That this attribution of the ineffectiveness of the legislation to the partiality of the magistrates, rather than to the admittedly defective nature of the Act, is justifiable is suggested by the outcome when appeals to the Court of Queen's Bench were made. A case arose against Crawshay Bailey, himself a magistrate in the Bedwellty division and one of the owners of the Deep Pit mine, where he was resident and which he actively supervised. This was dismissed by the Bedwellty Bench on the grounds that he was not the sole owner and that all the owners should have been summoned. At the rehearing, which was ordered by the Court of Queen's Bench, Bailey was convicted, paying a fine of 50s. and costs. On another occasion the Lord Chief Justice, Lord Campbell, remarked, 'I really feel it my duty to say that the magistrates had better consider whether an application of a criminal nature may not be made against them. This is not the first occasion in which the magistrates of Monmouthshire have acted in this way. It is most shocking to think how a salutory Act for preserving the lives of Her Majesty's subjects engaged in mining has been thus rendered entirely nugatory.'[1] The solution for this 'uncurbed despotism' in the ironworks valleys was that justice should be administered by stipendiary magistrates;[2] it was not until 1872 that it was made unlawful for any owner, agent, or manager of a mine (or his father, son, or brother) to adjudicate summarily on any offence committed under the mining code.

If the Act of 1855 was thus sometimes shorn of its power it nevertheless did help to promote progress towards safer

[1] MIR Mackworth's Report for 1857, p. 95.
[2] Evidence of Lionel Brough, *Report from Select Committee on Mines, P.P.* 1867 (496), xiii. 'In Glamorgan we have a stipendiary magistrate, and I never lose a case there; on the other hand I never win a case in Monmouthshire.'

working conditions. By introducing rules with legal force it both assisted the management in the maintenance of the necessary internal discipline of a colliery and helped the inspectors by giving them a definite safety code to enforce. At the end of the fifties a hopeful tone could be discerned, at least in the reports of Thomas Evans, the inspector for the South Wales district. Owners were trying to lay out mines with a fuller regard for safety, and improvements came as old collieries became exhausted and new ones took their place. Legislation 'has been the means of inducing a better system of management, and the employment of more competent viewers; the use of better machinery, greater supervision and a more regular supply of materials (timber &c.)'. As the law received stricter attention the decrease in the loss of life would become perceptible—'it is now a work of time'.[1]

The Mines Regulation Act of 1860,[2] to come into force in 1861 when the old Act expired, increased the number of general rules to fifteen. Wherever safety lamps were required to be used they were to be first examined and then securely locked by an authorized person; the inspector could require that cages used for lowering and raising persons must have an overhead cover; no single-link chain was to be used for raising or lowering persons; sufficient bore-holes were to be made when workings were approaching places likely to contain dangerous accumulations of water; all underground self-acting and engine planes were to have places of refuge at intervals not exceeding 20 yards. The penalty for violation of the colliery rules, in the case of an owner, agent, or viewer, was increased to a sum not exceeding £20. In addition, if the inspector considered that dangers not covered by the rules existed, he could give notice of such dangers and, if necessary, the matter could be referred to arbitration. No one under

[1] MIR Thomas Evans's Report for 1859, p. 116.
[2] 23 and 24 Vict., c. 151. Act for the Regulation and Inspection of Mines.

eighteen was to be in charge of an engine used for lowering or raising people to or from the mine. Also, after 1 July 1861, boys under twelve could not be employed in the mines unless they had a certificate saying either that they could read and write or that they were attending school for at least three hours a day on two days a week, Sundays excluded. This Act showed that legislative intervention had emerged from its probationary stage; its scope was extended to cover the ironstone mines in the coal measures, and no longer was a limitation of five years placed on its operation.

The practical effect of the education clauses of the Act was to exclude boys from work in coal-mines until they reached the age of twelve. The door boys were a link in the chain of production as essential as the hewer and they could not be released during the working day to attend school. The numbers employed under twelve had not been great, but once in the mines their education normally finished, the long hours leaving few with the energy to attend night school.

With the greater powers conferred on them by the more comprehensive safety code the inspectors were now better able to ensure that the mechanics of safety were achieved—that shafts were safe and well lined; that there were guides and overhead covers for the cages; that there were lifting guards or wickets at the shaft top; that adequate supplies of timber were made available for the colliers, and so on. In particular, efforts could be made to improve the winding arrangements which, primarily in the smaller collieries where capital resources were inadequate for the purchase of efficient machinery, were 'still very much behind the age, more especially in Pembrokeshire and the land-sale collieries in Carmarthenshire'.[1] But even in Crawshay's collieries men were still being raised and lowered by single-link chains in 1861 and it was only after a prosecution that all the eight or nine shafts were fitted with three-link chains—an expensive task so speedily completed that it earned a tribute in the

[1] MIR Thomas Evans's Report for 1861, p. 123.

inspector's report.[1] A year later Thomas Evans refused to descend Crawshay Bailey's balance pit at Aberaman colliery where a single-link chain was in use. Bailey was find £10, the chain replaced by a proper one, and by now such chains must have been rare, as Evans considered that this was possibly the last single-link chain in use in South Wales.[2] A safety precaution of a similar type was effected by the Act of 1862,[3] which made it illegal for any new mine to be opened without two shafts and which stipulated that, unless special circumstances could be pleaded, all old mines were to have two shafts by 1 January 1865. The existence of a second shaft helped to lessen the danger that an accident might derange the ventilation; it also gave the men a second escape route after an accident, and facilitated rescue operations.

But there remained the human element; owners willing to invest in safety, officials adequate in number and with the skill required for effective supervision, and a body of workmen alive to the necessity of incessant care and willing, as Mackworth had been fond of remarking, to observe discipline as scrupulously as a good regiment. Instances of completely careless management still figure in the reports of the sixties; Park colliery, near Neath, leased by Messrs. Thomas and Company, where six lives were lost in an explosion on 26 June 1863, may serve as an example of these. The colliery was inadequately ventilated by a small fan, and no provision was made for conducting the air to the working places, nor were these examined before the men went to work. Safety lamps were used, but most were unlocked. 'The whole colliery up to within a few yards of the shaft was in an explosive state. . . . It was not at all unusual for the men on entering their headings to find large accumulations of gas, which they were in

---

[1] MIR Thomas Evans's report for 1861, p. 127. One official claimed, for the firm, that in his eight years' experience he had never known a Crawshay single-link chain to break. *CG*, 9 Nov. 1861.

[2] MIR Thomas Evans's Report for 1862, p. 115. In 1873 the manager of Penrhiwceiber pit was fined £5 for raising men with a single-link chain.

[3] 25 and 26 Vict., c. 79. An Act to amend the law relating to Coal Mines.

the habit of removing by brushing it out with their coats.' Despite the verdict of 'Accidental Death' returned by the coroner's jury, proceedings were instituted and the owner and manager were each fined the maximum penalty of £20.[1]

Instances of management as negligent as this were, however, becoming rarer and accidents were now arising more from dangers inherent in the industry, such as deceptive roofs, which even careful management could not wholly overcome, and from incautious behaviour by the colliers themselves. Management and inspectors alike could do little to avert an accident such as that which occurred in a level at Tredegar in 1862. 'Holding back the tram in front, and his father holding on behind; the son lost his light, and the old man was not sufficiently powerful to retain the whole weight, consequently the tram "ran wild" and passed over the young man and killed him.'[2] While minor accidents of this type were numerous, another serious problem was the neglect of safety-lamp discipline. Thomas Wales could describe the newly-developing Rhondda Fach district as 'a virgin magazine of firedamp' and could consider this neglect as 'the crying evil of this most fiery district'.[3] The dangers were exemplified by the Ferndale colliery, where the occasional entry in the colliery log-book 'no blowers or falls today' suggests how frequent emissions of gas were. Ferndale was well ventilated by a furnace, having 'such a supply of fresh air as is seldom met with in the principality', yet, despite this, 178 men were killed by an explosion here on 8 November 1867, and a further 53 lives were lost on 10 June 1869.[4] The colliers had been allowed to buy their lamps at any shop they pleased and it had been reported to the manager before the first explosion that some men tampered with their locks. Nothing had been done; the manager confessed that 'he did not know what to do, they

---

[1] MIR Thomas Evans's Report for 1863, pp. 146–7.
[2] MIR See comments on tabular list of accidents in Lionel Brough's Report for 1862. [3] MIR Thomas Wales's Report for 1867, p. 138.
[4] For Ferndale, see MIR Thomas Wales's Reports for 1867, pp. 135 et seq., and for 1869, p. 107.

were a rough lot'. After the explosion several lamps were found unlocked, and keys or contrivances for opening safety lamps were found in the pockets of several of the deceased. That this dangerous practice did not stop when work was resumed is shown by the occasional instances of the prosecution and imprisonment of Ferndale men for smoking in the colliery or working with unlocked safety lamps in contravention of the special rules of the colliery.[1] Ferndale was not exceptional. The temptation to tamper with safety lamps to get more light was a strong one, particularly as there was usually no increase in the cutting prices when the use of locked safety lamps was made compulsory. These infringements of colliery regulations were difficult to detect, as fellow workmen were disinclined to act as informers, but in the sixties an effort was made to check such recklessness by sentencing the colliers who were discovered to two or three months imprisonment with hard labour.

A further attempt to improve the safety code was made by the Mines Regulation Act of 1872.[2] It was stipulated that in all mines where more than thirty persons were employed the manager must be certificated, possessing either a certificate of service granted to those who had been acting as managers before 10 August 1872 or a certificate of competency granted after examination. Boys under twelve years of age were not to be employed underground, while boys under sixteen were not to be employed at night or to work more than ten hours a day or fifty-four hours a week. The general rules were extended, and the Act entitled the workmen employed in a colliery to appoint two from their number to inspect it at least once a month. Whereas since 1860 an owner had been debarred from sitting as a justice when his own mine had been concerned, now the owner of a mine was not to act in any proceedings under the new Act. In addition an owner, agent,

[1] *MG*, 1, 29 Feb. 1868, 27 Feb. 1869.
[2] 25 and 36 Vict., c. 76. An Act to consolidate and amend Acts relating to the Regulation of Coal Mines.

or manager was liable to imprisonment if safety was endangered by any wilful 'personal act, personal default or personal negligence'.

In some respects the rate of progress towards greater safety had been disappointing, reforms being proposed often for almost a generation before they reached the statute book. Some of the Welsh practices, too, continued unaltered despite the criticisms of the inspectors. The final report of the Royal Commission on Accidents in 1886 condemned the Welsh custom of allowing the door boys to accompany the hauliers on their journeys; but it did not recommend any alteration to the system of the collier fixing his own timber in his working place, being convinced by the strong belief of all the witnesses from South Wales that their own system was best suited to local conditions.[1] Also the legal measures to punish owners or managers guilty of negligence and to provide the compensation for those affected by accidents remained only partially effective. Juries still showed unwillingness to return verdicts of manslaughter against the powerful coal-owners of their own neighbourhood, and on the rare occasions when officials were committed to the assizes on this charge they were invariably acquitted. Compensation for accidents might be granted, but it could seldom be obtained as a right. Mackworth's bitter comment—'I have yet to learn that a collier or his widow can obtain redress for the wrongful act, neglect or default, which breaks down his health, cripples him for life, or condemns him to a violent and needless death'[2]—still remained true. Lord Campbell's Fatal Accidents Act of 1846, permitting suit by near relatives of the deceased in the case of death caused by the neglect of others, was inoperative, as a collier's widow, even could she find a local solicitor willing to plead, had not the resources to maintain an action against a

---

[1] The Act of 1872 merely made the owner or agent responsible for seeing that the collier timbered his stall. This was a rule of dubious value as it was not possible to tell by examining a place after a fall if this responsibility had been neglected and those in a position to give evidence were interested parties.

[2] *MJ*, 7 July 1855.

wealthy company. No general Accident Fund had materialized in the South Wales coalfield before 1875, although the subject had been broached several times since the Cymmer disaster of 1856. The projected schemes always crumbled in the face of the opposition of the men, who feared that such a fund would lead to less care being taken by employers and who thought they saw, in the occasional willingness of the owners to participate and contribute, a sinister confirmation of their suspicions.

Throughout, the reports of the mines inspectors make sombre reading, with their record of injury and death in mines where difficult conditions tried even the resources of good management, and where ignorance, carelessness, and negligence brought their swift nemesis. Against this dark background gleam like silver the frequent glimpses of courage, such as that of John Dorman, overman at a colliery near Neath, who, on hearing a sudden inrush of water from old workings, tried to warn as many of the workmen as possible and, the inspector commented, 'preferred risking (indeed I may almost say sacrificing) his own life in attempting to save those of his unfortunate workmen'.[1] It would be wrong, however, to think that in the struggle for safety

> the tired waves, vainly breaking,
> Seem here no painful inch to gain.

Although the mines remained dangerous, by 1875 there was a better knowledge of mining, discipline was better, and more care was shown. In the South Wales inspection district, while there had been a death for every 42,421 tons of coal raised in the seven years ending 31 December 1862, in the three years ending 31 December 1875 88,890 tons were raised for every death.[2]

This reduction in the accident rate arose partly from the

[1] MIR Thomas Evans's Report for 1859, p. 111.
[2] MIR Thomas Wales's Report for 1875, p. 170. The risk of death for the miner had not decreased in quite the same degree, as productivity per head had risen during this period.

changing technique and structure of the industry. The change to the long-wall method of mining, for example, had made the mines safer, while the growth in the size of the average colliery had diminished the relative importance of the small concerns lacking the capital needed to adopt the safest techniques or to secure the services of skilled officials. But the most important single influence reducing the accident rate was the growing authority of the mines inspectors. The 'eyes and ears' of the government, they had, by their reports and activities, helped to establish and strengthen the mining code. Lionel Brough could write in his last report under the 1860 Act that, despite its limitations, it 'had a certain robustness that often enabled the Inspector to establish a principle or redress a wrong'.[1] Perhaps more important than the growth in the legal power of the inspectors was the change in the attitude of public opinion towards them. Inspection, starting in an atmosphere of prejudice, had by the 1860's become liberated from its unpopularity. The trade journals no longer maintained that safety could be left solely to the discretion of the coal-owners and the men; at the meetings of the South Wales Institute of Engineers the inspectors were clearly regarded with trust and respect; and the personalities and indignities once endured by Mackworth in carrying out his duties could, after the lapse of only a few years, no longer be understood.[2]

[1] MIR Report of Lionel Brough for 1872, p. 83.
[2] 'Ignotus', *The Last Thirty Years in a Mining District* (1867), p. 22.

IX

SOCIAL CONDITIONS

THE abiding impression that emerges from the accounts of observers of the social scene in industrial South Wales in the early forties is one of a neglected society. Seymour Tremenheere reported that he had found in 1839 'a people immersed in habits of sensuality and improvidence, earning very high wages, wasting nearly one week out of five in idleness and drunkenness; working their children in the mines and elsewhere at the earliest possible age'. He painted a drab picture of overcrowded houses, with refuse accumulating outside their doors and 'beset with stinking pools and gutters' owing to the deficiencies in drainage, and of a society where opportunities for civilized pleasures were few and, apart from the Sunday schools, educational facilities scanty. The prevalent feeling of the workers was one of 'disaffection towards the State, and of suspicion if not hostility towards their employers'. It was, indeed, to the negligence of the employers and of the landowner royalty-receivers that he attributed the unsatisfactory state of society.[1] This view was echoed by a commissioner investigating the state of education in South Wales in 1847. 'I regard their degraded condition as entirely the fault of their employers, who give them far less tendance and care than they bestow upon their cattle, and who, with a few exceptions, use and regard them as so much brute force instrumental to wealth, but as nowise involving claims on human sympathy.'[2]

---

[1] *Minutes of Committee of Privy Council on Education*, Appendix II. Tremenheere's Report on South Wales, *P.P.* 1840 (254), xl; *State of Population in Mining Districts*, *P.P.* 1849 (737), xxiv, pp. 31–32.

[2] *Report of Royal Commission on State of Education in Wales*, *P.P.* 1847 (871), xxvii, pt. ii, p. 293.

These comments, however, referred, not to the whole coalfield, but to the eastern region between Merthyr and Pontypool, where the population had increased, at least since the first census in 1801, with exceptional rapidity. While the population of England and Wales had increased by rather less than 80 per cent. between 1801 and 1841, that of Monmouthshire, where, significantly enough, the sale-coal industry had been progressing most swiftly and supplementing the influence on population of the growing ironworks, had almost trebled. In Glamorgan it had more than doubled.[1] This growth, marked though it was when expressed in terms of whole counties, was even more striking in the vicinity of the developing ironworks and collieries. The population of Merthyr Tydfil, the greatest iron centre and largest town in Wales, had increased $3\frac{1}{2}$-fold in this period; in the ten years alone, between 1831 and 1841, owing to the opening of new coal works, the population of the hamlet of Resolven had grown from 261 to 500, and that of the parish of Llanwynno from 1,094 to 1,614.[2]

This increase in population, accompanied by no corresponding development of social amenities, largely accounted for the degrading conditions which prevailed in this section of the coalfield in the early forties. Elsewhere in the coalfield, where no similar revolutionary expansion had occurred, the social problems were less acute. The various developments affecting the social life of the collier in the years between 1841 and 1875 form the subject of this chapter.

[1] The census of 1841 gave the following figures for the counties of South Wales:

Population of	1801	1841
Monmouthshire	45,582	134,355
Glamorgan	71,525	171,188
Brecknockshire	31,633	55,603
Carmarthenshire	67,317	106,326
Pembrokeshire	56,280	88,044

[2] See footnotes to county tables in the 1841 census.

SOCIAL CONDITIONS

One of the social problems first to engage attention was the employment of women and children in the collieries. As they worked hidden from the public view and often in isolated districts little was known about the extent and conditions of their employment until the publication of the reports of the Children's Employment Commissioners in 1842. These reports revealed, however, that it was no unusual thing for children to be employed in the collieries at the age of four, more examples of the employment of very young children being found in South Wales than in any other district. The agent to Sir Thomas Phillips's collieries in Monmouthshire observed that 'young boys are taken down as soon as they can stand on their legs'. One of the many was William Richards, only $7\frac{1}{2}$ years old, an air door boy in Buttery Hatch colliery, Monmouthshire. 'I have been down about three years. When I first went down I could not keep my eyes open; I don't fall asleep now, I smoke my pipe.' This boy, who earned 8d. a day when work was available for him, appeared an intelligent and good-humoured lad—'his cap was furnished with the usual collier candlestick, and his pipe was stuck familiarly in his button-hole'.[1] The employment of girls was less general, being confined to Pembrokeshire and, in the eastern sector of the coalfield, to the collieries attached to the ironworks. At the Plymouth collieries, for example, there was Mary Davis, nearly seven years old, who had been at work for eighteen months, 'a very pretty little girl who was fast asleep under a piece of rock near the air door below ground. Her lamp had gone out for want of oil; and, upon waking her, she said the rats, or some one, had run away with her bread and cheese, so she went to sleep.'[2]

The youngest children, up to the age of eleven generally, looked after the ventilation doors, opening them for the trams and hauliers to pass through. 'With his solitary candle, cramped with cold, wet and not half fed, the poor child deprived of light and air, passes his silent day.'[3] Other young

[1] *Children's Employment*, pp. 471, 534. [2] Ibid., p. 513. [3] Ibid., p. 475.

children might help their fathers, but their work was usually light as they did 'little more than pick up a few coals in loading the carts, and handing and looking after the father's tools'.[1] Where thin seams were worked young children might often be employed in hauling trams, as the making of roadways high enough for older workers or horses was expensive. At some places, as at Ynyscedwyn, the thinner seams were not worked, the limit there being 3 feet, but at Cyfarthfa an eleven-year-old trammer, Henrietta Frankland, was drawing trams containing 4 or 5 cwt. of coal to the main road from workings which were only 30 to 33 inches high.[2] In some parts of Monmouthshire boys had to drag skips of coal on all fours to the main roads from the narrow veins. The use of the girdle and chain was uncommon in South Wales, but Elias Jones, a carter aged fourteen, who drew coal in this way at Risca, near Newport, said 'it is very hard work indeed, it is too hard for such lads as we, for we work like little horses'.[3] Older children, generally from fourteen to seventeen years old, became horse-drivers or hauliers, driving the horse and trams along the main roads and, if the mine was entered by a level, getting an occasional glimpse of daylight. If the hauliers benefited from being more in the fresh air nevertheless the work was dangerous, as the risk of their being injured by the trams in the narrow roads was ever present.

The employment of children was no nineteenth-century novelty, being inherited from earlier generations. Some employers, however, were making efforts to exclude the youngest children from mining operations. At Esgyn colliery near Briton Ferry, owned by Messrs. Motley, Fussell and Co., no one under eight was employed, and at Vivian's Cwm Brombill colliery at Margam children did not start work until they were nine years old.[4] But the incentives to put children to work early were strong. They formed a source of cheap labour, attractive to employers, and particularly to those with limited

---

[1] *Children's Employment*, p. 529.   [2] Ibid., p. 505.
[3] Ibid., p. 548.   [4] Ibid., pp. 554, 558.

capital resources, and they could supplement the labour supply in regions where it was scarce or where the iron industry was competing with coal for the supply of adult male labour. To the workers the child's wage, small though it was, proved a valuable addition to family earnings. The usual daily rate of pay for a door boy was about 6*d*. or 8*d*. and as the boys grew older and stronger and capable of taking over other work in the pit so their wages rose. At Blaenavon, for example, the door boys earned from 10*s*. to 12*s*. a month, an amount they could earn in a week when they became hauliers.[1] The children could hardly be termed independent earners; 'the collier boy is, to all intents and purposes, the property of his father (as to wages) until he attains the age of seventeen or marries; his father receives his wages, whether he be an airboy of five years of age or a haulier of fifteen'.[2] Another incentive to the early employment of children was the ability of the hewer to claim an extra tram for a helper. William Richards, already a coal-cutter by the age of twelve, was first taken to work when four years old by his father 'because times were poor and he was worth an extra tram'.[3] This enabled a father to earn more, the justification for the custom being that it minimized the distress of depressed times for married men with families. It was only occasionally, as at Martin Morrison's collieries in Monmouthshire, where no parent could claim for a boy until he was seven years old, that restrictions were placed on this custom. When the eldest boy reached seventeen, regarded as the full age of a collier, he had a similar right to take a younger brother down.[4]

Where young workers were employed on operations aiding the general working of the colliery, such as the minding of ventilating doors or hauling on the main roads, they were usually employed directly by the owner; where they were more immediately helping a hewer or a small group of men,

[1] *Children's Employment*, p. 615.   [2] Ibid., p. 482.
[3] *Children's Employment Commission, First Report*, 1842, p. 32.
[4] *Children's Employment*, pp. 529, 545.

they were usually employed and paid by the men. Instances of the ill-treatment of young workers seem to have been rare and the rigours and dangers of life in the mines came to be accepted by them with an almost unconscious stoicism. But early employment tended to stunt growth, one witness telling the Commissioner that 'any one can distinguish a collier's child from the children of other working people'.[1] In some places schools were few, but even where they existed little use was made of them; 'as the children are taken down as soon as they can crawl, even in petticoats, ignorance is perpetuated' because education usually stopped when work began.[2] Instead of receiving instruction the children were immersed, at an impressionable age, in an environment where they were liable to be contaminated by the vicious habits of older workers. This was especially regrettable in the districts where girls were employed and where 'the parents, for the few shillings per week extracted from the labour of the girl, selfishly barter all the best attributes of the woman'.[3]

The employment of women was most general in Pembrokeshire. Here they screened the coal, sorting it from the culm, or did other work on the surface; but when they had arrived at full strength they usually went to work on the windlasses below ground. The seams of coal were often at a steep angle and two women might raise or lower about 400 loads of $1\frac{1}{2}$ to 4 cwt. each to the level by windlass and chain in a day's work of eight or ten hours duration. This labour was certainly severe but not so arduous and repellent as the work of the women coal-bearers in Scotland. Many districts in Pembrokeshire, however, offered no better employment for women and the unusually low wages earned by the male colliers in Pembrokeshire made the earnings of women's labour all the more valuable as a supplement. Possible alternative work in agriculture or in domestic service yielded not only lower wages but also less leisure than did work in the mines. Even at

[1] *Children's Employment*, p. 485.
[2] Ibid., pp. 488, 526. [3] Ibid., p. 633.

Merthyr, where the hours were longer, Charlotte Chiles preferred drawing, landing, and weighing coal at the Graig colliery for 40s. a month to her former work as kitchen-maid at Lord Kensington's near Carmarthen for wages of 60s. or 70s. a year with keep. 'I prefer this work as it is not so confining and I get more money.... I cannot save money now: but I get more dress and more liberty. I work 12 hours daily. ... The work, though very hard, I care nothing for as I have good health and strength.'[1]

The 1842 Act excluding women and children under ten from underground work in collieries thus marked a sharp break with the past in South Wales, and one which caused some immediate distress. One correspondent, who signed himself 'A South Wales Collier', informed the *Mining Journal* in 1843—a year of acute depression—that he had had the 'painful duty' of discharging a number of workers and that 'one old miner in particular, with a large family, all girls, told me if his three daughters, which he employed with him in the mine, were drawn out, the whole family must become inmates of the Union workhouse, as his own labour and exertions could not support them'.[2] It is thus not surprising to find that for some years evasion of the Act was not uncommon. When Seymour Tremenheere, the sole Commissioner appointed to secure enforcement of the Act, visited Wales at the end of 1845 he found that 'the main provisions of the Act had not been generally attended to', particularly in the collieries attached to the Monmouthshire ironworks.[3] Boys were employed without being required to provide a certificate of age and, some employers argued, it was difficult to prevent men from employing women helpers in collieries which could be easily entered by a drift or level. By the mid-fifties, however, evasion, even in the districts where it had been 'frequent and obstinate', had largely died out. Owners had succeeded in

---

[1] *Children's Employment*, p. 514.   [2] *MJ*, 27 May 1843.
[3] *The State of the Population in the Mining Districts*, P.P. 1846 (737), xxiv, p. 412.

stopping it by making the overmen, whose work took them daily into the collieries, responsible for securing compliance with the law. Moreover, the employment of women on surface work, even though quite legal, was rare; they were to be found at some ironworks collieries, but when Campbell and Needham, in 1857, started employing women as bankers at the top of the shaft of Hope colliery, Monmouthshire, this innovation could be stigmatized as 'a practice sufficiently reprobated at well-managed collieries'.[1] A practice that was dying out in the old districts was not adopted in the newly developing valleys. In 1866 a Rhondda collier said that women had never been employed at the collieries in his neighbourhood and that, even had employers wanted to employ them, the colliers would not allow it.[2] By the sixties, too, the attitude to child labour had changed, much of the pressure for raising the age of exclusion of children from the mines to twelve coming from the colliers themselves.

The reports of both Seymour Tremenheere and the Children's Employment Commissioners had expressed the view that, as colliers could earn good wages, the employment of women and children could not be justified by the plea of poverty. Certainly in periods of brisk demand, when employment was regular and cutting rates high, colliers could earn wages which far exceeded those of the impoverished agricultural labourers of Carmarthenshire and Pembrokeshire, for example, and could enjoy a standard of life that was surpassed only by that of the refiners and puddlers in the iron industry or by that of the skilled workers in the copper works. At other times, however, the collier's standard of life could be impaired by the wage reductions and the underemployment which periods of depression involved. Any account of the earnings of the colliers, therefore, must deal with these periodic

[1] MIR Mackworth's Report for 1857, p. 96.
[2] Evidence of John Griffiths, *Report of Select Committee on Mines*, P.P. 1866 (431), xiv.

differences; in addition, this general account must be modified to cover the disparities in wage levels which prevailed in different sectors of the coalfield and in the different branches of the industry. Statistical information about colliers' earnings is woefully incomplete, but their general pattern may be pieced together from the remarks of contemporary observers. In 1839, a year of high activity, the colliers connected with the ironworks in the eastern part of the coalfield were earning between 21s. and 25s. a week clear of deductions.[1] Two years later, in the more normal conditions of 1841, colliers' earnings, according to the numerous estimates cited by the Children's Employment Commissioners, averaged between 18 and 20s. a week in most of the collieries between Neath and Pontypool.[2] It is uncertain, however, how far this level of earnings represented an annual average. Some witnesses suggested that throughout the year the colliers' weekly earnings averaged only 16s., or even less, and as an advertisement for a colliery foreman at this time offered a wage of £1 a week (with a free house and garden) these lower estimates may not be far from the mark.[3]

In the few years immediately following the Commissioners' visit these earnings were further depressed by the general decline of trade. In the negotiations over the Monmouthshire stoppage, early in 1843, some of Thomas Powell's colliers claimed that their wages averaged less than 10s. a week, and the masters could only quote in rebuttal an average of 12s. and could merely offer an assurance that if the men accepted the reduced cutting rate they would earn an average of 15s. a week because of the more regular working that this would allow.[4] Not all Monmouthshire colliers were faring as badly —Thomas Prothero's colliers, when summoned for breach of

[1] Tremenheere's Report, 1840, p. 213.
[2] *Children's Employment, passim.* Many witnesses pointed out that deductions were made from these earnings to cover the cost of gunpowder and candles.   [3] Ibid., pp. 521, 534; *Cambrian,* 25 Aug. 1841.
[4] *Merlin,* 25 Mar. 1843.

contract, agreed that they had been earning between 18 and 20s. a week[1]—but the general level of earnings remained low until trade began to revive at the end of the year.

In the more prosperous year of 1846 Tremenheere assessed the colliers' wages—he cited particularly the colliers at Dowlais and Cwmavon—as ranging between 21 and 23s. a week;[2] this was possibly a generous estimate as the wage level of from 18 to 20s. is the one most frequently cited in the Report of the Education Commissioners. By 1850 the earnings of a good worker in the sale-coal collieries of the Aberdare district were between 24 and 30s. a week when regularly employed, but in the less favourable conditions before the strike of 1850 he had been receiving 18s.[3] In Monmouthshire, in the same year, the men claimed that a Bedwas collier who had earned £9. 6s. 3½d. in three months (a little over 14s. a week) could be regarded as representative of good workmen, although two of the strike leaders were shown to have earned 26s. a week in the month before the strike.[4]

The tendency for wage rates to fall came to an end by 1853 and there followed a period of high wages that was broken by the financial crisis of 1857. Addressing the Aberdare colliers during the strike of that year, H. A. Bruce (later Lord Aberdare) asserted—and the men did not correct him—that before the stoppage it had been difficult to get colliers to become overmen at a regular wage of 27s. a week.[5] The estimate of a local journalist at this time was that a collier working coal for export could earn between 30 and 35s. a week if he were a steady workman.[6] Earnings certainly fell in the period

[1] *Merlin*, 4 Feb. 1843.
[2] *State of Population in Mining Districts*, 1846, pp. 36, 45.
[3] *State of Population in Mining Districts*, P.P. 1850 (1248), xxiii, p. 70. In the Swansea district in 1848 colliers earned between 14 and 20s. a week, but work was uncertain. 'The Coppermen are well able to buy meat, the Colliers less so, and the farm labourers get little except the Pig they usually feed and kill in the Autumn.' Nevill MSS. 9. R. J. Nevill to G. de Tranqualez, 3 Apr. 1848.
[4] *MG*, 1 June 1850; *MJ*, 15 June 1850.
[5] *MG*, 12 Dec. 1857.
[6] Ibid., 5 Dec. 1857.

of drab trade that followed—the daily earnings of colliers in 1859 were estimated at 3s. 4d. in Carmarthenshire and at 4s. in Glamorgan[1]—but in 1862 activity was reviving again. At the height of the boom that followed colliers in South Wales, it was stated, could earn 35s. a week 'easily'.[2] Even in 1866, according to a Dowlais trustee, the colliers at Dowlais were earning 30s. a week, while a Rhondda collier gave his earnings as between 4 and 5s. a day.[3]

There followed a strong down-turn in earnings after the commercial crisis at the end of 1866 and a much stronger upturn that accompanied the great revival in industrial demand at the close of the Franco–Prussian war which culminated in the exceptionally high prices of 1873.[4] In the course of this cycle the average weekly earnings for a collier were placed by one authority at 24s. 5d. in 1869 and at 45s. 9d. in 1873.[5] In 1873 some colliers who were summoned to Swansea Petty Sessions for leaving their parents chargeable to the parish were all earning between 7s. 4d. and 7s. 9d. a day, while the colliers in various districts who were appealing for the support of the Amalgamated Association of Miners in their levelling-up campaign were earning between 5 and 6s. a day.[6] For 1874 reliable information about earnings may be derived from the coal-owners' books; in May of that year the wages of regular colliers in pits belonging to members of the Coal Owners' Association in the Cardiff District ranged between £2. 5s. and £2. 15s. a week. At a colliery near Neath individual colliers were drawing for the year 1874 (notwithstanding the two reductions of 10 per cent. which were enforced in the second half of the year as prices began to fall from their peak)

---

[1] *CG*, 5 Jan. 1861. [2] *MG*, 7 Oct. 1864.
[3] Evidence of G. T. Clark, *Royal Commission on Trade Unions, Fifth Report*, P.P. 1867–8 (3980 I), xxxix; Evidence of John Griffiths, *Select Committee on Mines*, 1866.
[4] The annual price of steam coal f.o.b. Cardiff during these years was: 1866 8s. 6d., 1868 8s. 0d., 1870 9s. 3d., 1872 19s. 3d., 1874 16s. 11d., 1867 8s. 6d., 1869 8s. 6d., 1871 10s. 6d., 1873 23s. 3d., 1875 14s. 3d.
[5] Thomas Brassey, *The Economist*, 4 Nov. 1876.
[6] *CG*, 5 Sept., 17 Oct. 1873.

amounts of £148. 9s. 5d., £198. 2s. 0d., £152. 16s. 4d., £127. 19s. 11d., and £132. 15s. 5d.[1] These sums might represent the earnings of a collier and at least one boy as his helper; but is tolerably certain that they do not represent the earnings of two adult colliers because they are, with one exception, less than double the earnings of the day-wage men, who came lower in the colliery hierarchy.[2] It is not surprising that periods of good trade should bring about a substantial increase in colliers' earnings; at such times cutting rates were increased, employment became more regular, and 'allowances'—for such things as wet places, soft coal, and hard top—were granted on a more liberal scale.

This general account of earnings, however, is subject to several modifications. There was some regional variation in wage levels, the outstanding example of this being the low wages which prevailed in Pembrokeshire compared with the rest of the coalfield. In 1841 colliers' earnings in Pembrokeshire were between 8 and 10s. a week, just half the general level, and this great gulf seems to have persisted. In 1849, according to some Pembrokeshire colliery accounts, wages ranged between 1s. 4d. and 1s. 8d. a day; they were estimated to be 2s. a day in 1859; in 1873 full time workers were receiving 3s. a day as daymen in some Pembrokeshire collieries, and between 4s. 3d. and 4s. 9d. as piece workers.[3] This persistently low wage level arose from the declining nature of the coal industry in Pembrokeshire, from its semi-agricultural character, and from the reluctance of the population to migrate to better paid districts. The Pembrokeshire collier had 'frequently a freehold or other interest in his cottage or hovel', and usually to the cottage a few acres of land were

[1] Coal Owners' Assoc. MSS. Miscellanea, Earnings, May 1874; Evans and Bevan Colln., Doc. 26, Pay Book, Gellia colliery, 1874–Aug. 1876.
[2] According to the Pay Book, Gellia colliery, the earnings of day-wage men were, for example, repairer (279½ days) £75. 14s. 1d.; rider (310¼ days) £92. 18s. 3d.; haulier (292½ days) £73. 5s. 8d.; engineman (341½ days) £109. 0s. 6d.; door-boy (265½ days) £27. 17s. 9d.
[3] *Children's Employment*, p. 573; NLW Lucas Collection, Doc. 134; *CG*, 5 Jan. 1861, 17 Oct. 1873.

attached. So that he could have some time free to devote to his land the collier in Pembrokeshire usually worked fewer hours than were customary elsewhere, and this helped to reconcile him to his lower earnings. His reluctance to sever his connexion with his land made him immobile, and this immobility was accentuated by his belief that employment in centres such as Merthyr involved—morally—'almost certain ruin'.[1]

Another wage differential was that which arose from the higher wage rates paid to colliers connected with the sale-coal pits compared with those paid to men doing precisely similar work in collieries attached to the ironworks. Sometimes these originated from the need to attract labour to remote and undeveloped areas. The account of one employer may serve as an illustration of this. He related how, when he had taken over a new tract of land, 'for the labour we had to get people from all parts; we took any who would come and put them into huts and various dwelling houses, wherever we could locate them for the time being, and we were of course obliged to pay a very high rate of wages in order to induce them to live in an uncivilized part of the country'.[2] This particular account represented the experience of an ironmaster, but it was primarily the coal-owners who were establishing themselves in new areas and who had to offer rates sufficient to compensate workers for the lack of amenities and for the higher cost of living in districts where shops and houses were scarce and transport facilities poor. In addition to this reason, the higher rates paid to sale-coal colliers also arose from the need to compensate them for the greater irregularities of work to which they were exposed. The great iron firms had the capital resources to produce iron for stock and by adopting this policy could provide employment which remained steady despite temporary fluctuations in demand. The sale-coal

[1] *State of Population in Mining Districts*, 1846, pp. 39-40; MIR Mackworth's Report for 1852-3, p. 184.
[2] Evidence of James Brogden, *Royal Commission on Trade Unions, Fifth Report*, 1867-8.

owners, however, sometimes because they had not the space available for storage but mainly because the value of the coal deteriorated rapidly with exposure, seldom produced coal for stock and instead met each recession in demand by offering only part-time employment to their men. Thus when a proposed contract and price-list was drawn up for the Bute collieries, for example, it was pointed out that it should be 'distinctly understood that the above prices are ample compensation for the occasional want of employment, and its greater uncertainty than in the collieries belonging to the Iron Works, where the price is less by 4*d.* and 6*d.* per ton'.[1] Accordingly in times of good trade the earnings of the sale-coal colliers reached a higher level than those of the colliers serving the ironworks, and fell beneath them when work was slack. The Bute agreement met the latter contingency by permitting colliers, with some restriction on numbers, to leave, even though their contracted term of service had not expired, when their earnings fell below an average of 55*s.* a month.

The figures of the collier's earnings, however, do not tell the whole story, as deductions were made from them to meet the cost of the tools, candles, and powder he used while at work. The effect of these deductions was not inconsiderable, judging from the instance cited by Tremenheere of a collier who, helped by a boy aged thirteen, earned £6. 10*s.* a month and spent 11*s.* 2*d.* on candles and powder.[2] Even the Monmouthshire coal-owners themselves, who were hardly likely to exaggerate the weight of deductions, estimated (in 1843) the cost of candles and powder at 4*d.* out of a daily wage of 3*s.* 6*d.*[3] Deductions of this type continued to be made in later years. In the 1870's colliers were charged between 3*d.* and 6*d.* for mandril helves, for example, and they usually had to buy their own safety lamps, although sometimes the employer was prepared to provide a Davy lamp, leaving the men who

---

[1] CCL Bute MSS. X. 8. Agreement with the colliers to end of Nov. 1850.
[2] Tremenheere's Report, 1840, p. 213.   [3] *Merlin*, 25 Mar. 1843.

preferred a Clanny lamp to buy it for themselves. On the other hand the almost universal custom of the coalfield was to allow all colliers who were householders a generous quota of free or cheap coal. Where they were available, too, company cottages were usually let to colliers at a rent below the market rate.

Whilst the evidence about wages is of too sketchy a nature to support precise quantitative statements it can, however, support the broad conclusion that during the years between 1841 and 1875, and more particularly during the latter part of this period, there was a rising trend in money wages. While the general level of the colliers' earnings in 1841—not one of the worst years—had been assessed at 18 or 20s., the corresponding estimate for 1869—a poor year for coal-mining— was 24s. 9d. a week. The position in the early seventies was abnormal owing to the boom conditions of 1873 but, even after the subsequent wage reductions, the wage level of 1875 showed an appreciable advance over that of 1869.[1] If, as many colliers' children followed the occupation of their fathers, the family earnings are taken as the basis of comparison, then the exclusion of female workers and boys under twelve from underground work involved some monetary— not social—loss, but the earnings of the youngest children had never been great and the employment of women never widespread. If, too, real earnings are considered rather than money earnings, it seems probable that any rise in the cost of living that occurred during the period was too slight to nullify the money gains.[2] The increase in the colliers' earnings

[1] A day-wage rate of 3s. 6d. paid to hauliers at fifteen bituminous collieries in South Wales in 1869 lends credence to the estimate of Sir Thomas Brassey that skilled colliers earned 24s. 9d. in that year; in 1875 the hauliers' rate stood at 4s. 6d. at the same fifteen collieries. Coal Owners' Assoc. Records, Scrapbook 5. For the assertions of two employers about the higher wage rates in 1875 compared with 1870, see *CG*, 19 Feb. 1875.

[2] See the discussion on the cost of living in Sir John Clapham, *An Economic History of Modern Britain*, vol. II (Cambridge, 1932), chap. xi, and in W. W. Rostow, *British Economy to the Nineteenth Century* (Oxford, 1948), chap. I. There seems no reason to believe that the trend in South Wales differed from that for Britain.

thus underlay a significant but indeterminate improvement in their standard of life, and it is worthy of note that the high rates which had been paid to induce colliers to work in isolated regions tended to persist even after amenities had been developed there.[1]

The welfare of the colliers depended not only on the amount of their wages but also on their method of payment. In 1841, it was stated, 'in many parts of Glamorgan and Monmouthshire the wages of the working collier population are very rarely paid in money, but a shop in the neighbourhood, not professedly in the hands of the proprietors of the works, advances goods to the workmen employed in the mine on account of the proprietors; the books of the shop and the books of the colliery are checked on the pay day at the same office, and the balance, if any, is handed over to the men. It very often happens, however, that the men unfortunately have nothing to receive for months together.'[2] Where these truck payments prevailed they were usually disliked by the men because they thought 'the prices high and the weights light' at the company shop. One collier at Aaron Brain's Hengoed colliery, for example, where the men had struck work in 1841 because of dissatisfaction with the employer's shop and had returned only on condition that they should be paid their money weekly and be left free to deal where they wished, thought that this would mean a saving of 3 or 4s. in the pound, an invaluable help, particularly when work was short.[3] The Monmouthshire coal-owners themselves echoed this view in 1843, conceding that real wages were reduced by 15 per cent. where truck prevailed—possibly an exaggerated admission as the abolition of truck was being offered by the

[1] A. Dalziel, op. cit., pp. 23–27. In 1871 general wage rates were higher (12½–15 per cent.) in the Aberdare valley than at Merthyr, and the Rhondda rates were 5 per cent. higher again.
[2] *Children's Employment*, p. 482.
[3] Ibid., p. 531. Hengoed colliery was in Glamorgan. Similar views were expressed by another Glamorgan collier, Benjamin Morgan, in his evidence to the *Select Committee on Payment of Wages*, P.P. 1842 (471), ix.

owners as the bait to induce the men to accept a general reduction in wages.[1] The problem of truck, however, is a complex one admitting of no simple one-sided verdict.

Truck was by no means universal. It was more likely to affect the colliers connected with the iron industry as the ironmasters, unlike the colliery owners who merely leased the mineral rights, usually owned considerable stretches of land and were able to control the setting up of competing stores, but, even so, Merthyr was free from truck. In some parts of the coalfield, too, notably Pembrokeshire, the truck-paying employer was the rare exception. There were, moreover, employers who were willing to abide by the spirit, as well as the letter, of the 1831 Act against truck; Sir Thomas Phillips, for example, paid his men in cash and would not allow a shop to be set up in connexion with his collieries in the Sirhowy valley.[2]

Even where truck existed it was, as the mixture of praise and blame by middle-class observers shows, not always to be condemned. A shop established by an employer who was developing a colliery in an isolated district remote from any market town could meet a real need of the workmen (and here the higher prices might merely be a reflection of greater transport costs). When the Bute Merthyr Company started operations at the head of the Rhondda Fawr valley in 1857 it decided to support someone in opening a shop near the pits to supply goods at fair prices to be controlled by the company, but the men were to be paid in cash and left to spend the money where they pleased.[3] At Cwmavon the company shop had been established to guard against the possibility that the local shopkeepers might charge extortionate prices. Here again the men were not compelled to deal at the shop and the company, to ensure that the supplies of cash were adequate to meet the wages bill, not only obtained gold and silver from Bristol to supplement the currency drawn from Neath but

[1] *Merlin*, 25 Mar. 1843.   [2] *Children's Employment*, p. 538.
[3] Merthyr of Senghenydd MSS., Doc. 386.

also paid the men in different batches on every week-day.[1] The fluctuations of trade, particularly if the period of active employment preceding a depression had been brief, often made it essential for the colliers to obtain credit, and this was provided more readily by the employer's shop than by outside shops. The collier of Waterloo colliery, in Monmouthshire, who complained that 'we run a little in debt in the winter season [when] we have no work; we are screwed out of every penny when work sets in again',[2] had nevertheless received an advance when he most needed it; thirty years later the Truck Commissioners could find many examples of humane assistance provided by the company shop. It is not surprising, therefore, that occasionally the employers established shops in response to requests from the men.[3]

As time passed some of these justifications for truck lost their significance—isolated collieries did not remain isolated for ever. Yet the company shops survived, even though the necessity for them had gone; the explanation of their survival must be sought in the 'long pays' and in the conditions on which advances between pays were made. A collier was normally paid monthly, with an intermediate fortnightly 'draw'; these payments were made in cash and, unless he considered it prudent to deal at the company shop, could be spent where the collier wished. Any further 'advance' between the pay and the draw was also made in cash, but was given only on the understanding that it, or most of it, would be spent at the company shop (which usually adjoined the pay office). The better paid and more provident men generally did not deal at the company shop—and in that lay its condemnation—but there were many who could not manage

---

[1] *State of Population in Mining Districts*, 1846, pp. 41–43. This shop was soon to be closed; by 1850 Tremenheere found many good shops, opened by persons from a distance, and a flourishing market day at Cwmavon.

[2] *Children's Employment*, p. 536.

[3] For example, see evidence of A. Macgregor, *Report of Select Committee on Payment of Wages Bill, P.P.* 1854 (382), xvi.

without advances. It was from these—the improvident, the men whose earnings were depleted by bad times, the fathers of families of young children—that the company shop drew its custom. A Cwmtillery collier observed that 'a man with a family of seven or eight children cannot stand a fortnight or three weeks without money or victuals',[1] nor was it easy for such a man to move from a truck-paying district. 'Advance men' who did not deal at the shop were liable either to become marked men, to be discharged at the first opportunity, or to be refused any future advances.

Once a store was established employers were anxious to continue it, partly from altruistic motives, partly because it was a source of profit, and partly because it gave them in- increased power over the men. Some, largely inheriting opinions their fathers and grandfathers had formed in the days 'when truck was a blessing',[2] sincerely believed that the company shop was advantageous to the men even at the end of the sixties. A large firm had the capital resources to buy goods of high quality at advantageous rates and could consequently give better service than a small retail store. But if a large company, for the sake of the reputation of the firm, tried to ensure that its shop was well run, it was also true that the shop offered a dependable source of profit. A shop could be started with comparatively little capital as goods could be bought on two or three months credit' and the money received from the men could be used to meet the bills when they fell due. The investment was a safe one as bad debts were rare, most sales being made against money already due to the men as wages; the advance men of necessity formed a constant clientele; and the prices in the company shop could be fixed without too close an observance of market rates. Not only could the shop through its profits, as a northern ironmaster pointed out, help the Welsh employers to compete in their legitimate business, but it also conferred on them greater

[1] *Report of Truck Commissioners, P.P.* 1871 (C 326), xxxvi, p. lvi.
[2] Evidence of Lionel Brough, *Report of Truck Commissioners, Minutes of Evidence, P.P.* 1871 (C 327), xxxvi.

control over their men.[1] The more wages were drawn in goods rather than in money the less would be the absenteeism of the men through drunkenness after pay day, while the debts that were contracted at the shop bound the colliers to their masters and this, in an expanding industry subject to recurrent labour shortages, was a useful help in keeping a labour force intact.

Thus while the long pay survived, so did the company shop,[2] and while men became partly accustomed by habit to dependence on it they never became fully reconciled to it. The Monmouthshire solicitor John Owen, who could speak with authority about the attitude of the workmen of South Wales, on being asked 'Have you ever known any workmen who were in favour of the [truck] system?', replied 'I never have.'[3] This answer summed up the general feeling of the workmen who, often with justification, regarded the company shop as a wage-reducing device and resented any feeling of being tied to an employer by indebtedness, and who felt a sense of grievance at the lack of success of their claim for weekly wage payments with freedom to spend their wages where they wished. Truck probably operated at its harshest where the colliers were working for a contractor. A barrister described how, at the small collieries near Ebbw Vale, 'a number of contractors undertook to work the coal and bring it to the bank at so much a ton for the large colliery owners. Those contractors begin without any capital whatever; they get three or four months' credit at Bristol for goods, and either set up a beershop or have some friends with whom they have

[1] *Report of Truck Commissioners*, 1871, p. vi.
[2] While the colliers connected with the ironworks were most affected by truck, the evidence given before the Truck Commission in 1870 shows that it was by no means confined to them.
[3] Evidence of John Owen, *Report of Select Committee on Payment of Wages Bill*, 1854. The opposition of the men was shared by H. A. Bruce (later Lord Aberdare) who, as stipendiary magistrate for the Merthyr district, had had wide experience of truck cases. His private comment on Richard Fothergill's attempt in 1851 to pay his workmen at Aberdare in truck was: 'I hope public indignation will abate this contrivance of fraud and iniquity—which more effectively impedes the march of improvement than any other villainy I know of.' NLW Clark MSS., 51/117. H. A. Bruce to G. T. Clark, 12 Apr. 1851.

such a connexion; they profess to pay the men once a month, and their policy is to supply them with everything and to pay as little money as possible. The hardships and inconveniences related to me were shameful.'[1] But even the large company shops were 'a little rough, some of them, at times in the way in which they treat their customers'.[2] John Owen in 1854 commented that women might 'stay perhaps from seven in the morning until six in the evening until they could be served';[3] seventeen years later the secretary of the Truck Commissioners paying a test visit to the Abersychan company shop on 'turn book day', at two o'clock one November morning, found women already waiting although it was four hours before the time for the opening of the shop.[4] It is not surprising that the hostility of the men to the company shop was shared by their wives.[5]

It was, however, difficult for the workmen to translate this antagonism to truck into effective action. Not only was trade unionism weak but also the practice of truck, affecting the more prosperous and provident section of the colliers least, seldom became the leading issue at stake in any strike. Recourse to the law courts—as will be seen in the next chapter—was of dubious value. While the illegality of truck eliminated the most blatant forms of it in time, practices survived which observed merely the letter of the law or slipped through its mesh. The decay of truck was gradual and is difficult to trace; some employers, sensitive to public opinion, abandoned it; some new employers did not adopt it; the unwelcome publicity it received during the inquiry of the Truck Commission hastened its decline. As one Welsh delegate told a miners'

[1] Evidence of D. T. Evans, *Report of Select Committee on Payment of Wages Bill*, 1854 [2] *Report of Truck Commissioners*, 1871, p. x.
[3] Evidence of John Owen, *Report of Select Committee on Payment of Wages Bill*, 1854.
[4] *Report of Truck Commissioners*, 1871, p. xii. On turn-book day, a day preceding the monthly pay, greater purchases on credit were allowed.
[5] Truck did not necessarily mean sober husbands as tobacco bought at the shop was accepted as currency at public houses. 'Packets of tobacco pass unopened from hand to hand.' *Report of Truck Commission*, 1871, p. xi.

conference in 1872: 'There has been an old lady in the Maesteg district for thirty years, but she is now dead, and her decease has been a further benefit to the men of fifteen per cent. The old lady was Mrs. Truck.'[1] It can hardly be doubted, in the conditions of the seventies, that her death, or her senility, marked an improvement in the condition and spirit of self-reliance of the mining population.

Another practice that had died out earlier was the custom of paying men their wages in public houses. The public house was a convenient source of small change, particularly when men were paid in groups,[2] and—more important—was often owned by a contractor or petty agent. Tremenheere commented on the prevalence of the custom of paying wages in public houses in 1846, and its evils were plainly voiced by the rector of Llanhilleth, a district where there were several small collieries. 'This state of things', he told the Education Commissioner, 'actually prevents the operative from being sober and thrifty, and holds out a reward to the drunkard, it being the interest of the employer or agent to have such men as will spend their all at his house: nor is he slow in intimating to such as are not in the habit of frequenting his house, that their services are not acceptable, and thus the more sober a man is, the more he is exposed to petty annoyance from his employer.'[3] The payment of wages in public houses had been declared illegal in 1842, and Tremenheere's efforts to enforce compliance with the law secured the support of employers, who were eager to repress a practice so provocative of absenteeism on the part of the workmen. In 1841 the Dowlais Iron Company started to pay the men individually through the office instead of through the contractors, although two further

---

[1] *Western Mail*, 4 Oct. 1872. Both Lionel Brough and T. A. Wales commented on the disappearance of truck since the inquiry of the Commission when they gave evidence to the *Select Committee on Dearness of Coal*, 1873.

[2] At Dowlais one collier deputed by a group to draw their weekly wages might take £20 or £30, some of it in £5 notes, from the cashier. Evidence of Thomas Evans, *Select Committee on Payment of Wages in Goods*, 1842.

[3] *Report on State of Education in Wales*, 1847, vol. ii, p. 299.

attempts, in 1844 and 1852, were necessary before this reform became fully effective.[1] Contractors and 'gaffers' were first told by the company that they would be discharged if they paid wages in public houses and later, in 1848, told that they must either relinquish their beer houses or give up their employment with the company.[2] The Crawshays at Cyfarthfa also debarred their contractors from owning beer houses in 1848 and subsequently started to pay their men direct, Robert Crawshay informing his father in 1859 that 'we now pay all the men, colliers and miners, separately so it takes more hands to do it, and it pays well'.[3] This lessening of the power of the contractors and the virtual disappearance of the practice of paying men in public houses both helped, as did the decline of truck, to improve the status and well-being of the colliers.

Another way in which the period after 1840 registered a gain for the collier was the reduction which took place in his hours of work. When the Children's Employment Commissioners visited the coalfield the usual working day—apart from Pembrokeshire, where it varied between eight and ten hours—was twelve hours. The piece-rate colliers, however, while the coal was worked from levels or shallow pits, were often free to leave when they wished; as one manager remarked, 'when paid by the job we do not look after their time'.[4] Even so, twelve hours were regarded as the normal day for these men, and the younger workers, the door-boys and hauliers, had to start work at the same time as the hewers and had to remain at work until the last tram of coal had been cleared from the

[1] *State of Population in Mining Districts*, 1846, p. 37; Evidence of John Evans, *Report of Select Committee on Payment of Wages Bill*, 1854.
[2] *MG*, 27 May 1848. The contract rules for the collieries of the Pontypool Iron Works in 1856 included a clause that 'No Contractor, Overman or Foreman, shall keep, or be beneficially interested in, any beerhouse for the sale of intoxicating liquors.' Mon. County Archives, Bythway Docs., No. 0067.
[3] Cyfarthfa MSS., Box IV, Bundle 13. R. T. Crawshay to W. Crawshay, 16 Apr. 1859.
[4] *Children's Employment*, pp. 480, 653.

colliery. During this working day there were no fixed meal times. 'The people working in the interior of the mines can scarcely be said to take any meals during the period they are at work—varying from eight to fourteen hours. They get their breakfast before they enter the works, and take with them a small bag of bread and cheese (their almost invariable fare), which they eat at irregular intervals during the day, as the circumstances of their work will allow, and as their appetite invites them.'[1] The most substantial change in these working hours came about only after the Mines Regulation Act of 1872. Before this Act, as the discussions during the sliding scale negotiations showed, the colliers worked on Monday from 7 a.m. to 6 p.m., from Tuesday to Friday from 6 a.m. to 6 p.m., and on Saturday from 6 a.m. to 4 p.m.; the Act, by restricting the hours for boys under sixteen to fifty-four a week, had the practical effect of fixing the hours for all at this figure.[2] During the discussions, too, it was assumed, both by the employers and by the men, that $1\frac{1}{2}$ hours were allowed for the midday meal.

While the change-over from the level to the pit as the characteristic production unit often meant that the collier, being tied to set periods for ascending and descending the shaft, was no longer free to start and leave his work when he wished, his general liability to irregularity of employment remained little affected by changing conditions. He derived some benefit from the improvement of dock facilities and the growth of steam shipping, which helped to reduce the number of days when he was rendered idle by congestion at the ports or by the prevalence of winds unfavourable for the passage of sailing-ships. In 1841 it had been remarked of the workers at Waterloo colliery in Monmouthshire, for example, that 'in winter they suffer much, as few vessels arrive for coal at Newport', and a

[1] *Children's Employment Commission. First Report*, 1842, p. 121.
[2] Coal Owners' Assoc. MSS., Sliding Scale Committee Minutes, 8 May 1877. In 1873 Lionel Brough said that hours averaged from nine to ten a day in Monmouthshire, and nine in Glamorgan, with Saturday a half-day. Brough's Evidence, *Select Committee on Dearness of Coal*, 1873.

few years later it was reckoned that the colliers who were dependent on the demand at Newport averaged ten days a month unemployed and often had no employment at all in the months of March and April when vessels were detained by strong winds.[1] The usual means of meeting recessions in demand which were expected to be purely temporary was by short-time working; John James, the owner of a colliery at Cwmllynfell at the head of the Swansea valley, said in 1857, for example, that in bad times 'we do not turn our hands off much; we work less'.[2]

In addition to the irregularity of work which resulted from conditions over which the colliers had no control there was also that which could be attributed to the behaviour of the men themselves. It was a common practice for men to absent themselves from work after the periodic pay. The manager of Dowlais, referring to the colliers, said that 'all might earn much more. Some of our men lose four days a month, others one week out of four. . . . We have offered 1*d*. or 2*d*. a ton extra to induce them to work regularly, but cannot succeed.'[3] The Dowlais men were not exceptional, other employers complaining that absenteeism forced them to keep more work open and employ more colliers than were strictly necessary. In addition, they had to use more horses and engage more labourers who were idle for part of their time. The evidence suggests that there was no change in this habit of the colliers in the fifties and the sixties. In 1861 a mineral surveyor, while commenting that the colliers in Neath were a sober and well-conducted body of men who seldom absented themselves from a day's work, contrasted them with the Aberdare colliers who generally kept two or three days a month holiday.[4] In 1868 a Dowlais trustee observed that 'the vice of the collier is

[1] *Children's Employment*, p. 536; *Report on State of Education in Wales*, 1847, II, p. 299.
[2] Evidence of John James, *Report of Select Committee on Rating of Mines*, 1857.
[3] *State of Population in Mining Districts*, 1846, p. 36.
[4] *State of Popular Education in England*, P.P. 1861 (2794 II), xxi, part II, Report of John Jenkins, p. 593.

to be idle; he will stay away on Monday and Tuesday, and then he comes in and makes the most of the remaining four days, and he sends out as much as he can'.[1] It seems probable that, because of idle days arising from one reason or another, the colliers worked on an average only about 4½ days a week.[2]

Usually the colliers of South Wales were engaged on a monthly contract. In 1841 the Marquis of Bute was urging the adoption of the northern practice of engaging colliers by the year with the object of lessening the risk of frequent strikes. The idea was revived in 1850, when it formed part of the owners' terms for the settlement of the Aberdare strike in that year.[3] The strike, however, was settled without the men agreeing to accept the annual bond and the coal-owners, recognizing defeat, made no further attempt to introduce it.

Whatever the final judgement about colliers' earnings, even when allowance has been made for truck payments and irregularity of work, it is clear that the wage rates and expanding opportunities of employment offered by the coal-mining industry continued to attract to it, with the single exception of the Pembrokeshire collieries, ever growing numbers of workers. This is shown by the following census returns:

Number of Male Coal-Miners

	Monmouth-shire	Glamorgan	Carmarthen-shire	Pembroke-shire	Brecknock-shire
1851	11,367	15,295	2,344	926	1,541
1861	10,701	23,791	2,829	853	1,802
1871	12,742	31,513	2,742	646	1,342
1881	14,656	44,435	2,666	477	2,092

[1] Evidence of G. T. Clark, *Royal Commission on Trade Unions, Fifth Report*, 1867–8.

[2] This was the estimate of John Nixon for the sixties and seventies in his evidence to *Royal Commission on Accidents in Mines, Preliminary Report*, 1881. In 1848 Nevill had estimated that the colliers averaged between 200 and 250 days' employment a year. Nevill MSS. 9. R. J. Nevill to G. de Tranquelez, 3 Apr. 1848.

[3] Bute MSS., Box 70, vol. 13. Bute to T. W. Booker, 19 Jan. 1841; vol. 14. Bute to Capt. Napier, 4 Apr. 1843. *MG*, 23 Feb. 1850.

While some of this increase came about through the sons of colliers' entering the industry some of it came from the attraction in of migrants from other counties and from other occupations.

The extent and nature of this influx of new population, drawn in by the prospects of employment offered by the various industries on the coalfield, may be illustrated by the figures for 1871, when in Glamorgan only a little over 62 per cent. and in Monmouthshire a little over 70 per cent. of the population had been born within the county. The immigrants came mainly from the neighbouring Welsh counties, the west of England, Ireland, and the rest of Wales;[1] for Glamorgan the most important source was the neighbouring Welsh counties, for Monmouthshire it was the west of England. It is not possible to say what proportion of these immigrants sought or obtained employment in the coal industry but, in general, the men most likely to be employed, except perhaps in Monmouthshire, were those who were Welsh speaking, and of these, in normal times, probably only the youngest would become skilled colliers.

The work of the hewer was regarded as a skilled craft. 'The collier of South Wales', it was remarked, 'has to cut the coal and fill it into the trams; he has to gob the rubbish, make and keep the working place safe and in order, he has to keep his stall road in travelling order, and do all the timbering necessary in his working place.'[2] This varied occupation was largely hereditary or only to be learnt by new-comers who started young—the sons of agricultural workers rather than the agricultural workers themselves. When H. A. Bruce was addressing the colliers of Aberdare in 1857, for example, he pointed out that many of them came from Carmarthenshire

[1]
	Glam.	Mon.
Total born outside the county, 1871 census	117,904	73,934
Born in Carms., Pembs., Brecs., and (for Glam.) Mon.	60,279	20,863
,, ,, Devon, Cornwall, Somerset, Glos. and Herefs.	22,562	26,586
,, ,, Ireland	9,478	6,920
,, ,, other Welsh counties	9,196	4,489

[2] T. Forster Brown, 'The South Wales Coalfield', *SWIE*, vol. ix.

and the Vale of Glamorgan where their fathers were bringing up families on 11*s.* and 12*s.* a week.¹ 'A man comes in and begins to labour', a mines inspector commented, 'and if he is a man turned of 30 years . . . I do not think that he ever goes to cut coal, but his family ultimately do.'² An older man might get employment at a colliery, particularly if he had a friend or relative there to speak for him, but might merely serve as a labourer, assisting with the timbering or helping to clear falls. But the usual pattern of slow graduation into the ranks of the skilled colliers was less rigidly adhered to in remote collieries or at times of active trade. The Welsh colliers complained, for example, that during the boom period of the early seventies inexperienced plough-boys and shoe-makers were being put straight on to cutting coal. The Amalgamated Association of Mineworkers, however, on the grounds that this was a problem peculiar to South Wales, declined to support a scheme to introduce a regular apprenticeship system into the Welsh collieries.³

Immigrants from outside Wales usually encountered the barriers of race and language. Peasants from the counties of Cardigan, Carmarthen, and Pembroke could get employment more readily than the Cornish miner, who spoke and thought in a different language from many of the colliers. Moreover the Cornishman, trained in a different type of mining, needed instruction for a month or two before he could venture to take a stall or his place at long work, and might find that he could not understand this instruction even when it was offered.⁴ The Irish immigrants did not generally penetrate to the colliery villages, but congregated more round the iron centres and there some were engaged in 'patching and unloading the coal'.⁵ Wherever the Irish appeared, owing to

---

[1] *MG*, 12 Dec. 1857.
[2] Evidence of T. A. Wales, *Select Committee on Dearness of Coal*, 1873.
[3] *CG*, 11 Oct. 1872.
[4] Ibid., 15 Sept. 1866. Cornish migration occurred on a considerable scale in 1866, an unfavourable year for new-comers to get employment in collieries.
[5] Evidence of T. A. Wales, *Select Committee on Dearness of Coal*, 1873.

SOCIAL CONDITIONS

their religious divergence and radically different standard of life, brawls and racial clashes occurred, particularly in years of bad trade. Instances can be found, such as the attempt to drive the Irish from the Rhondda valleys in 1857 or the serious clash at the Dunraven collieries near Pontypridd in 1866, where the hostility came wholly from the sale-coal colliers,[1] but they were infrequent compared with the disturbances at the iron centres. English migrants were absorbed most easily in the eastern part of the coalfield, which had long been exposed to the influence of such movement, but in the west, apart from a few overmen brought in for their technical knowledge, they were rarely to be found.

Besides this movement of population into the district there was also a considerable mobility of labour within the coalfield. Single men, unencumbered with families, had formed a large proportion of the immigrants with the result that a permanent feature of the population of the coalfield was an unusually low proportion of females to males, a disparity which was even more marked within the age group 15 to 35, which included most of the working colliers.

Number of Females per 1,000 Males

	Total population		Age group 15–35	
	1841	1871	1841	1871
England and Wales	1,046	1,053	1,088	1,075
Glamorgan	948	935	890	877
Monmouthshire	903	927	855	883

The existence of this substantial body of young unmarried colliers stimulated the mobility of labour as they had fewer local ties and could find housing accommodation more easily than complete families. Evidence of this mobility abounds. William Morgan had worked 'all over the hills, backwards and forwards, Glamorgan and Monmouthshire' in his fifty-

[1] *MG*, 12 Sept. 1857, 29 June 1866.

four years as miner and collier.[1] In the mid-fifties there were references to the 'migrating tide of colliers in pursuit of higher wages . . . flowing from west to east in the coalfield of South Wales', to the migration of colliers when trade was bad in the Swansea valley to the steam-coal collieries farther west, and to the general 'shifting population' about the collieries.[2] In 1869 about half the victims at Ferndale 'were strangers to the place, and unknown except by name',[3] and, at all times, the evidence given by colliers to the various Parliamentary Committees showed that many had seldom worked long in the same colliery or even in the same district. The attempts of the employers to control this mobility, valuable though it was in promoting the growth of the industry away from existing centres of population, provide further proof of its existence. Attempts were sometimes made to introduce contracts which restricted the number of colliers who could leave a colliery at any one time and, more generally, to prevent colliers from obtaining employment without a discharge note from their previous employer.

No doubt the groups of emigrants whose departure, mainly to Australia in the 1850's and to America in the following decade, excited regular comment in the local press included colliers in their ranks. In 1865, for example, an Aberdare correspondent, related how 'every week a large number of able-bodied men leave this neighbourhood for America, commencing the journey chiefly under the guidance and protection of the American emigrant company's local agent', and how such men could decide to go, auction their furniture, and be off almost before the neighbours knew.[4] Only a week or two previously the colliers from the Rhondda and Aberdare valleys had formed an Emigration Society to aid this outward

---

[1] Evidence of W. Morgan, *Select Committee on Payment of Wages in Goods*, 1842.
[2] H. Mackworth, 'On the Diseases of Miners', *Journal of the Society of Arts*, vol. iii (1845–5), p. 357; Evidence of John James and of Samuel Dobson, *Select Committee on Rating of Mines*, 1857.
[3] *CG*, 18 June 1869. [4] Ibid., 6 May 1865.

movement which might help to sustain the wages of those who remained behind.[1] 'We know perfectly well that the collier has America under his lee', a representative of the owners remarked;[2] but it is not possible to make any reliable estimate of how many colliers actually went.

For the housing of the growing communities of colliers good building materials were readily available, fire-clay often being found in conjunction with the coal seams and a brickworks being an adjunct to some of the collieries. The usual collier's cottage was solidly built of brick, contained three or four small rooms and, if not overcrowded, permitted a standard of comfort far superior to that of the hovels of rural West Wales. The Children's Employment Commissioner described the interior of one of a cluster of about twenty-five houses, known as the Land-level houses, occupied by a collier at Pentyrch, near Cardiff. 'The rooms were decently provided with articles of necessary furniture, a Welsh Testament was on the table, a clock hanging against the wall, and a good side of bacon and some bags of herbs added to a general appearance of cleanliness and comfort.'[3] A few years later the houses of the colliers in the Maesteg district were found to be 'expensively furnished', with a handsome chest of drawers and numerous coloured prints on the walls.[4]

In other respects, however, the colliers' houses, growing up in their drab rows along the hillsides, were less satisfactory. The same observers who praised the comfort they saw within them also pointed out their lack of drainage and sanitation and their imperfect supply of water. Even the twenty-five Land-level houses at Pentyrch, well built and provided with gardens though they were, had only one privy, and there were only ten for the large village of Blackwood.[5] The worst con-

[1] *MG*, 22, 29 Apr. 1865.
[2] Evidence of G. T. Clark, *Royal Commission on Trade Unions, Fifth Report*, 1867 8.   [3] *Children's Employment*, p. 520.
[4] *Report on State of Education in Wales*, 1847, i, p. 351.
[5] *Children's Employment Commission. First Report*, 1842, p. 170.

sequences of such neglect were felt by the colliers who lived in the larger towns, particularly those who formed part of the population of Merthyr. 'The vast majority of houses have no privies; where there is such a thing it is a mere hole in the ground with no drainage. Indeed, the town is in a very small degree drained at all. . . . There is also a most insufficient supply of water, especially at Dowlais.'[1] The enthusiasm of the account of the model town growing up round the Abercarn and Gwythen collieries in the Ebbw valley—with its effective sewerage and a privy provided for each house, its daily removal of rubbish, and with its public bakehouse, baths, and wash-house provided by the company for the use of employees free of charge—was occasioned because such amenities, like the freedom from cholera of Abercarn in 1849, were exceptional.[2] The general picture was one of neglect of sanitation, and for many decades to come the mining villages were to figure as backward areas in the reports of medical officers of health.

The houses of these growing communities were built either by the speculative builder or by the builder working to the orders of the employers or of the colliers themselves. While it was a common practice for the great iron firms to provide their workmen with company houses, in the sale-coal districts this was less customary. There were numerous exceptions where coal-owners, to help in attracting an adequate number of workmen, took the initiative in the provision of housing. One of the early decisions of the Bute Merthyr Steam Coal Company in 1857, when starting operations in the Rhondda valley, was to arrange for a contractor to build between fifty and sixty houses.[3] In 1860 Nixon and Company advertised that they would grant leases for 200 cottages at Mountain Ash, provide building materials at a reasonable price, and advance

[1] *Report on State of Education in Wales*, 1847, i, p. 304. Merthyr in 1850 still had no local act for paving, lighting, or cleansing, or for any sanitary purpose. T. W. Rammell, *Report to the General Board of Health on Sanitary Conditions of Merthyr Tydfil* (1850), p. 12.
[2] *MJ*, 29 June 1850.   [3] Merthyr of Senghenydd MSS., Deed No. 386.

money on the mortgage of the cottages at 5 per cent., and that they would take over the cottages when built for a term of years at a reasonable rent.[1] A further example is provided by the Ocean Coal Company which, by the end of 1871, had spent £6,193 on the provision of cottages.[2] But these were exceptions and when, during the course of the 1871 strike, the coal-owners evicted men from the company cottages the numbers involved were so small that this move had little effect, apart from the indignation it aroused and some subsequent difficulty in finding tenants for the cottages.[3]

More usual were the houses built out of the savings of the colliers or those built by the speculative builder. Even at Dowlais in 1842, where the company owned a considerable number of two- and four-roomed cottages, between 500 and 600 houses had been built by the men themselves, the company leasing the land for ninety-nine years and sometimes assisting by advancing on loan half the cost of building.[4] At Merthyr, too, it was 'colliers and miners and people of that class' who did much of the building. 'The general way of doing it is, that when a man has £50 or £60 he starts upon three houses directly; he builds as far as his money goes, and he will borrow £80 upon a small mortgage for two or three years; that is done to a very large extent.'[5] In the more purely colliery districts the same practice prevailed. 'Owners have never as a rule found houses', the mines inspector for South Wales commented in 1873, 'people, as private speculators, build houses and let them, it may be, in some cases, to the company and they receive the rent from the men; but in most cases they let them directly to the colliers themselves, and in those cases the masters have nothing to do with the houses'.[6] The rents

[1] *CG*, 31 Mar. 1860.
[2] NLW A. Stanley Davies MSS., Bundle 13.
[3] *MG*, 8 July 1871; A. Dalziel, *The Colliers' Strike in South Wales*, p. 76.
[4] Evidence of Thomas Evans, *Report of Select Committee on Payment of Wages in Goods*, 1842.
[5] Evidence of C. H. James, *Report of Select Committee on Payment of Wages Bill*, 1854.
[6] Evidence of T. A. Wales, *Select Committee on Dearness of Coal*, 1873.

of these private houses were often somewhat higher than those of the company houses[1]—'cottage property pays well, 8 or 10 per cent.', was the verdict of the same inspector—but the colliers in them enjoyed a sense of greater freedom. Nevertheless the supply of houses was often outpaced by the growth of population and many colliery households were overcrowded by the taking in of lodgers. At Maesteg in 1846 the cottages were found to contain an average of a dozen inhabitants each, and near some of the ironworks in Monmouthshire it was said to be not uncommon for nine or ten to sleep in one room.[2] While the presence of these lodgers, who still formed a numerous class in mining villages in 1873,[3] impaired the conditions of health and comfort in the collier's home, it brought some compensation by reducing the burden of rent payments.

The observers who had lamented the scant attention paid to sanitation in the early forties had also commented on the lack of educational facilities. Some attempt had already, before 1841, been made to remedy this deficiency: Sir Thomas Phillips had started a school for 400 children in the parish of Bedwellty, and a school connected with the Guests' works at Dowlais had been in existence for some years. Some collieries, too, had schools attached to them, supported by small sums stopped from the pay of the men; the deduction at Walter Coffin's Dinas colliery, for example, being 2*d*. in the pound.[4] But interest in education was becoming more widespread and employer after employer took steps to provide schools so that by 1859 it was 'the exception to find works of any magnitude unprovided with the means of education for their

[1] For example, colliers who left the employ of the Pontypool Ironworks Company could remain in company houses as tenants on sufferance, but at double the rent previously paid. Mon. County Archives, Bythway MSS., Doc. 0067, 1 Jan 1857. Colliers' rents varied greatly, but averaged between 2*s*. and 3*s*. a week, and seem to have risen little in the period 1840–75.
[2] *Report on State of Education in Wales*, 1847, i, p. 350; ii, pp. 292–3.
[3] Evidence of T. A. Wales, *Select Committee on Dearness of Coal*, 1873.
[4] *Children's Employment*, pp. 488, 520.

children'.[1] The ironmasters had set the pace, their large scale of operations permitting expenditure on schools and reading rooms in a way that was not practicable for the smaller coal-owners, but the coal-owners followed the same path, if more slowly. By 1871 out of thirty-six of the sale-coal collieries in Monmouthshire and in the Aberdare, Rhondda, and Ogmore valleys a deduction was made from the men's pay—usually 1d. in the pound—at thirty of them for schools.[2]

Medical attention was provided in the same way, the 3d. in the pound stopped for this from the men of Thomas Powell's Gelli-gaer colliery in 1841 being typical of many examples. The men at Risca, it was alleged, feeling that they should get some return for their money, attended the doctor to get medicine whether they needed it or not.[3] It was only rarely that the men were given any control over the medical fund or allowed any say in the appointment of the doctor—a lack of control which occasioned some resentment but seldom led to any active opposition. Consequently deductions from pay to finance medical aid and relief during sickness were general, although not universal—for example, in 1871 such stoppages, ranging from 1½d. to 3d. in the pound, were made at thirty-four out of the thirty-six sale-coal collieries referred to above.

Supplementing these arrangements, where the control and initiative lay largely with the employers, were the efforts made by the men themselves, through their benefit societies and clubs, to provide against the risks of sickness and accidents and the costs of funerals—the Welshman 'likes to be buried decently', G. T. Clark of Dowlais remarked. These societies had grown more numerous after 1834 owing to the impetus they had received from the prejudice against relief as administered under the New Poor Law. A preference was shown for those clubs which had 'badges, a peculiar uniform, offices with honorary titles and certain ceremonies of initiation, such

---

[1] MIR Report of Thomas Evans for 1859, p. 116.
[2] A. Dalziel, op. cit., p. 26.
[3] *Children's Employment*, pp. 527, 549.

as the Oddfellows, Druids and Ivorites',[1] while a further attraction to some, as clubs usually met in public houses, was the convivial evenings they provided. The Bedwellty Union Benefit Society, it was pointed out, spent on beer money for club meetings almost one-fifth of what it paid out in benefits.[2] Yet such clubs, besides satisfying a craving for pageantry, met a more fundamental need in a society where the danger of industrial accident and disease was never remote and where no general accident fund as yet existed. In the mid-fifties benefit clubs were described as being 'not only common, but ... universal' on the coalfield; in 1854 in Maesteg alone, a town of a few thousand people, there were thirteen separate clubs with over 1,300 members in all.[3] About a decade later there were about 5,000 members of the fifty societies at Dowlais.[4] There were, no doubt, in the history of the benefit clubs many instances of extravagant expenditure and financial mismanagement, yet their very survival shows that not all had been ill-managed; in their management workmen had been enabled to acquire valuable experience in organization.

The capacity for voluntary association amongst the miners was demonstrated even more forcefully in the religious field. The inadequacy of the Established Church, poorly endowed in Wales and with many of its incumbents absentees or non-Welsh speaking, contrasted strongly with the religious fervour of the Nonconformist miners. Tremenheere commented that the Dissenters were zealous and active, 'and their chapels and schools rise in all directions as soon as the population begins to accumulate'.[5] Thus while the Church of England in the diocese of Llandaff between 1849 and 1869 built thirty-nine new churches and rebuilt a further thirty-six, the three

[1] *Report on State of Education in Wales*, 1847, i, p. 481.
[2] *Children's Employment*, pp. 543, 567.
[3] Evidence of Wm. Llewellyn, *Report of Select Committee on Rating of Mines*, 1857; evidence of A. Macgregor, *Report of Select Committee on Payment of Wages Bill*, 1854.
[4] Evidence of G. T. Clark, *Royal Commission on Trade Unions, Fifth Report*, 1867-8.
[5] *State of Population in Mining Districts*, 1850, p. 68.

largest Nonconformist groups—the Independents, the Baptists, and the Calvinist Methodists—built in the same area 186 new chapels and enlarged 127, a contrast the more marked when it is remembered that the Establishment found more support among the higher social groups.[1] The chapels bore witness not only to the strength of nonconformity but also to the Welsh capacity for association, one neighbourhood readily assisting another, and the funds to build them, maintain them, and pay the salaries of the ministers, coming from voluntary subscription—often the savings of daily labour.[2]

Once built, the chapel exercised a considerable influence in raising the moral standard of the mining population. In the forties the vice of the colliers which had occasioned most adverse comment had been that of drunkenness; all had complained of this habit, Tremenheere commented, employers, clergy, and the families on whom the loss and suffering chiefly fell.[3] Similar complaints were reiterated to the Children's Employment Commissioners and a little later to the Education Commissioners. It would have been surprising had it been otherwise, as many circumstances combined to encourage the habit. Those who sought the 'colour and warmth and light' of life seldom had far to go if they could find it in the beer shop. In 1841 at Cefncoedycymmer, near Merthyr, with a population of about 1,500, there were thirteen or fourteen licensed houses, while there were seven to serve a population of about 200 in the colliery village of Tongwynlais, near Cardiff.[4] The irregularity of the collier's earnings tempted him to regard the gains from a prosperous month as a surplus which might be spent on drink, particularly when he received his pay in a public house; the public house, too, was often the headquarters of his benefit society. Moreover the collier

[1] *British Quarterly Review*, vol. liii (1871), 'The Established Church in Wales'. Reprinted in Henry Richard, M.P., *Letters and Essays on Wales*.
[2] For example, the colliers at Gilfach Bargoed agreed in 1840 to devote the £5 Christmas Box given them by their employer to the reduction of the debt of Salem Independent Chapel. *Merlin*, 1 Feb. 1840.
[3] Tremenheere's Report, 1840, pp. 214–15.
[4] *Children's Employment*, p. 489.

who got little rest at home owing to the presence of lodgers turned naturally to the public house, while to others it offered a refuge from 'vacuity of thought'.[1] There were few amenities to compete; the manager of Dowlais, when describing the night schools, reading rooms, playing fields, and works band that had been established there by the fifties, remarked that 'it is want of recreation of that sort that drives men to the public houses'.[2]

As a leaven, working against this, was the strength of religious feeling—almost always Nonconformist. Two comments from the Report on Education in Wales are instructive. 'I do not remember', said one of the commissioners, 'to have seen an adult in rags in a single Sunday-school throughout the poorest districts. They always seemed to me better dressed on Sundays than the same class in England.' 'Sabbath-breaking, or an absence from divine service', commented a Llanelly industrialist, with some exaggeration, 'would subject a man to more odium than, perhaps, any other offence.'[3] Accounts of later periods pay similar tributes to the strength of the influence of religion on the lives of the colliers. In the Neath district in the early sixties attendance at a place of worship on Sunday was almost invariable among the colliers, while on week-days their leisure was spent in their gardens or in recreations such as music and dancing. A few years later the trustee of the Dowlais Iron Company, himself an Anglican, remarked that the Nonconformist ministers exercised an influence over the workman 'far more than his master, and far more than the Catholic priest has with the Roman Catholics in Wales. . . . On any question such as an outburst of cholera or anything of that sort, you are perfectly certain you will have their support for doing the thing that is right.'[4]

[1] Tremenheere's Report, 1840, p. 214.
[2] Evidence of John Evans, *Select Committee on Accidents in Mines, Third Report*, P.P. 1854 (277), ix.
[3] *Report on State of Education in Wales*, 1847, i, pp. 4, 478.
[4] Evidence of G. T. Clark, *Royal Commission on Trade Unions, Fifth Report*, 1867-8.

There were limits to the influence of the chapels and of their ministers, and it was able to moderate rather than eliminate the attraction of the inn to the colliers. Nevertheless it is clear that the colliers were not without a sense of pride in their class. At the end of the strike of 1871 a Ferndale collier described the strike-breaking labourers who had been imported into that area as 'a herd of drunkards, pitch and toss players, bull-dog fanciers, &c., and we have been informed, and that on good authority, that only *one* of the whole gang attends a place of worship'.[1] Even if this description is coloured by the dislike generally felt for strike-breakers, it is patent that the writer of the letter believed that the low moral standard of the new-comers marked them off as a race apart from the typical Welsh collier. If the most important single reason for this difference is sought it was, undoubtedly, the influence exercised on the Welsh collier by his religious beliefs.

[1] *Western Mail*, 14 Sept. 1871.

X

INDUSTRIAL RELATIONS

THE uneasy nature of industrial relations in the Welsh coal industry—later a matter of notoriety—was already evident between 1840 and 1875. The opening of the period was heralded, in November 1839, by the march of the Chartists on Newport; it closed with the five months strike of Welsh colliers in the first half of 1875—the third major stoppage in the coalfield in four years. And not only was the period thus bounded by unrest; strife and conflict were also a recurring feature of the intervening years.

This is apparent even from a brief chronicle confined to the major strikes and lock-outs. Throughout the forties these centred mainly on the house-coal collieries of Monmouthshire. The decade opened with a succession of strikes early in 1840 arising from the refusal of the Monmouthshire colliers to work with those who had testified against the Chartists after the attack on the Westgate Hotel. The employers at the collieries concerned were not willing to lose trade for the sake of a few turncoats, and the men were given their way.[1] By mid-summer a more serious clash had developed. Falling iron prices had induced the ironmasters to enforce a 15 per cent. reduction in May[2] and its quiet acceptance encouraged the coal-owners to follow suit. But their proposal to cut wages by 2*d*. a ton encountered a resistance so stubborn that, after a fourteen-week stoppage and despite attempts to import labour, the employers gave way. Where the strike had spread to Glamorgan—mainly in the house-coal collieries of Gelligaer and the lower Rhondda—a similar result obtained. Only

---

[1] *Cambrian*, 22 Feb. 1840.
[2] NLW Bute MSS., Box 70, vol. 13. Bute to Marquess of Normanby, 28 Apr. 1840.

at Thomas Powell's Gelli-gaer collieries were the men defeated, the 2d. reduction being enforced, but the strike ending with an agreement that the cutting rates in future should be regulated by a sliding scale governed by the selling price of coal at Cardiff. The judgement of the Lord-Lieutenant of Glamorgan on this strike was that 'the Masters have been completely beaten by their men, in a way that never happened to them before'.[1]

A fresh attempt early in 1842 to impose a general reduction provoked a similar resistance and ended with a similar result. Starting in January the strike lasted till March, when the Monmouthshire owners—seeing their trade being diverted to Cardiff—allowed the men to return at the old rates.[2] The depression, however, steadily deepened. In the summer the ironworkers of Merthyr, who had suffered a steady decline in wages during the previous two years, made a brief stand and were joined by some of the colliers of the district. Struggling to exist on low wages, faced with widespread dismissals, and excited by the unrest and riots of the Midlands and the north, they resolved 'that it would be better for workmen to be idle without a sufficient quantity of provisions, than to be toiling twelve or fifteen hours a day without the common necessaries of life'. The strike lasted hardly a week, dying away as soon as news arrived announcing that the men in the north had returned.[3]

At the outset of 1843 the Monmouthshire coal-owners renewed what had almost become their annual offensive on the wages of their colliers. This time the larger coal-owners were more united and more vigorous in the pursuit of their aim. Convinced that the drift of trade towards Cardiff could be stemmed only by a substantial lowering of prices, they combined their demand for lower wages with pressure upon the

[1] NLW Bute MSS., Box 70, vol. 7. Bute to Captain Smyth, 24 Sept. 1840; vol. 13. Bute to T. W. Booker, 28 Oct. 1840; *Cambrian*, 23 Aug. 1840; *Children's Employment*, p. 526.
[2] *Merlin*, 12 Mar. 1842; NLW Tredegar MSS., 40/55. S. Homfray to Octavius Morgan, 12 Mar. 1842. [3] *MG*, 20, 27 Aug. 1842.

Canal Company for reduced charges. The men were told that the reduction would mean steadier employment and a more stable level of earnings. At the same time the courts were widely used to secure convictions against the men for leaving without notice and new workers were brought from Staffordshire and Merthyr. The men countered by intimidating those who continued to work and by marching into Glamorgan to stop the collieries at Gelli-gaer and in the Aberdare valley, but in both these tactics they ran foul of the law. By the end of March the men were forced to admit defeat and accept the cut of 3d. per ton, the masters promising—as they had done several times before in moments of crisis—to abolish all truck.[1]

These had been years of deepening depression; from 1839 into 1843 the trend of prices was downwards. During the strike of 1842 a Monmouthshire newspaper had commented that it was unreasonable of the men to expect the same wage rates when the price of coal was 9s. 6d. as they had received when it had been 11s.[2] By the last quarter of 1843, however, the signs of recovery in the district were unmistakable and, for a time, no further general disputes arose. At the end of 1845 advances in wages were still being conceded by the employers but with growing reluctance. The house-coal colliers of the lower Rhondda—whose wages were regulated by the price of coal—were forced to strike in November before their employers would grant an increase to which they were entitled, and these men struck again in July 1846.[3]

By 1847 the gradual decline began to give way to a more rapid deterioration, particularly as the railway boom demand for iron had been largely spent. The attitude of the employers stiffened, and a bid for an advance, based on the rising cost of living, by the Monmouthshire colliers and ironworkers was defeated after a nine-week strike.[4] The lack of demand was

[1] *MG*.; *Merlin*, Jan.–Mar. 1843.
[2] *Merlin*, 26 Feb. 1842.
[3] *MG*, 5 Dec. 1845, 19 Sept. 1846.
[4] Ibid., 15 May, 5 June 1847.

reflected in irregular working, the Duffryn colliers being employed for only two weeks in every month.[1] Ignoring this falling market, the Monmouthshire colliers fruitlessly endeavoured to stem the flow of reductions by a further long strike in 1848.[2]

Monmouthshire, through its geographic position and owing to the large number of English immigrants it had absorbed, was the sector of the coalfield most exposed to English influences. These probably played some part in making it the focal point of the turbulence that marked the decade, but it seems likely that they were of less moment than the more strictly economic forces that were operating. During the canal era the rapid advance of the coal trade of Newport had been based partly on its privilege of freedom from the payment of duty on much of its coastwise shipments; after this was removed in 1831 Newport could for a time maintain its lead on the basis of its goodwill and established position. But the lead of Newport was undermined by the railway and dock improvements completed at Cardiff by 1841, together with the growth in the production of house coal at the Gelli-gaer and Lower Rhondda collieries. The coincidence of this improved competitive position of its rival port with a period of general industrial depression caused not only a decline in Newport's relative share of the house-coal trade but, in the early 1840's, a fall in the absolute level of this—the most important—branch of its trade.[3] As the productive capacity of the Monmouthshire house-coal collieries had been expanded during the good years from 1837 to 1839 the Monmouthshire owners had every incentive to try and reduce

[1] *MJ*, 15 May 1847.
[2] *MG*, 19 Feb., 11 Mar., 15 Apr. 1848.
[3] This is concealed in the figures of the total shipments from Newport which were rising during these years, but these included the growing shipments of steam coal. The coal-owners told the men's delegates in 1843 that the shipments of house coal had fallen from 549,951 tons in 1841 to 454,042 tons in 1842 and that the trend was still downwards. *Merlin*, 25 Mar. 1843. The owners' estimate of house-coal shipments for 1841 exceeded the official returns for all coal shipments from Newport for that year, nevertheless their general point was certainly true.

their costs of production and, in particular, their wage costs.[1] At the same time the competition amongst the owners for a diminishing share of the market probably accounts for the early success of the men in resisting this pressure. Even in 1843, when the depression was deepest and the owners most determined, the struggle was soon confined to the larger coal-owners, the smaller producers abandoning the demand for a reduction to take advantage of the quick gains that could be made while the strike lasted.

By the close of the decade the Monmouthshire industry had become adjusted to the deterioration in its relative position in the Welsh coal trade, the secular increase in demand easing the major difficulties of this transition. It was in the expanding steam-coal district of Aberdare that the next major dispute occurred. During the slow recovery of activity in 1849 the men had succeeded by piecemeal strikes in winning back a reduction enforced in the previous year. At the close of 1849, however, the employers determined to recover this ground: the increase in demand had been more than met by the expansion of output and was thus not reflected in prices,[2] while the employers also felt that the sudden piecemeal strikes by the men were damaging to trade. In November, accordingly, they introduced a new agreement. This was to be binding for a year; involved a reduction in the cutting price; adopted the ton of 2,640 lb. instead of that of 2,520 lb. as the basis for wages; and placed severe restrictions on the mobility of the men. To resist these onerous terms the men went on strike at the beginning of December 1849, staying out until mid-April 1850 before they were finally overwhelmed by distress and the large-scale introduction of 'strangers'. The final blow to the Aberdare colliers came at a mass meeting held on 1 April when delegates from the Rhondda and Monmouthshire house-coal collieries refused to join them in the

[1] The coal-owners were also trying to secure reductions in the charges made by the Monmouthshire Canal Company.
[2] The average price of steam coal f.o.b. Cardiff was 8s. 3d. in 1848, 8s. 9d. in 1849, 8s. 6d. in 1850. W. G. Dalziel, op. cit., p. 108c.

strike. No sooner had the Aberdare men capitulated than the Monmouthshire owners gave notice for a reduction of 2d. per ton which was accepted after a five-week strike.[1] From 1850 to the beginning of 1852 steam-coal prices continued to fall and a further reduction of 5 per cent. was imposed in February 1852. During the next two years prices rose rapidly and by the summer of 1853 the colliers had obtained advances totalling 30 per cent.[2] Although prices steadied after 1854 the demand for steam coal arising out of the Crimean War gave buoyancy to the industry and it was thus not until the crisis of 1857 that the owners made any general attempt to reduce wages. At the ironworks, which were largely dependent on the American market for rails and hence strongly affected by the American crisis, a cut of 20 per cent. was made and accepted by the colliers. The colliers in the Aberdare and Rhondda valleys, however, when they were given notice in November of a reduction of 15 per cent. were unconvinced that the fall in the price of coal was enough to justify so large a reduction and, partly motivated by a vague intention of demanding a sliding scale to regulate wages, went on strike. Shortly afterwards, faced by a similar demand for a reduction, the men of the sale-coal collieries of Monmouthshire also came out on strike. In the Aberdare valley the colliers returned on the owners' terms before the beginning of February 1858, and by the middle of February the Monmouthshire men, too, had accepted the reduction. The Rhondda house-coal colliers vainly prolonged the struggle for a further month when the employers decided to impose an extra cut of 5 per cent.[3]

There followed a decade free from general stoppages. There were a few short, piecemeal strikes in 1864, but generally,

[1] *MG*, Dec. 1849–Apr. 1850, 1, 8, 29 June, 6 July 1850.
[2] Ibid., 23 Sept 1853; W. G. Dalziel, op. cit., p. 108.
[3] Ibid., Dec. 1857–Mar. 1858; *CG*, Jan. Mar. 1858. The men declared that the strike 'was in support of a great principle, which has existed in the sale coal collieries for many years, that of having 2d. in the shilling on the price of coal for cutting'. *CG*, 9 Jan. 1858.

with the rising activity, the threat of a strike was enough to win for the men most of the ground they had lost six years earlier. Even the heavy reductions of 1868 were accepted by the steam-coal colliers without any general strike, the men being content to limit their opposition to the owners' efforts to introduce double-shift working, and the owners being unwilling to make a major issue of this alone. In the house-coal collieries of Monmouthshire, Caerphilly, and the Rhondda, where this additional factor did not apply, the colliers stood out for three months before accepting defeat. It was during the rise and fall of the boom of the early seventies, however, that the greatest conflicts occurred. The severe stresses this boom occasioned in the coal industry coincided with two other prime sources of dispute: the efforts to smash the first general trade union that the coalfield had experienced, and the determination of the coal-owners to level down their wage rates to those paid by the ironmasters, now powerful competitors in the coal market, to their colliers. This explosive combination of circumstances led to large-scale stoppages of twelve weeks in 1871, three months in 1873, and five months in 1875.

The frequency and bitterness of these struggles over wage rates become more intelligible when the general conditions under which the industry was operating are examined. As has already been seen, the general conditions of supply and demand caused the price of coal to oscillate within a fairly wide range, and these price fluctuations reacted on industrial relations in several ways. Long before the practice of sliding-scale agreements was formalized it was customary for wage rates to vary roughly in accordance with the price of coal. The wide fluctuations in coal prices were thus matched by similar movements in wage rates. The changes in the cutting rate were not only frequent—in the Aberdare valley it was changed twenty-two times between March 1848 and May 1875—but they were also of considerable magnitude. All but four of the thirteen advances in the rate granted during these years were of 10 per cent. each time; of the nine reductions seven were of the order of from 10 to 20 per cent.

The resistance of the men to such acute reductions was heightened by their knowledge that the level of their earnings —as opposed to rates—was likely to be reduced by instability of employment. There was the seasonal element—though this was most marked in the house-coal trade—and there were the days lost by the occasional mishaps to winding, pumping, or ventilating machinery. Above all, the organization of much of the trade depended on the output being loaded direct into railway wagons at the pit-head and sent straight to port for shipment: a delay in finding customers, in getting empty wagons returned to the colliery, a weather hold-up at the port—all could cause discontinuity of working. The extent of this under-employment, too, was accentuated by the part-time working that was typical of years of depression, the very years when reductions in wage rates were likely to be enforced.

The employers showed determination in pressing for wage reductions when prices were falling and in delaying increases when prices were rising because wages formed so large an element in the cost of production. How large this element was, whatever the size of the colliery, may be illustrated by a few examples. At the small Rhigos level in 1837 the wage paid for cutting the coal accounted for 1*s*. 6*d*. out of a total cost per ton for delivering coal at the level's mouth of 2*s*. 5*d*. In 1841 at the Gelli-gaer collieries, which included some of the largest in Glamorgan at the time, the cutting price was 1*s*. 5*d*. per ton when the pit-head cost was between 2*s*. 9*d*., where the coal was worked by level, and 3*s*. 0*d*. where shafts were necessary. Between 1851 and 1869, at Messrs. Vivian's Morfa colliery, where production varied from 86,000 to 167,000 tons a year, wages formed from 42 to 55 per cent. of the total cost; at their smaller Goytre and Brombill colliery— where the annual output ranged between 9,000 and 37,000 tons—the wage bill represented from 38 to 58 per cent. of the production costs. At Nevill's Box colliery, near Llanelly, the wage cost in the period from 1839 to 1850 ranged from one-half to three-quarters of the total cost of producing between 9,000 and 19,000 tons.[1] This importance of the labour element in total working costs not only made the employers reluctant to concede wage advances but also made the men quick to demand them. At times of rising coal prices the colliers were well aware that the other elements in the cost sheet only partially filled the gap between the sale price and the cutting price which they received.

While the conditions under which the industry operated were thus always liable to lead to general disputes over wages they were equally conducive to the emergence of strife at individual collieries. This was most apparent when a new colliery or a new seam was opened and when negotiations arose over the basic cutting price—the chief determinant both of the level of earnings and of the profitability of the colliery. Even where the area had already been widely opened up and it was agreed to accept the normal price paid for working that seam in the valley or in the neighbouring collieries as the basis for negotiation there was still room for disagreement. The identity of the seam and its correlation with seams worked elsewhere were not always beyond dispute; the seam could be thicker (or thinner) than usual, contain more (or less) clod, have a better (or worse) roof and floor, make less (or more) small coal on working, and so on. Apart from the cutting price, the rates for 'dead work'—for setting cogs (i.e. roof supports), ripping floor and roof, driving headings—had also to be settled. The variations in geological conditions, which complicated the initial bargaining, could often give rise to further disputes even after an agreement had been reached.

[1] CCL Bute MSS. XVI. 4. Expense of working coal at Rhigos, 1837; VII. 44. R. Beaumont to Lord Bute, 5 Mar. 1841. Vivian MSS. IA; Nevill MSS. XLVIII. The total cost referred to is the pit-head cost. Besides cutting, &c., costs, it includes, generally, the cost of underground haulage, keep of horses, timber, ropes, maintenance of equipment, royalties, and rates. The Nevill and Vivian accounts are the most carefully drawn out; the others quoted are more in the nature of expert estimates.

INDUSTRIAL RELATIONS

If—to mention a few possibilities—the seam met a fault, became broken or split, thinned out or increased in gradient, the change was reflected in the men's earnings and soon led to demands for 'allowances' to compensate for these changes, or even for an entirely new price-list.

While the clear divergence of interests between employers and employed over wage rates made these the principal cause of friction, there were, from time to time, numerous other issues which strained industrial relations. There can be little doubt, for instance, that these were embittered in the early 1840's by the connexion that existed in the minds of many of those in authority between combinations of colliers and Chartist activities.[1] Reporting to the Secretary of State on the extent of Chartism in Glamorgan in 1839 the Marquis of Bute in his capacity of Lord-Lieutenant of the county asserted that 'it is with us principally among the Colliers'.[2] The Chartist march on Newport, a few weeks after this was written, served only to confirm this impression. The extent to which the Monmouthshire colliers were implicated emerged from the depositions taken before the trial of Frost and his companions. Lord Bute's own inquiries plainly suggested that the colliers from parts of Glamorgan had also been involved: 'I have been sitting today with Mr. Phillips, the former Mayor of Newport, and I find that the impression there is that a good many men came from the Gelli-gaer Collieries, not many from Merthyr, but that there were a good many from the Rhondda Collieries and that these were some of the best armed and most violent of the Chartist army who attacked Newport.'[3] Two of the Gelli-gaer colliers Bute designated as

---

[1] 'You know my opinion', wrote the Marquis of Bute to one of the Glamorgan coal-owners and manufacturers, 'to be that the groundwork of Chartism is the Combination of workmen for regulating wages etc. Political agitators have laid hold of this frame in order to work their own schemes upon it, and in this shape the Mischief has been introduced into your part of the Kingdom from the North.' NLW Bute MSS., Box 70, vol. 13. Bute to T. W. Booker, 28 Oct. 1840.
[2] Ibid., Bute to Marquess of Normanby, 17 Oct. 1839.
[3] Ibid., Bute to T. W. Booker, 7 Dec. 1839.

'Delegates, Captains and Intimidators. Frost in Monmouthshire—except in being a more educated man—was not more dangerous than Giles, nor so audacious as William Owen.'[1]

Once the connexion between the colliers and Chartism had been established it was difficult to eradicate. The magistrates were urged to action,[2] and the coal-owners informed that it was 'if possible, even more your interest than your public duty to find them out'.[3] The resultant suspicion with which combinations of workmen were viewed was aggravated by the continuance of Chartist activity in the district. In particular, the establishment of two Chartist periodicals, *The Advocate and Merthyr Free Press* and the Welsh *Udgorn Cymru* (*Trumpet of Wales*) further strengthened the conviction that the workmen of the area were imbued with revolutionary principles.[4] In this atmosphere every colliers' strike became easily designated as a Chartist plot. 'I received a letter from Captain Napier this morning informing me that Mr. Powell's colliers had returned to their work in Glamorgan', Bute informed the Home Secretary during the strike of 1843, and continued, 'I trust we shall be able to foil the Chartists in their endeavours to cause a general strike of the Colliers.'[5] In these conditions the dismissal of strike leaders assumed a new respectability: when designated Chartists their discharge was

[1] NLW Bute MSS., Box 70, vol. 13. Bute to Marquess of Normanby, 4 Dec. 1839.
[2] Ibid., Bute to T. W. Booker, 7 Dec. 1839. Bute to Sir John Guest, 6 Nov. 1839.
[3] Ibid., Bute to Walter Coffin, 15 Nov. 1839.
[4] Ibid., Bute to Marquess of Normanby, 26 Sept. 1840. The Rebecca riots did not cause a similar confusion. When Nevill was told, at the height of these riots in Carmarthenshire, that a military force was to be stationed at Llanelly he objected that, 'as a Magistrate long and very intimately connected with this part of the County and as a Trader employ^g all the Copper men and 2/3rds of the colliers of Llanelly I can speak with confidence of their peaceable and orderly habits and I am most anxious that they sh^d not be induced to infer that I have any reason unknown as it must be to them to require other support than that of the Civil Force'. Nevill MSS. 9. R. J. Nevill to Col. Love, 27 July 1843.
[5] NLW Bute MSS., Box 70, vol. 13. Bute to Sir James Graham, 25 Mar. 1843.

a public duty.[1] The shadow cast by the events of November 1839, however, was long but not endless. It faded considerably when trade improved in 1844 and gradually strikes for a penny increase in the wage rate became less confused with blows against the established order of society.

The efforts of the owners to introduce new techniques and working methods were another fruitful source of tension. In the change-over from pillar and stall to long-wall working the chief obstacle was always the reluctance of the colliers—ever intensely conservative in their attitude to their craft—to accept technical innovation. Even the introduction of the safety lamp into gaseous mines encountered opposition; not, as was sometimes asserted, because the men had a reckless disregard for danger, but because its poorer light meant that they could cut less, and this, in the absence of an adequate adjustment of wage rates, reduced their earnings. The introduction of 'Billy Playfair' was beset with similar difficulties. This was a machine to separate the small (for which the steam-coal colliers were not paid) from the large coal and so to determine accurately the amount for which the collier was entitled to payment. Previously a colliery official had arbitrarily 'cropped' from the weight of each tram the amount of small that he estimated it contained.[2] The use of the machine, however, aroused the opposition of the men, who were suspicious of the accuracy of the scales and felt that the width between the bars, which determined the amount of small, was too great.

It was, however, the desire of the owners to introduce some

[1] *MG*, 16 July, 10 Sept. 1842. In September over 100 men, dismissed from the Merthyr ironworks, paraded the town with placards proclaiming 'In England, a free and Christian country, we are turned out to starve for being Chartists.' They were prevented from begging and told to apply for aid to the Guardians.

[2] This meant that the men often had to fill much more than the stipulated 2,520 lb. before they could get payment for a ton. 'We are cropped most unfairly. When our trams go up, they are cropped just as they like. We do not know who crops them and can get no satisfaction at all', stated one collier who complained that the men had to cut from 24 to 27 cwt. to the ton. *Merlin*, 18 Mar. 1843.

form of double-shift working that generated the greatest friction. The schemes suggested, based on the practice of the north of England, required the colliers to work in two shifts of about seven hours each, while the hauliers and other grades, including boys, starting two hours after the morning shift of hewers, would work one long shift of twelve hours. The strength of the employers' feeling on this issue sprang from the changing nature of mining enterprise in the area. With deepening pits working larger takings, and involving higher sinking costs and more powerful and expensive machinery for haulage, winding, and ventilation, the capital expenses of colliery enterprise steadily rose. The most obvious way to offset these enhanced capital costs was to spread them over a larger output, and this the double shift promised to do. With two cutting shifts a much greater output could be maintained without the expense of opening up new working faces, while the more rapid advance would reduce the amount of timber used. Above all, the two cutting shifts would still be serviced by the same number of hauliers and other grades working the single long shifts.

The owners who attempted to introduce double-shift working in the later 1860's, however, found the way to the attainment of these economies barred by the steadfast opposition of the men.[1] There were several reasons for this opposition.

[1] John Nixon, the chief advocate of the double shift, sent several of his colliers to the north of England to study the working of the system there but, even though these reported in its favour, he could not induce twenty out of more than 1,000 men he employed to give it a trial. Not all employers favoured the scheme. Both David Davis of Ferndale and George Elliot felt that it involved too serious an interference with the habits and comforts of the men. Elliot, however, hoped to produce much the same result as Nixon in a different way. He pointed out that each collier in Wales had up to 12 yards of face to himself, a distance that was occupied by five or six hewers in his native Durham. The Welsh method, he claimed, increased his working costs by £40,000 a year because of the much greater amount of face that had to be opened and maintained to secure a given production. Elliot proposed that three men should work in one stall. Acting on the advice of men more familiar with the Welsh collier than he was himself, he discussed the change fully with his men before introducing it; he also altered a demand for a wage reduction of 15 per cent. to one of 5 per cent. His men started working on the new plan, but stopped after the

The double shift involved a sharing of working places and the colliers, individualistic as workmen, were reluctant to have their working conditions and earnings partly dependent on others, albeit fellow colliers. In the steam-coal collieries in particular, coal that was undercut at the end of a working day was likely, under the pressure from the roof, to have fallen and be ready for loading by the next morning. A collier would be reluctant for another man to reap the benefit of this. The double shift threatened to deprive the collier of leisure at the most convivial hours since the first shift would have started at 4 a.m. and the second would not have finished till 7 p.m. Also, since most households included lodgers besides the men of the family, it involved a considerable extra burden for the women-folk as meals and baths would be spread over a much longer period. Moreover, the colliers, though this was never explicitly stated, were apprehensive about the effects of the extra production on prices and, through them, on wage rates.

While these considerations largely determined the attitudes of the employers and of the men to the double shift, much of the argument about it centred on the issue of safety.[1] The employers argued that the double shift not only reduced by half the number of hewers likely to be endangered in the event of an explosion, but also, by reducing the length of face and the number of road- and air-ways to be maintained for a given output, facilitated inspection and ventilation and thus minimized the risk of explosions and roof-falls. Against this

colliers had held a mass meeting. They stated that they preferred to work at the full reduction rather than alter a custom against the general feeling in the district. *Double and Single Shift Working Compared* (Aberdare, 1868). Evidence of George Elliot, *Royal Commission on Trade Unions. Sixth Report, P.P.* 1867–8 (3980–II) xxxix; evidence of George Elliot, *Select Committee on the Dearness of Coal*, 1873.

[1] After the Ferndale explosion of 9 Nov. 1867, when 178 men were killed, Nixon advocated the double shift in a letter to the *Mining Journal*. Nixon also issued a pamphlet under the title *The Single Shift System the Cause of Double the Loss of Life* (Cardiff, 1867). The miners, in reply, issued the pamphlet *Double and Single Shift Working Compared* (1868). Nixon was sincere in his use of the safety argument, but the colliers believed that greater safety depended not on the double shift but on the greater willingness of the owners to incur the expense and take the trouble it required.

the men argued, principally, that these advantages were offset by the inconvenience of the greater congestion and by the increased danger arising from the more rapid working of gaseous seams. Even if their argument was not convincing, the men, by taking their stand upon the issue of safety, made it difficult for their employers to force the double shift on them. The consequent exasperation and frustration of the owners was matched by the conviction of the men that their employers were being insensitive to their comfort and intent on securing economies by attacking their standards. A few years later a mines inspector pronounced the epitaph on these early attempts to introduce the double shift: the men 'will not have it; utterly reject it'.[1]

The atmosphere of antagonism and suspicion engendered by the numerous possibilities of conflict in the industry was, moreover, accentuated by the tactics that were employed by both sides when disputes broke out. In almost every general strike and in many of the isolated individual disputes it was a standard reaction of the owners to introduce outside labour to weaken the men's position. During the Monmouthshire strike of 1840 the owners seem merely to have advertised for 1,000 colliers;[2] in the strike of 1871 the method was less haphazard, the Owners' Association utilizing the services of an agent—Paul Roper—to recruit men, paying him 6s. per head for those he obtained and paying the cost of transporting the strangers from Staffordshire and Cornwall.[3] Often the various firms took their own action, the owners of the Abercarn colliery, for example, bringing men from Neath during the 1850 strike, while Thomas Powell, in the 1857 strike, secured coal-trimmers from Newport and Cardiff.[4] But however the operation was conducted, it usually inflamed the men and

---

[1] Evidence of Lionel Brough, *Select Committee on Dearness of Coal*, 1873.
[2] *Cambrian*, 25 July 1840; *MG*, 25 July 1840.
[3] A. Dalziel, op. cit., pp. 85–90; *MG*, 5, 12, 19 Aug. 1871.
[4] *MG*, 10, 24 Aug. 1850; *CG*, 2 Jan. 1858.

frequently led to riot and violence. In March 1843, for instance, when the agent of Thomas Powell's Gelli-gaer colliery brought men from Merthyr to work the pits during a strike, these men were subjected to continual hooting and jeering by the villagers for the two days that they worked. When the agent returned with a further batch of blacklegs he was met by a threatening and noisy mob, given half-an-hour to get rid of the intruders and forced to promise to bring no more.[1] When Hezechiah Morgan and his three brothers came from Monmouthshire to replace strikers at Powell's Dehewy colliery they were met by some 150 colliers and women who loudly demonstrated outside the house in which they took refuge. As they were not actually injured, however, the jury at the Quarter Sessions acquitted the two men arrested for their part in the affray. Nevertheless, despite the opinion of the jury that the brothers had no reasonable cause to fear maltreatment, it is not difficult to believe the statement of one of the brothers that 'people are still afraid to go there to work'.[2] Hostility easily passed from noisy derision into actual rough usage. When English workmen were brought in during the strike of 1850 they were beaten by gangs of men armed with sticks and, in addition, all their furniture was destroyed.[3] The reception accorded to the men brought from Ebbw Vale to break a strike at Abercarn in 1861 started with hooting and shouting, passed quickly to the hurling of stones and ended with the destruction of the houses in which the blacklegs were quartered.[4]

The effects of the tactics employed by the owners and men are hard to assess. The occasions when the importation of outside labour during strikes led to violence are those which have left most records and there is less information available

[1] *MG*, 25 Mar 1843.
[2] Ibid., 24 Oct. 1845.
[3] *Report on State of Population in Mining Districts*, 1850, p. 71. The Aberdare colliers had threatened to pull up the railway lines if the Taff Vale Railway did not stop bringing 'strangers' into the valley *MJ*, 16 Feb. 1850.
[4] *MG*, 21 Sept. 1861, 5 Apr. 1862. Two of the men concerned were sentenced to twelve months' imprisonment.

for the instances when the presence of strike-breakers was merely resented but not vigorously opposed. Certainly these events left a feeling of bitterness which lingered long after the strikes which had occasioned them were settled. There were the memories of the prosecutions of the men who were arrested as a result of the disturbances, while the presence of those new-comers who remained in the valleys, and were accepted only slowly by the close-knit mining communities, served as a constant reminder of the divergence of interest between the collier and his master.

A further weapon in the owners' armoury was the discharge note. This was a certificate given to each worker who satisfactorily completed his contract of service at a colliery and which had to be produced before he could be engaged at another pit. While it could serve as a legitimate check on colliers who left work without notice and as a certificate of competence for a collier seeking work, it could also be used in a more oppressive way as a device to victimize individual colliers and to break strikes. Some informal agreement about the use of the note already existed between employers before 1841. 'I am afraid', wrote Lord Bute in that year, 'that within the last five or six years, viz. since the great increase in demand for Coal and Iron, the managers of Ironworks and Collieries have admitted men without enquiring into their characters, and without looking for the marks upon their discharges according to the former understanding.'[1]

Even before the establishment of formal Employers' Associations such agreements were not without their effect. A Monmouthshire collier complaining about truck to the Children's Employment Commissioner said that 'if a man gets a pound in debt he can't get his discharge, and it is useless to attempt to get work without a discharge'.[2] In 1843 John Owen, a Monmouth solicitor, criticized the employers for leaving too much to their 'gaffers', saying that if any man

[1] NLW Bute MSS., Box 70, vol. 13. Bute to Sir Charles Shaw, 15 Feb. 1841.
[2] *Children's Employment*, p. 531.

went to law against his employer he was sacked. His discharge was not withheld, but a black mark was put against his name and his character transmitted to the other 'gaffers'.[1] A decade later John Lewis, a miner, related how, after he had won a truck case with Owen's help, he received a discharge, but it had a notch in it. A master told him he could have work 'but as soon as he saw my discharge, he said "No, we do not want you"'. Lewis was unemployed for nine months, had to enter the workhouse, and succeeded in getting work only after he had, on Owen's advice, cut the notch off his discharge.[2]

During times of unrest the discharge note acquired an added significance, particularly because it was taken for granted that 'agitators' and strike leaders would be victimized. It was not without reason that the delegates of the men, when negotiating the terms of settlement of the strike of 1843 in Monmouthshire, insisted that no one should be dismissed simply because he had played a prominent part in the dispute.[3] Both after the strike of 1850 and after that of 1857 it was asserted that the men's ringleaders would certainly not be employed again; referring to the latter dispute, one colliery overman stated that 'No man going out on strike had a discharge. . . . It is the practice not to give discharges in Aberdare on such occasions.'[4]

After the strike at Abercarn in 1861 had once more drawn attention to the discharge note one newspaper commented 'let the Company withhold this discharge, and the collier might just as well try to work his passage to the moon as attempt to obtain employment on these Welsh hills'.[5] This was undoubtedly an exaggeration. James Darby, for instance, who said that he had been sacked from Risca colliery after he had complained of the danger from gas, had not been

[1] *MG*, 18 Mar., 1 Apr. 1843. The Truck Commissioners reported in 1871 that any workman who prosecuted was liable to be dismissed and black-listed.
[2] Evidence of John Lewis, *Select Committee on Payment of Wages Bill*, 1854.
[3] *MG*, 1 Apr. 1843. [4] Ibid., 30 Mar. 1850, 6 Mar. 1858.
[5] *The Reformer and South Wales Times*, 27 Sept. 1861. (Our attention was drawn to this reference by Mr. A. L. Trott.)

given a discharge note yet had obtained work at the Abercarn colliery.[1] Also, when a strike occurred at Coedcae colliery in 1867 most of the strikers found work in other collieries, many of them perishing in the Ferndale explosion.[2] Even during the strike of 1871, when the owners had an association of some strength, their attempts to prevent men from finding employment at non-associated collieries and ironworks were a complete failure. While the possession of a valid discharge no doubt opened out wider opportunities to the collier seeking work, the lack of unity and the competition for labour among employers reduced its value as an instrument of repression. The principal heritage from the history of these early years was the colliers' lasting suspicion of the discharge note; a suspicion which led to the defeat of any subsequent attempts to impose it.

The employers also tried to increase their hold over the men by making free use of the law courts. Until 1875 breach of contract by manual workers constituted a criminal offence. In the Welsh collieries the normal contract—or the custom where no written agreement existed—required a month's notice on either side for its termination. High feelings, impetuosity, and ignorance frequently led the men to strike without giving this notice and on such occasions, more often than not, the owners brought some of the strikers before the courts.[3] Men so charged were liable to a sentence of up to three months' imprisonment but, as the motive for the prosecutions was more to bring strikes to an end than to secure convictions, the owners usually offered to withdraw the charges if the men would agree to return to work. Nevertheless, while neither the requirement of a month's notice nor its enforcement was harsh, the frequent recourse of the owners

[1] *CG*, 26 Jan. 1861.   [2] *MG*, 1 Feb. 1868.
[3] For one example, typical of many, see *MJ*, 20, 27 Apr., 11 May 1867; *MG*, 25 Jan. 1868. The first eight colliers charged had their wages confiscated; later twenty-six men were sentenced to fourteen days hard labour. W. P. Roberts appealed, mainly on the grounds that no one had signed the colliery rules, but the appeal was dismissed.

to the law served merely to impair industrial relations. The men resented the inequalities of the master and servant law and the possibility that the unpaid magistracy, drawn from the same class as their employers, might, even if unconsciously, not administer justice fairly.

When faced with a charge of leaving without notice, intimidation, or riot, the colliers of Monmouthshire and East Glamorgan invariably, until his sudden death in 1863, turned for help to John Owen. Setting up as a solicitor in Monmouth in 1828, and later adding an office at Abergavenny, Owen soon acquired a local reputation as the 'Poor Man's Friend'.[1] Inevitably, cases involving colliers and miners came to form a large part of his practice and, by the vigour, persistence, and skill with which he conducted them, he gained the full confidence of the men. 'The general nature of my practice', Owen himself said, 'is arranging differences between working men and their employers.'[2] He was chosen by the Monmouthshire colliers to present their grievances to the owners at a meeting held to negotiate a settlement of the 1843 strike.[3] Colliers outside his own county, too, were soon in search of his services. In 1847 he was said to be the legal representative of the Rhondda colliers' union and two years later he was also appearing on behalf of the Aberdare colliers.[4] Owen's prominence as legal adviser to the colliers naturally exposed him to the accusation that he was stirring up the trouble-making element among them. Such a charge, however, was unfounded. The view of the Glamorgan magistrates that Owen's influence on the men was wholly salutory[5] lends credence to his claim that he never interfered in a strike unless his opinion was asked, and that then he always urged moderation on the men. 'When I first went amongst them', he asserted in a

[1] *MG*, 17 Apr. 1863. Owen, this obituary notice stated, had often given unpaid professional help and pecuniary assistance to people 'too poor to pay, yet thought by him to be unfairly accused'.
[2] Evidence of J. G. H. Owen, *Select Committee on Payment of Wages Bill*, 1854.   [3] *Merlin*, 25 Mar. 1843.
[4] *MG*, 18 Sept. 1847, 3 Nov. 1849.   [5] *Cambrian*, 8 Apr. 1843.

letter to the press in 1843, 'riot and disturbance extended through the coal districts of this and the adjoining county of Glamorgan. I told them I could not assist them unless they were peaceable, and kept within the pale of the law.'[1]

Owen's pleadings in the courts met with some measure of success. In 1846, for example, he succeeded in obtaining compensation of £120 from the magistrates who had committed seven Rhondda colliers to Cardiff gaol on informal and incorrect warrants of arrest.[2] In 1849, when some of Insole's men were being prosecuted, Owen's defence—that the men who had signed the contract could not have understood that it not only bound them to work for a year without a strike but also stipulated that all disputes between them and the employers were to be settled by the employers—led to the cancelling of this contract after it had been referred to arbitration.[3] To defend the collier was one thing; to attack the owners and their agents, however, was another, as Owen's experience in truck cases soon led him to discover.

'So far as the truck system is concerned', Owen wrote in 1843, 'I have found it much easier to convict a poor man for going into a gentleman's preserve and stealing a pheasant, than it is to convict a gentleman for charging a poor man 11*d*. for a pound of bacon that is only worth 6*d*.'[4] Owen had good cause for disgust. In the previous year, for example, out of seven truck cases he had undertaken he had been able to secure a conviction in only one, most of the remainder being dismissed when the magistrates upheld some technical objection to the charge.[5] There had been little change in the position a decade later. Truck existed mainly in forms which did not contravene the letter of the law, but even where solicitors considered that the facts justified prosecution their efforts

---

[1] *Merlin*, 8 Sept. 1843.   [2] *MG*, 19 Sept. 1846.
[3] Ibid., 11 Aug. 1849. For one of the later examples of the defence of the colliers by Owen, see *MG*, 1 Jan. 1862. In addition to his court cases Owen also frequently appeared at inquests on behalf of the relatives of men who had been killed in accidents.   [4] *Merlin*, 8 Sept. 1843.
[5] See issues of *MG* and *Merlin*, 30 July–17 Sept. 1842.

usually ended in failure. By most of the magistrates on the hills, Owen told the Committee of 1854, 'it is not considered honest to prosecute an information for truck'. Another solicitor, Charles James of Merthyr, commented on the 'extreme particularity' required in drawing up an information as 'you always in a truck case have a very wealthy company to meet, who bring counsel down'. He had lost a case against the Rhymney Iron Company concerning a coal agent, David Humphreys, who, on being given a list of names by the pay clerk, called men to him and told them that they did not deal enough at the company shop. It could not be proved that Humphreys, in giving orders about the shop, acted as an agent for the company: his authority, in the eyes of the Court of Queen's Bench if not in those of the men, was confined to giving orders about work in the colliery.[1]

The colliers could not fail to contrast the effective use that their employers made of the law courts with their own lack of success when they had recourse to them in their struggle against truck. Even if they were mistaken, as H. A. Bruce, a former stipendiary magistrate of Merthyr, asserted that they were, in attributing the rarity of convictions 'to the leaning of the magistrates towards the course of the rich and powerful' rather than to the imperfections of the law,[2] the result of their experience tended to increase their belief that their main hope for securing redress of their grievances lay in the strength of their own trade unions.

Nevertheless strong trade unionism was slow to develop. This was only partly a reflection on the organizing abilities of the Welsh workmen. Their numerous friendly societies and their voluntary exertions to build and maintain their chapels led the English manager of Dowlais to comment that 'The Welsh . . . have great capacity for organization and self-

[1] Evidence of Owen, and of James, *Select Committee on Payment of Wages Bill*, 1854.
[2] *Hansard*, 3rd series, vol. 13c, 16 Feb. 1864. Payment of Wages Bill.

government.'[1] In the field of industrial organization, however, there were several obstacles to overcome. The geographical division of the area into deep valleys between which intercommunication was difficult retarded any unified growth.[2] Another force creating disunity was the varied quality of the coal of the area. The South Wales coal industry consisted virtually of three broad industries dealing with anthracite, steam, and bituminous coals respectively, each confronted with its own market conditions, customs, and labour problems. There was also the influence of the existence of a large body of colliers at the ironworks, whose wages were determined by the variations in the iron market rather than by those in the coal market and whose employment was also markedly more regular than that of the sale-coal colliers. This divergence of interests was a disintegrating factor whenever efforts were made to establish strong unions. There was, finally, the difficulty of absorbing into the coalfield large numbers of immigrants, many of whom came from non-industrial districts where no organized trade unionism existed.

A unity that was slow to appear spontaneously the colliers sometimes tried to impose by force. The brutal methods employed during an earlier period by the Scotch Cattle to terrorize colliers who continued at work on terms unacceptable to the majority lingered in Monmouthshire into the 1840's.[3] The funerals of the relatives of the men who worked during the Aberdare strike of 1850 were 'saluted . . . with the most heartless yells and laughter and by discordant sounds from the beating of frying pans, kettles etc.' Two of the

[1] Evidence of G. T. Clark, *Royal Commission on Trade Unions, Fifth Report*, 1867–8.
[2] The Amalgamated Association of Miners had a large number of small geographic districts as the basis of its organization in South Wales. 'Small districts were the most workable in South Wales, and the most calculated to increase the members', the Union conference at Walsall was told in 1872. *CG*, 4 Oct. 1872.
[3] See, for example, *Merlin*, 25 Feb. 1843. In 1847, at Coalbrook Vale in Monmouthshire, the house of a worker who accepted a wage reduction was wrecked and a young child 'brutally dashed against the wall'. *MG*, 5 June 1847.

blackleg colliers were shot at and a third died from wounds received when a few pounds of powder, wrapped in a sock and with a fuse attached, were thrown into his bedroom after he had been warned several times 'by the union' to cease work.[1] These instances of brutality serve as a strong commentary on the weakness of the colliers' organizations at this time. Nevertheless, even if there was no sustained and widespread unionism, some brief unity and degree of combination emerged at times of crisis. The determined and recurrent resistance of the Monmouthshire house-coal colliers in the 1840's, for example, would have been impossible without some form of organization. The *Monmouthshire Merlin* asserted that the men had a union which distributed strike pay,[2] but whatever the truth of this the men were sufficiently unified to act together, to bring out those who continued working, to appoint delegates to state their case, and to secure the services of Owen. In 1847 all the Rhondda colliers—except those at Dinas—were stated to be in a union. Each colliery had its own committee of management and sent delegates to general meetings, the finances being raised by a levy of 1*d*. per week from every man and boy.[3] Under the stimulus of the strike of 1850 the Aberdare colliers also came together to form the 'Glamorgan Union of Colliers', which was to have branches at every colliery where there were at least forty colliers and a subscription of 4*d*. per month. Perhaps in view of the attempt of the owners to impose a contract that was to be binding for a year, the union declared—rather ambiguously—that its aim was 'to prevent all kinds of strikes, especially all kinds of sudden strikes, except when justice on the part of the workmen calls for them'.[4]

There is nothing to suggest that these combinations, the response to periods of crisis, were other than ephemeral. The efforts made, too, from time to time by delegates from England

---

[1] *State of Population in Mining Districts*, 1850, pp. 70-71.
[2] *Merlin*, 18 Mar. 1843.
[3] *MG*, 18 Sept. 1847, 11 Aug. 1849.   [4] Ibid., 16 Mar. 1850.

to establish a more durable organization in South Wales achieved only a transient success before the end of the 1860's. The visit of Twiss to Wales in 1831, for example, to urge the cause of the Friendly Society of Coal Mining was remembered chiefly because he had absconded with the union funds. In Monmouthshire in 1850 two 'strangers' sentenced to one month's imprisonment for breach of contract claimed to be organizers for a national miners movement.[1] Their activity was probably on behalf of the Miners' Association of Great Britain which under the forceful leadership of Martin Jude flared up briefly in that year after its collapse in 1848.[2]

The attentions that English unionists paid to South Wales in the 1860's, however, were less fitful. Welsh delegates had been present at the Leeds Conference of 1863 at which the Miners' National Union, the product of several years of devoted work by Alexander Macdonald, had been set up.[3] The connexion with this union, however, was broken off in the following year owing to dissatisfaction caused by the refusal of the Executive Council to grant support during a truck case at Blaina and by restlessness over Macdonald's limited and pacific policies. Contact with England was none the less maintained, at first through the short-lived National Association of Practical Miners that was formed by the break-away elements from the Miners' National Union, and later by visits paid to South Wales by prominent English unionists.[4] Roberts, the 'Miners' Attorney General', appeared in the district to demonstrate the advantages of union by defending the colliers in the courts during 1865, and Pickard and Halliday, officials of the Miners' National Union, came to represent the widows and children at the inquest on the Ferndale explosion of 1867.[5]

Despite this, for five years after the break with the Miners' National Union in 1864, such combination as existed had only

[1] *Merlin*, 15 June 1850.
[2] S. and B. Webb, *History of Trade Unionism* (1920 edn.), pp. 182, 299.
[3] *CG*, 14 Nov. 1863. [4] Ibid., 19 Nov. 1864.
[5] Ibid., 22 Apr. 1865; *MG*, 21 Dec. 1867, 1 Feb. 1868.

a narrow local basis, and there was little sign of the existence of formal unions with a permanent organization financed by regular contributions. In 1866 John Griffith, a Rhondda collier, stated that 'we did try to organize ourselves but we saw it was useless, and it all went abroad. The men would not come together and would not join.'[1] A year or so later George Elliot commented on the absence of organized unions in South Wales: 'I do not think that they have any union except the spontaneous combination which arises if there is the least interference with them.'[2] The opinion of the Truck Commissioners, too, was that trade unionism had no hold among the miners and colliers of South Wales. In 1869, however, a fresh impulse towards unionism came from England with the formation in Lancashire of Thomas Halliday's Amalgamated Association of Miners by the more militant wing of the Miners' National Union. In August, after a visit from Halliday himself, the colliers of Monmouthshire and Glamorgan, feeling more enthusiasm for an organization that was prepared to deal with the issue of wages, agreed to form a union and join the Association.[3] In the relatively unorganized district of South Wales there was ample scope for the union to grow in strength; a strength that was to be tested to the limit between 1871 and 1875 by three major disputes.

More free from violence than the earlier rifts in industrial relations, these struggles were nevertheless bitter. In the course of them the issue of the disparity between the wage rates paid to colliers by the ironmasters and by the sale-coal owners assumed a new prominence; a stronger Association of owners was born; leaders who were to dominate the councils of employers and employed for the next generation emerged; and settlement was reached only when it was agreed that a sliding scale be adopted as the regulator of wage rates.

[1] Evidence of John Griffith, *Select Committee on Mines*, 1866.
[2] Evidence of George Elliot, *Royal Commission on Trade Unions, Sixth Report*, 1867-8.
[3] *CG*, 20 Aug. 1869; *MG*, 4 Dec. 1869.

XI

INDUSTRIAL RELATIONS (*CONTINUED*)

THE most potent cause of association among the owners was the need to present a united front in their dealings with the men. Joint action of an informal nature was doubtless a frequent accompaniment of large-scale strikes or lock-outs, but only slowly was this formalized by the establishment of permanent organizations for this purpose. The ironmasters, long accustomed to consult each other on trade matters, set the pattern. Although their combination for the regulation of prices and output that had functioned during the first quarter of the nineteenth century[1] was not revived, they met as occasion warranted to discuss matters of wage policy and labour control. At a meeting in London in 1847, for example, they agreed to support each other in resisting further demands for wage advances, undertaking to contribute iron, in quantities proportionate to their own output, to fulfil the orders of any firms affected by strikes, to employ no new workmen unless they possessed a written discharge, and to employ none of the men involved in a strike. Their success on this occasion was celebrated at a dinner in the following year and a presentation of plate was made to Samuel Homfray, the chairman of their meetings.[2] In 1853, too, the Merthyr ironmasters agreed to support the Dowlais Iron Company, in its resistance to a demand for a 10 per cent. increase by its colliers, by subsidizing Dowlais to the extent of £1,350 or 1,350 tons of iron a week.[3]

During the 1860's, however, even on the restricted topic of wage changes, unanimity was rarely achieved. The chief

[1] T. S. Ashton, *Iron and Steel in the Industrial Revolution* (Manchester, 1924), pp. 177–8.   [2] *MG*, 20 Mar. 1847, 5 Aug. 1848.
[3] Dowlais MSS., Section C, Box 5. Minutes of Meeting, 26 July 1853.

obstacle, generally, was that some of the ironmasters were deeply involved in the coal trade and found it difficult to impose reductions on their colliers if the sale-coal owners were not following a similar course. Both in 1861 and in 1866 the unity of the ironmasters foundered on the problem of reducing the pay of the colliers. In 1861 when wages were reduced in the iron industry but not at the steam-coal collieries Richard Fothergill of the Aberdare Ironworks refrained from reducing the wages of his colliers. This defection led G. T. Clark of the Dowlais Iron Company to comment that 'having failed so signally in acting together we had better, now and in future, act separately'.[1] Five years later the ironmasters agreed that 'Fothergill's Aberdare Colliers (not his Plymouth) and Crawshay Bailey's Aberaman Colliers are excluded from any notice of reduction at the present moment, as owing to their situation in the midst of the sale-coal Collieries, the reduction could not now there be carried', and the Dowlais Company also decided to exempt its colliers.[2] The wages policy of the ironmasters was thus exposed to a double complication; the course of action of some was guided primarily by the signpost of the price of iron, while that of others, owing to their participation in the sale-coal trade or to the proximity to their works of sale-coal collieries, depended more on the price of coal. There is, accordingly, every reason to accept the statement of G. T. Clark that, although a South Wales Iron Masters' Society existed, 'it has not worked particularly well'.[3]

It was in the early 1860's that the coal-owners turned to

---

[1] Dowlais MSS., Section C, Box 5. G. T. Clark to R. Fothergill, 15 Apr. 1861. Fothergill wrote that 'it has not been our custom to reduce the wages of our colliers unless supported by the Coal Trade, seeing that we sell more than half the coal we raise'. Fothergill to Clark, 22 May 1861.

[2] Crawshay MSS., Box 7. H. A. Withers to Wm. Crawshay, 28 June 1866. A year earlier, in a similar situation, Crawshay wrote: 'I do not intend to reduce the Colliers if Dick Fothergill does not.' Wm. Crawshay to R. T. Crawshay, 19 Jan. 1865.

[3] Evidence of G. T. Clark, *Royal Commission on Trade Unions. Fifth Report*, 1867–8.

formal association, the steam-coal proprietors resolving, at a meeting held at the Windsor Hotel, Cardiff, on 14 March 1864, to form the Aberdare Steam Collieries Association. The objects of this Association were 'the care of all matters connected with the working of the Steam Coal of the district' and 'the protection and benefit of the trade generally'. This organization was undoubtedly formed partly in response to the more active interest the men were evincing in trade unionism and to the numerous demands they were making during the period of active trade in 1863 and 1864. That its primary function was to lie in the field of industrial relations was confirmed both by the resolutions of the initial meeting and by the careful Deed of Association that was drawn up subsequently. The Association was provided with funds by a levy based on the tonnage of large coal raised by each colliery as determined by the various parish returns. The amount of each levy was decided as occasion arose, but as security for payment each member had to give a promissory note, payable on demand, for an amount equivalent to 3d. per ton. The funds were to be used to cover the general expenses of the Association and to compensate any member for loss of profit and other expenses that arose out of any stoppage that he suffered through resisting, with the prior approval of the Association, the demands of his workmen. A member qualifying for compensation had the option of claiming payment either in coal or in cash. In the event of any member failing to provide his share of the requisite coal or cash levy his promissory note was to be cashed and used instead.[1]

Several considerations made the Association a formidable organization. The various rights and obligations of the members were clearly set out in a detailed and binding Deed of Association; its membership, confined to the Aberdare valley, was geographically compact, and included—in the Powell Duffryn Company, Nixon's and David Davis—several of the most influential firms in the industry; and its members were

[1] W. G. Dalziel, op. cit., pp. 3–5.

working the most famous of the Welsh steam coals. Nevertheless, the restricted scope of its membership was a fundamental source of weakness. Its eleven members controlled twenty-one collieries producing, in 1863, 1·6 million tons or just under 15 per cent. of the total output of the coalfield, and even in the market for steam coal Aberdare in the late 1860's was being strongly challenged by the developing Rhondda valleys. In 1870 this weakness was partially remedied by the reconstitution of the Association as the South Wales Steam Collieries Association to include some of the most important producers in the Rhondda valleys. Even so, its membership comprised only thirteen firms controlling twenty-six collieries with an output of just over 2 million tons, still only a bare 15 per cent. of the production of the coalfield.[1]

The steam-coal owners were not, however, the only group of employers that was mobilizing to counter the spread of unionism during the sixties. The Rhondda house-coal owners were also active. In June 1866, when food prices were rising, the house-coal colliers agitated strongly for a wage increase; their employers, with an uneasy eye on the disordered state of the money market that had followed the failure of Overend, Gurney and Co. the month before, were convinced that the time had come for a reduction. To strengthen their hand in this situation the owners resolved to form the South Wales Bituminous Collieries Association, basing its organization on that already adopted by the steam-coal owners.[2] There is no clear evidence that this body remained in existence as a formal organization, but the house-coal owners appear to have acted in concert on numerous occasions in the ensuing years.

These different groups of employers were to be brought together by their experiences during the major stoppages that marked the early 1870's. In 1871 the price of coal began to rise sharply; at the same time the coal-owners resisted a

[1] W. G. Dalziel, op. cit., pp. 6, 8.
[2] *MG*, 16, 23 June 1866.

demand for a wage advance which the ironmasters had already granted. For some time the coal-owners had been becoming increasingly uneasy over the higher wage rates which prevailed in their pits compared with those paid by the ironmasters to their colliers. The main justification for this difference—the greater irregularity of work in the sale-coal collieries—lost its relevance as soon as the ironmasters began to invade the coal market on a significant scale. The coal-owners now saw only that the labour cost of some of their competitors was distinctly lower than their own and became anxious to eradicate this difference. As the disparity remained even after the ironmasters had given a 5 per cent. advance the coal-owners decided to impose a 5 per cent. reduction. Encouraged by Halliday, the President of the A.A.M., the men came out on strike on 1 June 1871.[1]

The twelve weeks dispute that ensued was a test of strength both for the Union of the men and for the Association of the steam-colliery owners. Although the finances of the Union made nonsense of Halliday's excessive promise of 10s. a week strike pay,[2] and although the resistance of the men was aided more by their ability to get work at the ironmasters' pits than by the A.A.M., the union none the less emerged from the conflict greatly strengthened. Its financial assistance, though small, had played some part and had been distributed to all— unionists and non-unionists alike—and had impressed all with the need for greater funds. The union executive had also done much to make the owners' attempts to introduce black-legs unsuccessful and had fostered a wider degree of solidarity among the men by impressing on those still at work that 'should we be obliged to go to work at the reduction, you may depend on it that all those that are now working at the advance will be reduced also'.[3] Above all the owners were

[1] *CG*, 26 May 1871; *MG*, 22 Apr., 3 June 1871.
[2] In the twelve weeks of strike the men received only £1. 5s. 7d. each. *MJ*, 23 Sept. 1871.
[3] AAM manifesto dated 29 June 1871, quoted in A. Dalziel, op. cit., pp. 51–52. It was stated that the house-coal colliers were devoting 3s. in the pound

induced to submit the dispute to arbitration, as the men desired, and the final settlement not only avoided the reduction that the owners demanded but gave the men a 2½ per cent. advance—half the advance they had requested. This favourable result really rested on the considerable revival in trade and on the disharmony between the ironmasters and coal-owners, but it was the union that reaped the harvest. By the time of the annual conference of the A.A.M. in October 1871, held significantly at Merthyr, the fillip that the struggle had given to the union was abundantly clear. In Aberdare alone membership increased from 310 in February to over 6,000 in July and other areas exhibited a similar expansion.[1] The boom conditions of 1872-3 enabled the A.A.M. to consolidate its position and by the beginning of 1873 its membership in South Wales was probably at least 30,000 and still rising.[2]

The dispute, however, had also demonstrated the solidarity of the Association of the steam-coal owners. All the associated firms, together with two non-members, adhered firmly to the decision to resist the demands of the men and to make no separate settlement. The coal-owners, too, by conceding an advance of only 2½ per cent. compared with the 5 per cent. granted by the ironmasters, had reduced the wage differential slightly. This gain they endeavoured to perpetuate by a clause in the strike settlement which stipulated that in future the sale-coal colliers' wage rates were to vary only with changes in the rates paid—not simply to the colliers—but to all employees at the ironworks. Nevertheless, the strike had also revealed some of the weaknesses of the owners' organization. Their Association controlled some 75 per cent. of the output of steam coal from the Aberdare and Rhondda valleys, but the market had received considerable quantities during the

of their wages to help the steam-coal colliers on strike. *MG*, 24 June 1871. The colliers at steam pits still working also refused to fill trucks belonging to members of the Owners' Association.

[1] A. Dalziel, op. cit., p. 77.
[2] W. G. Dalziel, op. cit., p. 171.

strike not only from the other sale-coal collieries in these valleys and from the Monmouthshire and the north of England steam-coal collieries, but from the ironworks pits, where large numbers of the strikers were also given work.[1] The power and funds of the Association were well-fitted to deal with strikes restricted to one or a few collieries in its own region, but for a large-scale stoppage a wider support was needed in face of the growing power of the men's union.

The terms of settlement of the 1871 strike produced merely a short period of uneasy peace. The colliers were restive because they could not secure full advantage of the sharp rise in coal prices which soon took place and which greatly outstripped the rise in the price of iron. The union leaders, however, had been closely associated with the negotiations leading to the settlement and felt bound to oppose any unilateral renunciation of its terms by the men once it had become clear that the coal-owners would not accede to any relaxation of them. The agreement was thus still in force when, at the end of 1872, a temporary recession in the iron trade led the ironmasters to demand a wage reduction of 10 per cent. If they had been allowed to enforce this then the coal-owners would have been entitled, under the agreement, to impose a similar cut on their workers. The demand for the reduction was, however, resisted by the colliers at the ironworks, who came out on strike on 1 January 1873. Once the dispute had started the sale-coal owners, as the selling prices of coal were still rising, argued that, so long as the ironworks were not actually working, the agreement did not require them to take any steps to enforce a reduction themselves. The Amalgamated Association of Miners, then at the height of its power in South Wales, could thus use its full resources to assist the colliers at the ironworks and was on this occasion able, at a fortnightly cost of nearly £8,000, to honour its promise to pay 10s. a

[1] Before the strike the ironmasters had agreed not to employ strikers and to sell to the associated coal-owners all coal surplus to that required for their contracts. Both undertakings were largely ignored. A. Dalziel, op. cit., pp. 36–44.

week strike money to its members. With this support the men were able to resist until nearly the end of March when a settlement was reached which was substantially a victory for them. The ironmasters were allowed to save a certain amount of face since the reduction was imposed, but it was to last only for five days and then the wage rates of December 1872 were to be restored.[1] Once again, however, it had been the buoyancy of trade that had helped the men to maintain their union intact and to withstand the demands of their employers.

Nevertheless the dispute of 1873 once again brought the owners face to face with the weaknesses of their own organization. In 1871 the coal-owners had felt that their resistance had been undermined by the advantage the ironmasters had taken of the strike to press their coal sales; in 1873 the ironmasters felt that they had been left to fight the coal-owners' battle. Yet many amongst both sections of employers now believed that the time had come to bury their mutual resentments and recriminations and, instead, to present a united front to the men. An opportunity for reconciliation presented itself with the need to adopt a common policy over the introduction of the weighing clauses of the Mines Regulation Act of 1872. These came into force in August 1873 and involved the substitution of the imperial ton of 2,240 lb. for the long ton of 2,520 lb. as the basis for the payment of wages. The owners were resolved that the cutting prices should be reduced in the same proportion, while the men hoped to get a wage increase by demanding the same wage for the imperial ton as had been paid for the customary ton. A series of meetings of employers held during July and August concerning this issue led to the decision to establish an organization that would embrace, as far as possible, all the coal-producers of the district—ironmasters as well as sale-coal owners; house-coal and anthracite as well as steam-coal producers.[2] The new

[1] For a full account of the 1873 dispute see W. G. Dalziel, op. cit., pp. 162–74. For an instance of the widespread belief that the aim of the employers was to crush the men's union see, e.g., *MJ*, 23 Jan. 1873.
[2] Coal Owners' MSS. First Minute Book.

Association based its regulations on those of its predecessors and thus restricted its activity principally to the field of industrial relations, but it surpassed its predecessors in size and strength. Its membership, at the start, consisted of eighty-four firms, included the most prominent iron and coal companies of the district, and controlled over 70 per cent. of the output of the coalfield. The new Association, too, possessed stamina as it was destined to survive for over eighty years—until 1955, when the final tidying-up operations after the nationalization of the coal industry had been completed and the continued existence of the Association became superfluous.

Just as the growth in unionism and improved trade had been contemporaneous in South Wales, so did the break in prices reveal the temporary nature of this growth. Two successive reductions of 10 per cent. in wage rates, imposed in May and August 1874, started the decline in trade union support. There had been some undercurrents of dissatisfaction with the A.A.M. as it had refused to give assistance in some local strikes on which men had embarked without securing prior approval and had given no financial help to men who were unemployed owing to the use of the discharge note by the employers.[1] This dissatisfaction became stronger after Halliday had given the unpalatable advice that resistance against the reductions would be unwise and the closing months of 1874 were marked by the secession of some districts from the Amalgamation.[2] Already losing numerical strength, and with its finances undermined by the support it had given during the strike of 1873, the Amalgamation was ill-equipped to embark on a further struggle. Yet a new bitter dispute, which was to last for five months before a settlement was reached, started on 1 January 1875 when the men struck against a further reduction of 10 per cent. The employers had declined arbitration and had refused to set up a joint committee to investigate colliery accounts to determine if the state of trade justified a reduction. 'It appears that it has

[1] *CG*, 22 Aug., 26 Sept., 10 Oct. 1873.   [2] Ibid., 16 Oct. 1874.

come to this', Halliday declared in a manifesto to the men, 'that you must now accept the reduction of ten per cent. on the mere word of the employers to the effect that the price of coal has very much decreased. No proof that this was the case was adduced nor will the employers adduce any.'[1] Not only were the men on this occasion attempting to fight the owners on a falling market but by February the owners decided on a general lock-out to prevent the strikers from being supported by men who remained at work. Even so, the men held out and a settlement was not reached until 29 May, when it was agreed that work should be resumed at a 12½ per cent. reduction in wages and that the future course of wages should be governed by a sliding scale supervised by a joint committee of owners and men.

The men emerged from the struggles of the early 1870's with their union enfeebled and poverty-stricken, and with the problem of building up an effective organization unsolved. Yet the disputes had given experience of negotiations on more than a narrow, local scale to their leaders, and particularly to William Abraham ('Mabon'), who rose to prominence in these years. Gifted with powers of oratory which soon gave him a reputation extending beyond his own district of Loughor, Abraham was appointed with Halliday as Parliamentary agent of the A.A.M. in 1874 and also chosen to represent the Amalgamation at the Trades Union Congress; in 1875, when the workmen selected their representatives for the sliding scale discussions, Abraham was their first choice.[2] He was to remain the leading figure of the colliers of South Wales for a generation. The acceptance of a sliding scale by the employers, too, was regarded by the men with satisfaction.

[1] CG, 1 Jan. 1875.
[2] Ibid., 17 Apr., 16 Oct. 1874, 9 July 1875. Subsequently William Thomas Lewis (later Lord Merthyr), while renouncing any claim to having pioneered the scale, wrote that he had done 'the lion's share' of the six months' work involved in working out the intricate details of the scale on behalf of the owners. Merthyr of Senghenydd MSS., No. 388.

Such a device had been frequently suggested by them, and as recently as June 1874 Henry Mitchard of Blackwood had proposed to the Employers' Association that the practice which had long prevailed in Monmouthshire of advancing and reducing wage rates by 2*d*. per ton in accordance with variations of a shilling in the market price of coal should be generally adopted.[1]

The men welcomed the sliding scale because they believed that it removed the level of the wage rates from the arbitrary control of the employers and averted the possibility that reductions which had no justification in a fall in the selling price of coal might be demanded. The mere erection of a scale, however, did not alter the essential fact that the wage rate formed a substantial proportion of total costs; it meant merely that in future the struggle would centre largely on the details of the construction of the scale. Slowly, too, the men became aware that in accepting the sliding scale they also implicitly accepted the principle of an identity of interests between owners and men, and that in debating the technical minutiae of the scale they might fail to secure their broad aim of a minimum standard of life for all the workmen. For the moment, however, the scale was enough, and the relief of the men was shared by the employers, who welcomed any device which seemed to promise freedom from the turbulence of the years that had just elapsed. 'Reason has asserted her sway', commented H. H. Vivian, 'and a very desirable scheme has been adopted both by employer and employed. We shall no longer be a byword; we shall no longer be pointed at; and no longer will it be said "Look how they quarrel amongst themselves in the South of Wales district".'[2]

[1] *CG*, 12 June 1874.   [2] Ibid., 18 Feb. 1876.

INDEX

Aberaman colliery, 107, 193, 202, 266.
Aberdare parish, 188.
Aberdare valley, 5, 64; and steam-coal trade, 94, 98, 104 ff., 142, 250, 252-3, 299; and explosions, 63, 182, 183, 188.
Aberdare Coal Company, 20 n., 29, 106, 164.
Aberdare Iron Company, 84-85, 275.
Aberdare Steam Collieries Association, 276-7.
Abraham, William ('Mabon'), 283.
Absenteeism, 228, 233-4. *See also* Colliers.
Accidents, 180, 181, 187, 195, 196, 204, 206; death-rate from, 194, 207; Landshipping colliery, at, 181; Tregob colliery, at, 188. *See also* Explosions.
Admiralty: coal contracts of, 23-24, 28, 29, 37, 81; trials of coal by, 34-41, 101, 107, 122.
Anthracite, 2, 31, 77, 92-93, 137; demand for stagnant, 43-46, 92, 96; new uses for, 6, 42.
Associations of owners: coal-owners, 33, 174-8, 276-7, 279, 281-2; ironmasters, 274-5.

Bailey, Crawshay, 114, 131, 158, 161, 275; and safety in mines, 199, 200, 203; and railways, 98.
Banks, 143-4; provision of capital by, 144-7.
Bargoed Coal Company, 155, 159.
Bèche, Sir Henry de la, 34, 45, 184; quoted, 52.
Bedlington, Richard, 60.
Bettws Llantwit Company, 157.
Bevan, David, 132.
Beynon, Thomas, 132, 154, 166
'Billy Playfair', 259.
Blackwell, Kenyon, 183, 185.
Blaenavon Iron Company, 68, 152; sales of coal by, 84.
Blewitt, Reginald James, 29, 127, 164, 175; and railways, 99.

Brough, Lionel, cited, 73, 190 n., 208, 232 n.
Bruce, H. A. (later Lord Aberdare), 86, 131, 218, 235; and truck system, 228 n., 269.
Brunton fan, 65, 66.
Bryn Colliery Company, 141.
Burnyeat, Brown and Company, 142.
Bute estate, 102, 113, 120, 123-4.
Bute, Marquis of, 86, 123, 141, 164-5; and colliers' unrest, 234, 257-8, 264; and docks, 101, 103.
Bute Merthyr Steam Coal Company, 153, 225, 240.

Calvert, John, 110.
Cameron's Coal Company, 148-9.
Canals, 3, 7, 11; Aberdare, 11, 106; Glamorganshire, 11, 13, 99, 100, 106, 110; Monmouthshire, 11, 99-100, 102; Neath, 10; Swansea, 10, 93.
Capital: requirements, 14, 16, 115, 137-40, 149; sources of, 12, 137, 140-1, 147 ff. *See also* Banks.
Cardiff, 123, 132, 251; coal trade of, 3, 4, 5, 11-12, 20, 25-26, 27, 32, 91, 97-98, 100-1, 103-4, 109, 173, 175, 177; banks at, 143-4. *See also* Docks.
Cardiff and Swansea Steam Coal Company, 153, 156.
Carr Bros. and Company, 142.
Chapels, 245, 247.
Children, employment of, 194-5, 211-14, 216; legislation concerning, 179-80, 202, 205, 215.
Clark, G. T., 15, 16, 86, 243; quoted, 246, 275.
Clark, W. S., 50 n., 113, 114.
Coal-cutting machines, 71-72.
Coal, shipments of, 10, 11, 91, 95, 97, 100, 104; coastal, 2, 8, 32-33, 111; overseas, 3, 8, 18, 25-26, 30-33, 42; duties on, 30, 42 n.
Coffin, Walter, 13, 20, 47, 109-10, 112, 139, 140; and Taff Vale Rail-

286 INDEX

way, 97, 112; public activities of, 131, 132; religion of, 128.
Collieries, scale of, 13–15, 134–7, 208.
Colliers: alleged unrest of, 88, 209, 258; cheap coal for, 8, 120, 223; health of, 181, 190; hostility to technical change, 61, 259–62; irregularity of work of, 75, 221, 222, 232–4, 255; numbers of, 73, 74, 234; work of, 235–6.
Commons, Committee of, 1835, 179.
Cope, Matthew, 168.
Copper industry, 47, 131; coal requirements of, 2, 7–8, 10; coal sales by, 82–83.
Cory Bros., 157, 166, 167; John, 132, 154, 166; Richard, 132, 166; Thomas, 166.
Cory, William, 142, 166.
Crane, George, 6, 44.
Crawshay: family, the, 104, 110; Richard, 12; Robert, 90, 129 n., 231; William, 90, 129, 146 n., 202; quoted, 71, 85, 275 n.
Cwmneol colliery, 107, 151, 161.
Cwmsaerbren colliery, 66, 114.
Cyfarthfa Ironworks, 9, 152; coal sales of, 84, 89–90; methods of wage payments at, 231; water balance pits of, 70.
Cymmer colliery, 110, 111, 194, 195.

Davies, David (Ocean), 128, 131 n., 132, 144.
Davis, David (Blaen-gwawr), 108, 128, 129, 132, 140–1, 147, 276; and double shift, 260 n.
Davis, David (Maesyffynnon), 131, 132.
Deep Duffryn colliery, 107, 142, 166.
Demand for coal, 2–8, 16, 41; for household uses, 7, 45, 77; for railways, 46–47; for steamships, 5, 18, 27–28, 35–41, 45, 167; variations in, 77–80.
Depths of working, 51, 53, 65.
Dinas colliery, 14, 109, 111, 112, 121, 180, 242.
Discharge note, 264–6, 274.
Dobson, Samuel, 55, 57 n., 187, 197 n.
Docks, 26; Briton Ferry, 94, 124; Cardiff, 4, 5, 26, 101–2, 103, 124; Llanelly, 4, 95–96; Newport, 4, 26, 102–3, 124; Port Talbot, 4; Swansea, 94, 103, 124.
Double shift, 260–2.
Dowlais Ironworks, 9, 45, 152, 192, 233; and employers' combinations, 177, 178, 274–5; and long-wall working, 60; coal sales of, 85–89, 90; coal used at, 7, 48; company houses, 241; earnings at, 218, 219; friendly societies at, 244; Fochriw pit, 53, 67, 87; mechanical haulage at, 69; methods of coal sales, 162, 167, 168–70, 171, 172; methods of wage payment at, 230–1; output of collieries of, 233; producing steel, 48; school, 242.
Dunraven United Collieries Company, 154, 155.
Dylais Coal and Iron Company, 154.

Eaglesbush colliery, 64, 146 n., 147, 182, 183.
Ebbw Vale Company, 12, 150, 153; coal sales of, 84; producing steel, 48.
Elliot, George, 55, 127, 131 n., 142, 159–60, 161; and double shift, 260 n.; and price control, 177 n.; humble origins, 126; on trade unions, 273; quoted, 79.
Emigration, 238–9.
Employment: contracts of, 234, 266; statistics of, 75, 234.
Evans, Thomas (Mines Inspector), 198, 201, 203.
Explosions, 54, 184, 188; Coalbrookvale (1856), 198; Cwmnant-ddu (1856), 199; Cyfyng (1858), 188; Cymmer (1856), 194, 195, 207; Dinas (1844), 180–1; Duffryn (1845), 182; Middle Duffryn (1852), 65, 189, 195; Eaglesbush (1848), 64, 183; Ferndale (1867, 1869), 204, 266; Lletty Shenkin (1849), 183; (1852), 187, 194; Park (1863), 203; Risca (1846), 183.

Ferndale colliery, 71, 114, 137, 170, 204, 238.

INDEX

Fforchaman colliery, 71, 107, 151, 161.
Firms, scale of, 13–14, 134–7.
Fothergill, Richard, 131, 228 n., 275.
Friendly societies, 195, 243–4, 245.
Gelli-gaer colliery, 13, 20, 65, 139, 192, 243, 249, 250, 255, 257.
Glamorgan Coal Company, 137, 159.
Glamorgan Iron and Coal Company, 158.
Graigola collieries, 10, 13, 21, 82.
Great Western Colliery Company, 154.
Guest, Sir John, 86, 131; and railways, 97, 98.

Hadley, Leonard, 110.
Halliday, Thomas, 272, 273, 278, 282, 283.
Haulage, methods of, 51, 53, 68–70.
Hendreforgan colliery, 63, 68.
Hill, Anthony, 90, 144.
Homfray, Samuel, 28, 175, 274.
Hood, Archibald, 55, 127, 142.
Hours of work, 74, 231–2.
Houses, 239; company provided, 223, 240–1, 242 n.; insanitary condition of, 239–40; overcrowding of, 209, 242; private building of, 241–2.

Insole, George, 13, 110, 164, 165; and London coal sales, 19–20.
Insole, James Harvey, 142.
Inspectors of Mines: appointed, 184; call for appointment of, 181, 184; work of, 54, 196, 202, 208. *See also* Mackworth, Herbert Francis.
Iron industry, 106, 112, 131, 138; demand for coal by, 2, 6–7, 44–45, 48–49, 109; Employers' Associations in, 274–5; ironworks, location of, 8–10; sales of coal by, 83 ff., 278; use of anthracite by, 5–6, 44–45.

Joint Stock Companies, 118; advantages of, 149–50; failures among, 156–9; growing importance of, 151–3; mobilization of capital by, 153–6; registrations of, 151.

Jones, Edward, 128, 132.
Jones, Mordecai, 108.
Joseph, Thomas, 129–30, 141, 154, 155.

Landore: colliery company, 13, 14; steelworks, 48.
Latch, Joseph, 132.
Legislation: 1842, 179, 215; 1850 Inspection of Coal Mines Act, 180, 184–5, 191; 1855, 196–201; 1860 Mines Regulation Act, 201–2; 1862 Coal Mines Act, 53, 67, 203; 1872 Mines Regulation Act, 82, 200, 205–6, 232, 281.
Lewis, William Thomas, 128, 283 n.
Llanelly, 4, 10, 17, 258 n.; and copper industry, 2, 10; banks at, 143; coal trade of, 11–12, 21, 25–26, 27, 28, 32, 91, 95–96, 172. *See also* Docks.
Llangennech: coal, 29, 33; Coal Company, 21, 22 n., 25, 26.
Llansamlet collieries, 10, 13, 51, 63.
Lletty Shenkin colliery, 107 n., 143, 183, 187, 193, 194.
London, coal sales in, 2, 19–23, 29–30, 32, 43, 44, 46.
Long-wall mining, 59, 208; date of introduction of, 60–61; limitations of, 62; resisted by colliers, 61.

Mackworth, Herbert Francis: appointed inspector, 54, 185, 198; quoted, 79, 203, 206; work as inspector, 186–90, 191, 192, 193, 196, 197, 199, 200.
Maesteg: friendly societies at, 244; housing at, 239, 242.
Medical attention, 243.
Menelaus, William, 56, 69, 87–89.
Merthyr Tydfil, 4, 9, 11, 249, 257; and coal trade, 21; banks at, 143; housing and sanitation, 225, 240, 241; population of, 210.
Merthyr Vale colliery, 53, 55, 142, 166.
Migration into coalfield: from Wales, 235–6; from outside Wales, 235, 236–7.
Milford, coal trade of, 32, 91, 93.
Mobility of labour, 221, 237–8.

INDEX

Monmouthshire and South Wales Coal Owners' Association, 135, 219, 381–2.
Morgan, Charles (of Tredegar Park), 123, 124, 127, 130, 175.
Morris, George Byng, 150.
Morris, Sir John, 60, 150.

Navigation colliery, 55, 65, 108, 142, 166.
Neath, 94, 132; and copper industry, 10, 92; coal trade of, 21, 25, 91, 172, 173.
Neath, Vale of, 6, 9, 44, 92, 96.
Nevill, R. J., 60, 164, 171, 172, 174, 258 n.; and early coal trade, 22–26.
Newcastle, *see* North of England.
Newport, 5, 132, 248; banks at, 143–4; coal 'ring' at, 174–6; coal trade of, 3, 11–12, 25–26, 32, 91, 97, 98–101, 181, 251; irregularity of trade at, 231–2. *See also* Docks.
Newport Abercarn Black Vein Steam Coal Company, 150, 154, 166.
Newport Coal Company, 174.
Nixon, John, 32 n., 37, 53, 55, 141–2, 182, 183, 197 n., 276; and double-shift working, 260 n., 261 n.; and long-wall working, 60–61; and ventilation, 65, 67; sales by, to French market, 5, 31–32.
Nonconformity: and owners, 128–9; and workmen, 244–7.
North of England, 135, 181, 191; competition with, 2, 28, 31–32, 33–43, 45–46, 176; influence on technique, 53, 54–55, 260.

Ocean Coal Company, 137, 147–8, 241.
Output: from Aberdare valley, 108–9; from Rhondda valleys, 115; of anthracite, 46; per miner, 73–74; the coalfield, of, 8, 18, 75–76, 77.
Owen, Col., 13, 127.
Owen, John: and discharge note, 264–5; and truck, 228, 229, 268–9; men's legal adviser, 267–8, 271.

Pembrokeshire, 225; decline of coal industry of, 92–93, 234; employment of women and children in, 68, 211, 215; lower earnings in, 218–19; size of collieries in, 13, 15.
Penrose and Evans, 146 n., 147, 182, 183.
Phillips, Sir Thomas, 128–9, 211, 225, 242, 257.
Pillar and stall mining, 57–59.
Playfair, Dr. Lyon, 34, 45, 184.
Plymouth Iron Company, 9, 14, 85, 90.
Port Talbot, 47.
Powell, Thomas, 20, 29, 31, 37, 55, 65, 110, 128, 135, 142, 147, 151, 164, 174, 185, 217; and strikes, 249, 258, 262–3; alderman at Newport, 132; coal trespass by, 130; death, 159; mismanagement of colliery of, 192; on Taff Vale Railway Board, 97; pits in Aberdare valley, 5, 106–7; scale of operations, 13, 14, 125–6, 140; self-made man, 126; start in coal trade, 13; supports victims of accidents, 182 n.
Powell Duffryn Company, 69, 109 n., 137, 140, 142, 151, 152, 159–62, 276.
Price, Joseph Tregelles, 128.
Prices, steam coal, of, 80–82, 219 n.; reasons for fluctuations in, 77–80.
Prothero, Thomas, 13, 130, 135, 140, 217.
Public houses, 245–6.

Raby, Alexander, 22, 22 n., 23 n., 24.
Railways, 15, 26, 93, 98, 102–3, 124; Aberdare, 98, 107; Great Western, 43; Llanelly, 4, 93, 95; Newport–Pontypool, 100; Rhymney, 36, 124; South Wales, 43, 95; Swansea Vale, 94; Taff Vale, 4, 5, 88, 97, 98, 100, 102, 107, 111, 113, 114; Vale of Neath, 94–95.
Rhondda valleys, 98, 104, 109 ff., 204, 237, 253, 279.
Rhydydefed Colliery Company, 150, 153.
Rhymney Iron Company, 9, 85, 152; and truck system, 269.
Richardson, Joshua, 50 n., 54, 184, 197 n.
Risca colliery, 6, 13, 29, 66, 71, 183, 192, 243.

INDEX

Roberts, W. P., 266 n., 272.
Roper, Paul, 262.
Royalties, 179 ff.
Russell and Company, 5, 13, 29.
Russell, John, 151, 198.

Safety lamps, 14 n., 15, 52, 184, 189, 201, 203, 204–5, 222, 259.
Sale of Coal Committee, 1871, 178.
Schools, 242–3.
Schools, Sunday, 209.
Sirhowy tramroad, 11, 99.
Sliding scale, 253; at Gelli-gaer, 249; of 1875, 283, 284.
Small coal, 58–59, 171–2; and copper industry, 83; and iron industry, 88; royalties, 117.
South Wales Bituminous Collieries Association, 277.
South Wales Colliery Company, 151.
South Wales Institute of Engineers: membership and influence, 56–57; discusses long-wall working, 60–62.
South Wales Steam Collieries Association, 277, 279–80.
Strikes, 247, 278; Abercarn, 1861, 263, 265; Aberdare, 1849–50, 252, 265; 1857–8, 253, 265; in eighteen-forties, 248–51, 267; outside labour brought in, 262–4; 1871, 254, 277–8; 1873, 254, 280–1; 1875, 152, 254, 282–3.
Struvé, W. P., 64, 65, 66, 67, 197 n.
Swansea, 5, 10, 94, 188; and coal trade, 11, 21, 25–26, 28, 30, 32, 91, 172; and copper trade, 2, 10; banks at, 143–4, 145. *See also* Docks.
Swansea Coal Company, 13, 83.
Swansea and Neath Colliery Company, 154, 156.

Thomas, Lucy, 13, 19–20.
Thomas, Samuel, 107, 128, 139, 141, 147.
Thomas, William (of Brynawel), 126, 127, 133.
Tinplate industry: demand for coal, of, 2, 7; location of works, 47, 92.
Trade Unions: Amalgamated Association of Miners, 219, 236, 270 n., 273, 278, 279, 280, 282, 283;

Glamorgan Union of Miners, 271; in Aberdare valley, 1850, 271; in Rhondda valley, 1847, 271; Miners' Association of Great Britain, 272; Miners' National Union, 272; slow growth of, 269–71.
Tredegar Coal Company, 18, 84.
Tredegar Iron Works, 9, 84, 152, 192.
Tremenheere, Seymour, 180, 209, 215, 216, 218, 230, 244, 245.
Troedyrhiw Coal Company, 168.
Truck system, 224–9, 250; decline of, 229–30; legal case concerning, 268–9.

United Merthyr Colliery Company, 151, 161.

Ventilation, 15, 50, 53, 54, 179, 181, 182, 188–90, 197, 199; and long-wall working, 59; improvement of, 67; mechanical, 64–67; primitive methods of, 51–52, 62–64.
Vivian, Henry Hussey (Lord Swansea), 54, 63, 131, 154, 156, 212, 284.

Waddle fan, 65, 66, 67.
Wages: as element in costs, 255–6; changes in rates of, 254–5; children, of, 213; colliers, of, 217–21; colliers in iron industry, of, 221–2; deductions from, 222, 242–3; paid in public houses, 230–1; rising trend of, 223; women, of, 214–15.
Wayne: family, the, 5, 106, 113, 128; Matthew, 29, 182; Thomas, 182.
Wilkinson, George, 55.
Williams, David, 107, 126, 141, 142, 160, 182, 193; and public affairs, 131, 133.
Winding: legislation concerning, 197, 201, 202; steam, by, 71; water balance, by, 70.
Women, employment of, 214–15, 216.

Yeo, Frank Ash, 132, 166.
Ynysawdre Coal Company, 154.
Ynyscedwyn Ironworks, 5, 6, 7, 9, 44, 45, 212.
Ystalyfera Ironworks, 6, 44, 45.

PRINTED IN
GREAT BRITAIN
AT THE
UNIVERSITY PRESS
OXFORD
BY
CHARLES BATEY
PRINTER
TO THE
UNIVERSITY